JUMPING THROUGH HOOPS
Autobiographical Stories by Modern Chinese Women Writers

Jumping Through Hoops is a collection of nine intense and dramatic stories that sheds new light on the experiences of Chinese women during the Second World War. Originally published in Chinese in 1945, as part of Xie Bingying's classic anthology *Nu zuojia zizhuan xuanji* (Selected autobiographical writings by women writers), the extraordinary narratives reveal the writers' personal struggles during the years of turmoil between the Republican and Communist eras. Whether the contributors are internationally acclaimed or just rediscovered, most of these narratives are seldom found in other collections, either in Chinese or in translation.

Jing M. Wang is an Assistant Professor of Chinese Literature and Language at Colgate University. She specializes in twentieth-century Chinese women's autobiographical writings and modern Chinese literature. She is the co-author of *Yingshi rumen* (How to read English poetry, Shanghai Translations Publishing House, 1990).

"Informative and fascinating. A 'must read' for anyone interested in China … " — *Adeline Yen Mah, author of* Falling Leaves: The True Story of an Unwanted Chinese Daughter

"Anyone interested globally in autobiography would do themselves an immense service by reading these texts. For the Western reader … reading these remarkable stories will be like stumbling upon an undiscovered country. These stories serve as a valuable and enormously entertaining lesson in cultural and political history. The opening pages of Bai Wei's 'Jumping Through Hoops', are as powerful as anything I have read in autobiography … " — *Dr Patrick Riley, Department of Romance Languages and Literatures, Colgate University*

"This collection represents an invaluable source as to how women thought and lived their lives during the Resistance War. Their voice not only needs to be heard by the Chinese people but also by Western audiences who are interested in both Chinese culture and women's lives during that period." — *Dr Yanfang Tang, Associate Professor of Chinese, College of William and Mary*

"We have seen short stories written by some of the contributors in this collection, but in contrast … their autobiographical writing is less sentimental, contains far more personal experiences … and delves deeper into individual lives and psyches … Scholars and students of modern Chinese women writers will find this book an essential reference for the biographical information contained therein and the inner world of women writers it reveals." — *Dr Lily Lee, Department of Chinese Studies, University of Sydney, and editor of* Biographical Dictionary of Chinese Women

JUMPING THROUGH HOOPS

To Mimi

JUMPING THROUGH HOOPS

Autobiographical Stories by
Modern Chinese Women Writers

Edited by
Jing M. Wang

Translated by
Jing M. Wang & Shirley Chang

香港大學出版社
HONG KONG UNIVERSITY PRESS

Hong Kong University Press
14/F Hing Wai Centre
7 Tin Wan Praya Road
Aberdeen
Hong Kong

ISBN 962 209 582 8 (Hardback)
ISBN 962 209 583 6 (Paperback)

British Library Cataloguing-in-Publication Data
A catalogue record for this book is available from the British Library.

Secure On-line Ordering
http://www.hkupress.org

Printed and bound by Condor Production Ltd., Hong Kong, China.

Contents

Acknowledgments

My sincere gratitude goes to Julia Watson. Without her insight and support, it would have taken much longer for this book to take shape. I am indebted to Patrick Riley and Yanfang Tang for their valuable suggestions. I also thank Tani Barlow, Xiaomei Chen, Jinhua Dai, Perry Link, and Patricia Sieber for their encouragement. Especially deserving of my acknowledgment is Hao Yan, who showed endless patience in helping me find rare sources needed for annotation. Special thanks also extend to the Research Council of Colgate University, Case Library at Colgate University, Kroch Library at Cornell University, Beijing University Library, Nanjing Library, and Shanghai Library.

I genuinely appreciate the warm love from my families and friends.

About the Translators

Jing M. Wang is an assistant professor of Chinese at Colgate University, Hamilton, New York. She specializes in twentieth-century literature with a focus on women's autobiography. She earned her doctoral degree in Chinese from The Ohio State University, Columbus, Ohio, in 2000. With her MA and BA in English, she has a passion for poetry, drama, and fiction by British as well as American writers. She co-authored *Ying shi ru men* [How to read English poetry] (Shanghai, 1990), which has been adopted as a textbook and is in its second reprint.

Jing Wang is also the editor of this volume.

Shirley Chang grew up in Taiwan, receiving her BA in Chinese Literature from National Cheng-chi University. She received her MA in Chinese from the University of Iowa and Ph.D. in Chinese literature from the University of Wisconsin-Madison. She is the author of *Tang chuanqi zhong de "yiren zhuan"* (Stories of the unconventional characters in Tang dynasty chuanqi stories)(Taipei, 2001). Her other projects include translating thirteen Tang dynasty (618–907 AD) *chuanqi* stories written in classical Chinese into English, and translating Susan Sontag's "Project of a Trip to China" into Chinese. Currently, she is teaching at Shih Hsin University in Taiwan.

Introduction

This collection of autobiographical narratives produced in China during World War II testifies to the diverse ways in which modern Chinese women writers tell the stories of their lives. It showcases the nine writers' extraordinary experiences included in Xie Bingying's (1906–2000) classic anthology entitled *Selected Autobiographies of Women Writers* (*Nü zuojia zizhuan xuanji*, 1945). Published at the initiative of Xie and the female editor Huang Baoxun, the original collection represents one of the rare concerted efforts to gather women's life stories in one volume in China in the first half of the twentieth century and for a long time to come. It is noteworthy particularly because the anthology came out when it had become increasingly difficult for women writers to make their personal voices heard. Highlighting the unconventionality of these narratives, the front cover of Xie's book features the portrait of a Western woman wearing long curly hair, earrings, and a low-neck dress. She looks half submissively and half defiantly to her lower right, with her right hand on her heart, as if full of stories that she hesitates and yet strongly desires to confide in the reader. This portrait gracing the cover of the book embodies the complicated connection between modern Chinese women's autobiographical practice and its Western "model" which I attempt to unfold in this introduction.

The narratives in the translated collection include: An E's (1905–1976) "How I Left My Mother" (Wo zenyang likai de muqin, 1944), Bai Wei's (1894–1987) "Jumping Through Hoops" (Tiao guan ji, 1944), Chu Wenjuan's (1907–?) "Imprints of Life" (Shengming de yinhen, 1943), Lin Beili's (1916–?) "A Journey of Twenty-Seven Years" (Er shi qi nian de lücheng, 1943), Peng Hui's (1907–68) "A Brief Autobiography" (Jian dan de zizhuan, 1943), Xie Bingying's "Midpoint of an Ordinary Life" (Pingfan de ban sheng, 1943), Ye Zhongyin's (1912–?) "My Autobiography" (Wo de zizhuan, 1943), Zhao Qingge's (1914–99) "Can This Also Be Called an Autobiography?" (Ye suan zizhuan?, 1943), and Zi Gang's (1914–88) "Self-Criticism and Self-Encouragement" (Zi kui yu zi mian, 1943). Through the personal lives of the autobiographical subjects, these narratives index the historical and political turbulence in early twentieth-century China and during the War of Resistance against Japan. They are very seldom, if at all, found in other collections of Chinese women's writing that exist in Chinese or in English.

Instead of using the title of the original Chinese book, I call this anthology *Jumping Through Hoops: Autobiographical Stories by Modern Chinese Women Writers*. I employ Bai Wei's "Jumping Through Hoops" as part of the book title, because her metaphor brings to life all the female subjects' struggles for independence and the frustrations they had encountered as women in their careers and family life. Bai's vivid image of the hoops also clinches my argument about the tremendous cultural and political hurdles that stood in the way of autobiographical storytelling in China since the 1930s, as I will elaborate below.

It is my hope that this translated anthology will play multiple roles in promoting modern Chinese women's autobiography as a genre. Because many English editions of women's book-length autobiographies from the Republican period (1911–1949) have long been out of print, this book will help make up for the loss and expand the existing body of Chinese women's life stories in English. It is also intended to direct critical attention to modern Chinese women's autobiographical narratives and to add a new dimension to the current criticism and theorizing of autobiography in a global context. In the meantime, in spite that Chinese women's writings from most major periods in twentieth-century China have become available in English in recent years, self-representations during World War II remain severely underrepresented. This anthology will fill the gap. Furthermore, the book contributes to the rediscovery and rejuvenation of Xie's original book.

In order to help the reader better appreciate these narratives, I will give an overview of the Chinese autobiographical tradition in the pages that follow. I will first discuss the Chinese cultural inhibition against and the desire for self-representation through an examination of some examples of autobiographical writing in traditional times. Secondly, I will investigate the historical and intellectual circumstances in early twentieth-century China that compelled women writers to engage in life writing, identify the unique features that mark women's autobiography from traditional biographies of women written by men, from women's fiction, from Chinese male writers' autobiographical narratives, and from women's autobiographies in the West. I will also discuss the anxiety women writers exhibited in their endeavors of self-expression. Lastly, by way of critically appraising the narratives included in the present anthology, I will try to show how they add to the existing gamut of Chinese women's life stories in English.

The Inhibition of Early Chinese Autobiography

Georges Gusdorf (1956) insists that autobiography "expresses a concern peculiar to Western man" (p. 28) and that the genre "is not possible in a cultural landscape where consciousness of self does not, properly speaking, exist" (p. 30). Roy Pascal (1960) also holds that autobiography is "a distinctive product of Western, post-Romantic civilization, and only in modern times has it spread to other civilizations" (p. 180). Feminist critics of women's autobiography in the recent two decades have already successfully refuted these claims, so the genre is no longer considered an essentially Western, male phenomenon. Nevertheless, the ways in which Chinese writers over the centuries practiced, conceptualized, and re-conceptualized autobiography remain to be introduced to audiences and brought to critical attention outside China.

The Chinese term *zizhuan*, structurally and semantically equivalent to the English term "autobiography," appeared in China around AD 800 (Koozoo 1999, p. 6). But self-representation had various other nomenclatures before and after the appearance of the word *zizhuan*. Chinese scholar Guo Dengfeng (1965) organizes traditional autobiographical writing in China into the following categories: self-preface (*zixu*), self-written biography (*zizhuan*), self-written funerary inscription (*zizuo muzhiming*), epistolary self-narration (*shuduti zixu*), versified self-narration (*cifuti yu shigeti zixu*), elegiac and miscellaneous self-narration (*aijiti zajiti zixu*), self-written account of conduct (*zizhuang*), self-indictment (*zisong*), and self-eulogy (*zizan*) (pp. 1–6). In Pei-yi Wu's (1990) analysis, likewise, traditional Chinese autobiography includes self-written biographies (*zizhuan*), autonecrologies, such as self-written tomb notices and inscriptions (*muzhiming*), grave notices (*kuangzhi*), dirges (*lei*), sepulchres (*shou cang zhi*), epitaphs (*bei*), and obituaries (*zhuang*), annalistic autobiographies (*zixu nianpu*), and authorial self-accounts and prefaces (*zixu*) (pp. 15–67).

Lexically, the Chinese word *zizhuan* is quite straightforward, *zi* meaning "self" and *zhuan* "biography." Thus, *zizhuan*, or autobiography, is simply a self-written biography. The close affiliation with biography, a major form of historiography in traditional China, not only renders autobiography invisible as a genre but also imposes on it constraints of history writing, such as "impersonality of tone," "suppression of an individual voice," and "opacity as to the yearnings of heart or the inward workings of mind" (Wu 1990, p. 6). As a vehicle of didacticism, a biography in traditional times mostly commemorates the subject's public deeds, moral virtues, and literary accomplishments. As autobiography eked out a precarious existence in the shadow of biography, writers experienced enormous formal and psychological difficulty in writing their lives. The formal obstacle is "the lack of a suitable literary form," and the psychological hurdle the "inhibition" (p. 3) against self-disclosure. Consequently, biographical accounts were much more common than life stories written about and by the same subject. Hence perhaps the prevalent view that only a hero deserved to write an autobiography.

Now, such restraint might have derived from the problematic position of the individual in traditional Chinese society. In the Confucian system of thought, all persons were properly organized into the five basic human relationships: ruler and subject, father and son, husband and wife, brothers, and friends. A man's value was determined by how well he played his designated social and familial roles. By the same token, a woman's worth rested with the fulfillment of her duties as daughter, daughter-in-law, wife/widow, and mother. In the meantime, everyone's well-being depended on the general state of the society at large, whether a country, a family, or an interpersonal relationship. This reciprocity created a mutually supportive and fostering relation between a person and the surrounding social network. Intertwinement with the society at large and contribution to one's community define a person's significance. Such interdependence between the self and other people can easily lead to the invalidation of the individual.[1] As the self was not considered a self-contained entity that defined its own importance, autobiography, a genre that apparently celebrates the achievement of the autonomous individual, was tantamount to unabashed self-exaltation. The interconnectedness between a person and society provides an angle from which we can understand why ancient Chinese writers experienced tremendous impediment in writing their life stories.

Paradoxically, I think it is because of, not in spite of, the cultural veto against the writing of autobiography that Chinese writers sometimes fell hopelessly into self-glorification once they overcame their cultural and psychological obstacle. After all, they had to set off their most shining qualities and catalogue all their accomplishments to prove worthy of an autobiographical account. A notable example is Qu Yuan's (ca. 343–277 BC) "Encountering Sorrow" (Li sao), a narrative poem in which the speaker extols his highborn ancestors, celebrates his birth, lauds his moral and personal integrity, laments his disfavor with King Huai of Chu, and vents the frustration of his political ambition. To someone not familiar with a traditional Chinese scholar official's sense of self-worth and his loyalty to the ruler, the amount of self-adoration that informs the work can turn into distasteful narcissism.

The impulse of self-representation persisted in other writers, too, who often tucked into larger texts their usually very sketchy self-portraits in the forms of prefaces and postfaces,[2] two common forms of autobiography in ancient China. "The Self-Account of the Grand Historian" (Tai shi gong zixu), the postface to Sima Qian's (145?–90? BC) Records of the Grand Historian (Shi ji), for example, continued the autobiographical tradition established by Qu Yuan and was acclaimed as "Encountering Sorrow without rhyme" (wu yun zhi Li sao). In the narrative, Sima Qian refers to himself self-consciously as the Grand Historian instead of using the first person singular pronoun. His self-account gives a rather lengthy genealogy and works up to a self-vindication. It is a well-known fact that Sima Qian completed Records of the Grand Historian in prison. When General Li Ling was captured by the Huns, enemy of the Han empire, Sima Qian praised in front of the emperor Li's great deeds in defending the Han. However, when Li's treason was later revealed, Sima Qian was sentenced to death for deceiving the emperor. But Sima Qian chose castration and imprisonment in order to complete his work. It is not hard to see from this case that telling one's personal story needed justification not only by family history and official history, but also by a work of larger significance.

"Self-Record" (Zi ji), the last chapter in Wang Chong's Critical Essays (Lun heng, pp. 27–91) embodies overt and unabashed self-assertion. In this third-person narration, instead of praising his ancestors as contemporary cultural etiquette dictated, Wang commends his own personal virtues, such as careful choice of company, uprightness in office, and frequent, conscientious moral self-examination. Most importantly, he dwells on his precocious talent for learning during childhood and proudly names the classics that he studied. Pei-yi Wu (1990) highly commends Wang's "freedom from historiography" and recognizes his work as "the first untrammeled autobiographical expression in China" (pp. 45–6). Breaking the pattern of ancestral eulogy, Wang's work fully exemplifies the tendency of self-aggrandizement in ancient Chinese autobiographical writing.

Self-narration in the first person did not occur in China until Cao Pi's (187–226) substantial autobiographical preface to his prose work *Heavenly Discussions* (*Tianlun*). Moving beyond Wang, Cao makes no mention of his book, includes no genealogy, and focuses exclusively on self-eulogy: his excellence in horsemanship, archery, swordsmanship, and even parlor games. His self-reference as "I" is the most notable innovation in distinguishing the personal voice in early Chinese autobiographical writing.

The above account demonstrates that autobiography was an age-old tradition in China in spite of the cultural etiquette of reserve and reticence. Undoubtedly, by preventing many from writing about themselves, the interdiction succeeded in stunting autobiography at large and keeping the genre in subservience to the respected biography. In certain situations, however, the taboo stimulated the desire for self-expression, effecting a dichotomy between humility on the one hand and self-glorification on the other. That explains why writers sometimes felt too humble to tell their life stories at all; yet once they broke the taboo, they could fall completely in love with their ego and become quite obsessed about their accomplishments.

If the cultural milieu in traditional China did not encourage male writers' autobiographical practice, women encountered more formidable obstacles in writing their lives for the lack of education and the more demanding gender requirement of reticence. The majority of women conventionally remained objects of male representation in biographies rather than narrators of their own life stories. Biography had been an established genre since Sima Qian first employed it as an important technique in his *Records of the Grand Historian*. His style and format provided models for later historians writing biographical entries in the standard histories of each dynasty. Alongside public biographies, i.e., life accounts included in the *lie zhuan* (biographies) section in the standard histories, private biographies existed written by individual writers about their relatives often in the forms of birthday celebrations and funerary inscriptions. Women's biographies were called *lie nü zhuan*. Women's biographies can also be divided into the public and the private. Han Confucian scholar Liu Xiang's (77 BC – 6 BC) *The Biographies of Women* (*Lie nü zhuan*)[3] contains the earliest life stories of women in the public form. Liu categorizes women into seven types as his chapter titles indicate: Biographies Illustrating the Correct Deportment of Mothers, Biographies of the Virtuous and Wise, Biographies of the Benign and Wise, Biographies of the Chaste and Obedient, Biographies of the Chaste and Righteous, Biographies of Those Able in Reasoning and Understanding, and Biographies of the Pernicious and Depraved. It is important to note the regulatory function of these categories, as they explicitly prescribe terms of ideal motherhood and womanhood by providing positive as well as negative role models. As gender norms that dominated women's lives, these representations were to shape the Confucian education of women for centuries to come.

Following Liu's example, all the later official histories contain a section called "Biographies of Women," which portray and eulogize women's excellence in moral behavior. However, historians continued to tighten the gender codes. As sexual chastity gradually became a predominant theme running through women's public biographies, standards of chastity grew increasingly demanding. For instance, in *History of the Jin Dynasty* (*Jin shu*), *History of the Northern Dynasty* (*Bei shi*), and *History of the Southern Dynasty* (*Nan shi*), women were included for a variety of virtues, such as filial piety, female chastity, reasonableness, courage, and even capability in leadership. Since *History of the Yuan Dynasty* (*Yuan shi*), however, the biographers not only almost exclusively emphasized female chastity, but also concentrated on, and therefore encouraged, increasingly violent physical demolition, such as disfiguring and cutting off body parts, as testimony of their determination to preserve their chastity. The demand for female chastity reached its peak in *History of the Ming Dynasty* (*Ming shi*), in which nothing short of gory self-immolation would satisfy the male historians.[4]

Private biographies also participated in the construction of women's images in traditional China. Here I cite a few composed by male writers in the Ming dynasty (1368–1644) and the Qing dynasty (1644–1911). "The Epitaph of Fang Mu Zhang Ruren"[5] by Gui Youguang (1507–1571) portrays his widowed mother's devotion to his childhood education by evoking scenes of the mother weaving under the same light at night as the son studied and making the son kneel for doing a mediocre job in an exam. Wu Meicun (1609–1672) wrote "The Epitaph of Wang Mu Zhou

Taianren"[6] in memory of a good friend's mother. The author remembers his own mother as a filial daughter-in-law, dedicated mother, and industrious wife. Zhang Xuecheng's (1738–1801) mother in "The Epitaph of Pei Mu Cha Yiren"[7] resembles the selfless and public-spirited women portrayed in both Liu Xiang's work and some of the earlier dynastic histories. The images of women in the official histories and private accounts all reflected and contributed to the formation of gender codes in traditional China. Most representations of women in the past came from the extensive body of women's biographies written by male historians and writers.

Given the conventional status of women as objects of male imagination and portrayal, the culturally induced humility as virtue prohibited women more than it did men to expose themselves publicly. As a result, only a very small number of women had the opportunity to write the stories of their lives. The first existing self-narration written by a woman is allegedly Han scholar Ban Zhao's (45–115) preface to *Admonitions to Women* (*Nü Jie Xu*). She makes three points in her self-account: apologizing for her worthlessness and obtuseness, describing the humility and piety with which she served her husband's family, and stating her purpose for writing *Admonitions to Women* — to educate her young daughters and prepare them for married life. The self-image projected here fits neatly with the traditional roles of a woman. Representation of herself as a person would have been quite out of place here.

Existent literature shows that almost ten centuries elapsed before Song dynasty (960–1279) poet Li Qingzhao (1084–1151) told her story in the postscript to *A Catalogue of Bronze and Stone Inscriptions* (*Jin shi lu hou xu*). Both literary and art scholars, Li and her husband Zhao Mingcheng (1081–1129) collected books, paintings, and antiques with great enthusiasm and particularly enjoyed making rubbings of ancient stone or bronze inscriptions. The 1126 invasion of Kaifeng by the Jurchens from the north disrupted their idyllic life. The manuscript of *A Catalogue of Bronze and Stone Inscriptions*, a collaborative work of husband and wife, survived the turmoil. Writing the postscript to commemorate their conjugal happiness, their shared passion for art and books, and their work, Li had enough justification for her narrative act. In the text, she starts with her marriage and briefly introduces the financial status of her own and her husband families without making it a genealogy. She focuses on the vivid, and occasionally sensuous, details of life with her husband, such as perusing art works and eating fruit. She also describes a game they played of giving the exact textual locations of literary allusions. Because of her excellent memory, she often won these games. Li shows little interest in the feminine virtues expected of her sex, economizing only to buy books, enjoying simple clothing, and avoiding jewelry and decorations. Although being a woman and a writer of *ci* (a genre quite permissive of uttering emotions) might have enabled her to reveal her private life, she conceals her autobiography surreptitiously in a postscript, an account of the much larger work that she mostly attributes to her husband.

These instances, out of the sundry varieties of autobiographical writing produced in traditional China, show that women's self-representations were largely void of the self-congratulatory tone that characterizes mostly autobiographical narratives written by men.

The Inevitability of Modern Chinese Women's Autobiography

With Shen Fu's (1763–c.1808) *Six Records of a Floating Life* (Fu sheng liu ji)[8] standing out as one of the rare life stories, full-length autobiography as a genre did not appear in China until the twentieth century. Chinese women writers began to engage in autobiographical practice in the 1930s. Some of the prominent texts include *An Autobiography of Lu Yin* (*Lu Yin zizhuan*, 1934)[9] by Lu Yin (1898–1934), *Autobiography of A Female Soldier* (*Yi ge nü bing de zizhuan*, 1936)[10] by Xie Bingying, *My Tragic Life* (Beiju shengya, 1936)[11] by Bai Wei, and *My Life* (*Wo de shenghuo*, 1967)[12] and *Ninety-Four Years of a Floating Life* (*Fu sheng jiu si*, 1991) by Su Xuelin (1897–).[13] Other life stories were published in English, such as Chen Hengzhe's (1893–1976) *Autobiography of a Chinese Young Girl* (1935)[14] and Su Hua Ling Chen's (1904–1990) *Ancient Melodies* (1953).[15] Still others became accessible in English through translation, not the least of which is Xie Bingying's *Girl Rebel: The Autobiography of Hsieh Pingying* (1940) and Buwei Yang Chao's (1889–1981) *Autobiography of a Chinese Woman* (1947).[16] These by no means exhaust the list.

Prior to the twentieth century, writing was mostly a male endeavor. As shown abundantly clear in Dorothy Ko's study, only gentry women in the seventeenth century Jiangnan area had the privilege to publish their literary creations, facilitated by commercial print culture.[17] For all the traditional women's writings that exist today,[18] it remains true that most women then wrote for leisure and rarely made a living with the pen. Except for increasing their desirability on the marriage market, women's literary accomplishment did not count in the real world. As Qing literary historian Zhang Xuecheng remarks:

> In my opinion, wherever official honors are proffered, the wise and the talented will vie for them. In that sense, the scholar pursues learning for the same reason that the farmer tills his fields, and there is nothing at all unusual about it. But a woman's writing is not her vocation, and so when a woman happens to excel as a result of her own natural endowment, she needs not compete over style, nor be stirred by the promise of fame and reputation. (Quoted from Mann, 1992, pp. 44–5)

According to this view, women's writing amounted to nothing more than pastime, having no practical purpose to it. Nor was it a painstaking endeavor, as their natural endowment needed no cultivation. Therefore, women did not achieve worldly fortune and fame through writing.

In the early twentieth century, however, educated Chinese women began to write seriously for publication and pursue literature as a career. The autobiographical sentiment most saliently characterizes women's writing at that time. What, then, were the circumstances that compelled female writers to take up the writing of their life stories? How did autobiography fare in modern China? A brief account is in order here of the social, political, and intellectual context that provide a backdrop against which we can explore these issues. The first and foremost factor that enabled women to write was their access to modern education in the public space of school vis-à-vis traditional gender education in the private home. Missionary girls' schools were established China toward the latter half of the nineteenth century, first in southern and then in the northern provinces. Western-style textbooks for liberal arts education combined with Confucian classics. These new educational institutions freed girls from the walled domain of the Confucian home and opened an avenue to literacy for them.[19] After secular Chinese girls' schools came into being during the first decade of the twentieth century, co-educational schools followed within the next ten years. Literacy empowered Chinese young women, liberated them from their traditional confines, and prepared them to take the new intellectual challenge in the 1920s.

The New Literature Movement, with the May Fourth Movement as its highpoint, most directly impacted the first generation of educated

Chinese women in their choice to write professionally. In 1915, Chen Duxiu (1880–1942) started in Shanghai a journal called *Youth Magazine* (Qingnian zazhi) which became *New Youth* (Xin qingnian) in 1916. *New Youth* condemned Confucianism and acclaimed Western thought as China's way to cultural, literary, and political modernity. The year 1917 saw the publication of Hu Shi's (1891–1962) famous essay "Some Modest Proposals for the Reform of Literature" (Wenxue gailiang chuyi) in *New Youth*. The eight guidelines of writing laid down in his essay include: 1) Writing should have substance, 2) Do not imitate the ancients, 3) Emphasize the technique of writing, 4) Do not moan without an illness, 5) Eliminate hackneyed and formal language, 6) Do not use allusions, 7) Do not use parallelism, 8) Do not avoid vulgar diction. The promotion of candid expression of one's true feelings without superfluous ornaments and formal constraint fostered a new literature more easily approachable by writers unversed in traditional learning and untrained in conventional forms of composition. In the meantime Hu Shi's Literary Revolution established the vernacular language (*baihua*), as opposed to classical language (*wenyan*), as the major form of literary discourse. Pushing beyond Hu Shi's ideas of reform, the more radical Chen Duxiu published "On Literary Revolution" (Wenxue geming lun) in *New Youth* in the same year. In the essay he unreservedly advocates "a plain and lyrical nationalist literature," "a fresh and sincere realist literature," and "a clear and common social literature" (pp. 140–45). In 1918, through Hu Shi's translation, the heroic Nora in Henrik Ibsen's *A Doll's House* (Wan ou zhi jia) took China by storm for her rebellion against patriarchal oppression and confinement of the home. This act of self-assertion inspired many young women, as well as young men, to break away from parentally arranged marriage in search of the freedom to choose their own spouse. Thus, the stress on "substance" and "genuineness" in New Literature gave unprecedented sanction to self-expression in literature.

Under the auspices of the New Literature Movement, educated women began to make a living by writing. The establishment of the vernacular as a respectable means of written discourse, the ethos of individualism, and the creative space provided by literary journals, all led to a proliferation of women's autobiographical fiction. Notice, however, that educated women camouflaged their life stories as fiction during the May Fourth period (1917–1926). They made their interior experience, romantic love in particular, the major subject matter. For a while, writing one's personal life/love stories came into vogue and satisfied what Leo Ou-fan Lee calls the "autobiographical mania" (1973, p. 285) of Chinese readers and writers. The legitimacy of women's autobiographical fiction rested with its discursive power that endorsed the individual's rebellion against diverse institutions of oppression, most characteristically, arranged marriage and conventional hierarchical human relationships in the family and society. Through the discourse of love and personal liberation, women writers joined forces with their male contemporaries in their strife against feudalism.

Endorsement of the autobiographical sentiment, however, turned out to be transient. After the shaky coalition between the Nationalist and Communist Parties broke down with Jiang Jieshi's (1887–1975) massive purging of leftist forces in 1927, most intellectuals, deeply disillusioned, turned to Marxist and Communist ideologies as a collective choice. Under the auspices of the Chinese Communist Party, the Chinese League of Left-Wing Writers (Zhongguo zuoyi zuojia lianmeng) was formed in 1930 to promote proletarian literature. With leftist literature on the rise, women writing their lives even in the disguise of fiction became a risky affair, for the "autobiographical" had been divested of the discursive power that it had possessed during the May Fourth period and had come to be viewed as "bourgeois" and "self-indulgent." In the 1930s, with increasing Japanese aggression, literature for national defense made it politically disabling for a writer if his or her work was labeled "autobiographical." The ideal of individualism that prevailed during the May Fourth period yielded to a preoccupation with China' internal political conflict and national survival. The leftist literary ideology, the new mainstream, demanded that writing represent social realities and the nation's struggle in its crises, denouncing literature that centered around individual thought, emotion, and lifestyle. The subjective and the personal came to be severely criticized as lacking in social consciousness. The new literary ideal of social and political application took many women writers to task for their inability to move beyond their private concerns to a broader vision of social reality,[20] leading to what Wendy Larson calls the "demotion of gendered literature" (1993, p. 59). The suppression of a gender specific literature precluded the possibility of women's continued self-articulation in fiction.

Paradoxically, however, full-length autobiography as a genre, vis-à-vis traditional Chinese short self-narrations appended to more important texts, emerged at the very historical juncture when individual expression yielded to collective action. I contend that the leftist literary ideology of social engagement and removal of private sentiments presented an opportunity as well as crisis for women's writing. It channeled women's impulse toward self-representation into openly proclaimed autobiography without the mask of fiction. After all, autobiography was a genre still in the making and too marginalized to carry any critical weight and assume any social responsibility in the eyes of the intellectual mainstream. Therefore autobiographical storytelling provided a fissure, a space, in which women writers continued to articulate their personal concerns.

In the meantime, I challenge the assumption that the leftist ideology monolithically controlled the Chinese literary scene. At the height of leftism Western autobiography came to China through translation, which gave great impetus to Chinese women's autobiographical practice. Rousseau's *Confessions* (1782–1789) stands out as one of the most indisputable examples. Rendered into Chinese by Zhang Jingsheng[21] (1888–1969) for the first time in 1928 as *Chanhui lu*, Rousseau's unrestrained, unapologetic preoccupation with the growth of the individual self captured the imagination and set the trend for both female and male writers of China at the time. In the preface to *My Life*, for instance, Su Xuelin (1967) confirms the enormous impact of Rousseau's work in early twentieth-century China:

> At that time, a French saying spread to China that the most beautiful literature in the world is autobiography. A part of Rousseau's *Confessions* was translated into Chinese. Under such influence, many writers started writing autobiographies or confessions. Urged by the trend of the time, I also took this path. (Preface, p. 3)

Western women's autobiographies were also rendered into Chinese and inspired Chinese women writers to pursue the same literary goal. Xie Bingying claims that when she wrote *Autobiography of a Female Soldier* (1936), she looked to Isadora Duncan's (1877–1927) *My Life* (1927) and Agnes Smedley's (1892–1950) *Daughter of the Earth* (1929); (1936, Preface, p. 4),[22] as sources of inspiration. Western autobiographies translated into Chinese rekindled the autobiographical desire in women's writing and helped prize open a space in which Chinese women writers continued to utter what mattered to them personally.

Under Western influence, liberal intellectuals in China strongly encouraged the writing of autobiography. Hu Shi, who promoted the individualistic ideal as well as the vernacular, urged people to write their lives. Women writers responded to his call and began to come forth with their life stories. Su Xuelin remembers Hu Shi's support of (auto)biographical writing and regards his *Self-Narration at Forty* (Sishi zishu, 1933) as a role model in the preface to *My Life* (1967, p. 1). In "How I Came to Write My Autobiography," Buwei Yang Chao also attributes her autobiographical effort to Hu Shi's personal inspiration (1967, p. 1). Yuenren Chao points out that Hu Shi's "The Biography of Li Chao" (*Li Chao zhuan*, 1919)[23] and *Self-Narration at Forty* set examples for Buwei Yang Chao's autobiographical endeavor (1947, Foreword, i). Thus, we can see that the desire of self-representation, suppressed in fiction in the 1930s, found outlet in a different genre fanned by Western autobiographical culture and Chinese liberalism. As no other available means of representation permitted and contained women writers' impulse to tell their personal histories, the advent of full-length autobiography was a matter of necessity, a historical inevitability.

What did women writers accomplish in autobiography? My research shows that as the requirement of social and political application in literature compelled them to redirect their self-representational desire from mainstream fiction into the less noticeable autobiography, women writers did not just fill the new niche with the same plot of romantic love that had informed their fiction. In their fiction, the female protagonists often appear as lovers in a self-chosen relationship or wives in the modern, nuclear family, new identities vis-à-vis traditional gender roles in the conventional household. In their autobiographies, however, they changed their strategy of self-expression and emerged as writers, repressing and sublimating romantic love into literary creativity. Through the celebration of themselves as writing agents, pursuit of the freedom to love with their bodies gave way to aspiration to create with their intellect. They successfully established the unprecedented female identity unequivocally as writers.

The new female identity rendered women writers at least three services: it counteracted traditional portrayals of women as martyrs of male-defined, physically constituted virtues; it clearly marked the autobiographical subjects in terms of self-definition from the lovers and wives in women's (often their own) fiction; it also set them off from their contemporary male writers' autobiographies. The key to investigating this distinct identity pivots on intellectual disembodiment, a gesture to break away from women's conventional definition based on biology and to rein1vent themselves through literary talent. As I remarked earlier, women's talent did not count in the real world in traditional times. What did count for women was feminine virtue performed through the body, such as sexual chastity, foot-binding, self-mutilation, and widow suicide. For example, countless traditional biographies of women by male writers and historians focused narrowly on women's willingness to hurt and destroy their own bodies to earn a good name. Such representation defined women as nothing more than corporal beings. More often than not, female writers in the past accepted and complied with the gender norms imposed on them. In contrast, women writers in the 1930s celebrated themselves as tellers of their own stories and carved out a brand-new image away and against conventional views of women as somatic beings with little intellect. This new identity also obtained for women writers a subject position vis-à-vis traditional women's status as object of male representation.

The same cerebral turn clearly distinguished women's autobiography from their fiction. In fiction, female protagonists, lovers and wives so to speak, spill their grievances into the more private forms of diary and letter but never aspire to the status of the public writer, and writers are gendered as male rather than female. As Wendy Larson incisively points out, "Never did [women writers] depict women who are directly and unproblematically writers" (1998, p. 147).

In their autobiographies, however, women writers no longer accepted the positions of lovers and wives, but redefined themselves as professionals, most often as writers, without ambiguity. They often concentrated on their pursuit of education, their paths to independence, and their literary accomplishments, minimizing, and in some cases eliminating, details of marriage, sexuality, and childbearing. A professional image unencumbered by family relationships and household chores, this self-reinvention constituted a significant revision to the gendering of the writer as male in women's fiction.

It is worth noting that, quite unlike many of their contemporary male writers' self-representations, the newly refashioned self in women's autobiography by no means embraced the role imposed on writers by the leftist literary trend to represent contemporary practical issues and social realities since the 1930s. While male writers of the time portrayed literary work negatively and sought to apply themselves in socially and politically more significant ways in their autobiographies (Larson 1991, pp. 1–10), many women writers did not share this tendency. Instead, women writers held fast to their literary identity, as writing meant to them nothing less than "an existential art of self-definition" (Feuerwerker 1975, p. 158). The difference in self-perception as writers between Chinese female and male writers finds a parallel in the way that some Western feminist critics of autobiography resisted the postmodern skepticism about self and authorizing. As Nancy K. Miller (1988) insists, "… the postmodern decision that the Author is Dead and the subject along with him does not … necessarily hold for women, and prematurely forecloses the question of agency for them" (p. 106). By the same token, it was impossible for modern Chinese women writers to squander their new privilege as writers, simply because taking up writing as a profession and means of livelihood was an unprecedented accomplishment and an avenue to emancipation from traditional profiles and gender roles.

Placed in a global context, modern Chinese women's life writing adds a different dimension to the current theorizing and study of women's autobiography. Feminist theorists of women's autobiography in the late 1970s, such as Mary G. Mason and Estelle C. Jelinek, already began to debunk the myth of autobiography as a linear narrative on the development of Western white male subjectivity (Smith & Watson 1998, pp. 8–10). In the years that followed, diverse new conceptions of women's autobiography proliferated. Of reference value to Chinese women's autobiography, Françoise Lionnet's concept of "autoethnography" refers to "the defining of one's subjective ethnicity as mediated through language, history and ethnographical analysis" (Smith & Watson, p. 177). Domna C. Stanton's coinage "autogynography" draws attention to a whole spectrum of characteristics of some women's autobiographical writing — narrative discontinuity, domestic details, female bodily desires, and what not (Smith & Watson, p. 137). To assist the reader in better understanding women's self-representation as opposed to men's, Sidonie Smith (1993) contrasts the traditional autobiographical male self, typically depicted as unencumbered by the body, with the ways in which many Western women writers take up the body in negotiating their gender, cultural, and racial identities (pp. 1–24). Feminist autobiography critics, such as Susan S. Friedman and Mary Mason, observe that Western women's autobiographies typically feature female identity defined in relational terms (Smith & Watson, pp. 72–82, 321–24). The single-minded emphasis on intellectual pursuit and literary accomplishments in Chinese women's autobiographies most conspicuously differs from the use of life writing as a means of achieving ethnic or sexual identity in the multi-cultural West. Chinese women writers first and foremost avoided the rhetoric of embodiment and family relation as parameters of self-definition, a strategy sometimes employed by Western women writers. Still more intriguingly, modern Chinese women writers' self-conscious erasure of their marriage, family, and children in their autobiographies much resembled the physically unencumbered identity established in Western male writers' autobiographies, as remarked by Smith. Indeed, almost all the Chinese women autobiographers tended to deny their gender identity and tried to identify with male rather than female literary predecessors. With their salient feature of intellectual disembodiment, autobiographies by modern Chinese women contribute importantly to the rich tradition of women's life writing worldwide.

The Anxiety of Modern Chinese Women Writers' Autobiography

So far, I have attempted to show how modern Chinese women's autobiography grew out of its historical circumstances and what women writers accomplished in the genre. I hasten to point out that they shared with Chinese ancients the sense of taboo about self-exposure, which revealed itself in the process of their storytelling. Most of them displayed a considerable amount of psychological hindrance in writing their personal history and usually resorted to prefaces or other means to rationalize, defend, and apologize for their autobiographical acts. For instance, Su Xuelin's life writing most clearly exhibits such tension. In the preface to *My Life*, Su invokes Hu Shi's appeal for autobiography in order to legitimize her act. She felt embarrassed about writing her life, because she thought she had little literary and academic attainment to deserve it (Preface, pp. 1–3). Su performs the same ritual of modesty in the preface to *Ninety-Four Years of a Floating Life*, where she insists that she was "compelled by circumstances" to write it. To the repeated invitations of the editor and publisher, she replied: "I have *Love for My Mother*[24] … and *My Life* … Besides, only a person of historical importance deserves to write an autobiography. I am an unworthy and unaccomplished person. If I do the same, wouldn't I be a laughingstock? Let's just forget about it" (Preface, p. 1). Su's misgiving confirms the Chinese historical notion that an autobiography should be an account of the subject's public deeds, not their private life, just as traditional biography focused on a person's communal services, literary achievement, and moral virtue. The fact that she shared this idea sheds much light on the ways that her contemporary female writers chose to concentrate on their career and omit details of their family life.

In Xie Bingying's case, her foreword to the 1936 edition of *Autobiography of a Female Soldier* reveals that writing her autobiography also proved to be a difficult process. Although by 1930 she had completed the narration of her life in elementary and middle schools, she would not have thought of publishing it but for the urging of a publisher. At the end of the foreword, she acknowledges her debt to Western role models that she found in modern dancer Isadora Duncan's *My Life* (1927) and leftist journalist Agnes Smedley's *Daughter of the Earth* (1929). It was due to the inspiration she found in these two women's courageous acts to write their life experiences that Xie's determination prevailed over psychological hurdle and cultural etiquette (Foreword, pp. 1–5). By this, however, I do not intend to create a binary opposition between Chinese reserve and Western candor, for many Western women writers also tried to rationalize their autobiographical acts, even Isadora Duncan and Agnes Smedley who inspired for women writers in China.

Chen Hengzhe's *Autobiography of a Chinese Young Girl*, an account of the young female subject's unbending will in pursuing education against the odds of her time, was written in English and published in 1935 in the United States under the name of Chen Nan-hua. According to her own explanation, she concealed her real identity so that the story "might be taken as a kind of specimen" of her generation of women who struggled in the "whirlpool of cultural and social conflicts" of China and "attempted to shape their own lives from that whirling current" (Foreword, p. vi). Here the writer's individual history embodies the untold stories of numerous women in China's agonies and convulsions of modernization. In spite of her explanation, the writer's decision not to use her real name in this narrative of outspoken feminism insinuates a need for invisibility that resonates with the traditional Chinese dilemma created by the desire for and the taboo against self-representation.

Unlike many of its contemporary works, Lu Yin's autobiography does not depend on a self-written preface to justify its existence. However, it took repeated efforts on the writer's part to eventually come forth with her story. According to Lu Yin's biographer Xiao Feng (1982), Lu Yin started writing her life story entitled *A Brief Biography of a Girl Named Yin* (*Yin niang xiao zhuan*) in 1919 while she was at college. Instead of publishing it, however, Lu Yin destroyed it (p. 25). In her autobiography, Lu Yin (1934) recalls how anxious she felt in the writing process:

> But this kind of experimental work should be kept as quiet as possible. Otherwise, if it came out bad, I would be a laughingstock. Therefore, I stayed away from everybody everyday, hiding in a corner in the library and writing secretly. A few days later I read over my writing and found it disorganized and unsystematic. Discouraged, I put it away at the bottom of my suitcase. This unfinished draft was never completed. Two years ago I burned it. It is nothing now but a trace of memory in my writing career. (p. 80)

The secrecy and shame might well have derived from a pang of conscience against acting as one's own historian. Her figurative self-destruction might also be a manifestation of guilt about the "immodest" project of self-commemoration. She imagines writing another autobiography at an older age and hopes to earn the right to it with "one or two literary masterpieces" (p. 88).

However, modern Chinese women writers' self-representational complex compelled them to tell their individual stories despite the repressive literary ideology of their time and cultural disapproval in general. Leaving behind the images of romantic lovers and frustrated wives in their fiction, women writers adopted textual work as the term of self-definition and portrayed themselves as the first generation of women writers and other professionals in the space of autobiography.

The Variety of Modern Chinese Women's Autobiography

Given the tremendous amount of cultural, historical, and political difficulty, Chinese women writers performed feats in pouring out the stories of their lives at a time when China could least afford to foster the writing of autobiography. These stories told in the unique voices of the writers during the war years will throw new light on the Chinese autobiographical tradition and play a vital role in enriching and redefining the study of Chinese autobiography. In the following pages, I will briefly discuss the writers and their narratives represented in this volume.

Set in Beijing during the May Fourth period, An E's "How I Left My Mother" plays out the silent psychological drama between the female subject and her mother in the daughter's struggle to leave the confines of home and become an active patriot. The daughter was a college student actively involved in the May Fourth Movement. One day she was shocked and humiliated to find that her mother had personally come to school to take her home. When they reached home, she lost freedom. Mother and daughter never confronted each other, each reading the other's mind exactly. They possessed equally strong wills, so neither gave in to the other. In this mental, unspoken enmity, their mutual love became mingled with frustration and hatred. The mother felt that she would rather see her daughter die than let her trespass traditional rules of propriety, and no one knew better than the daughter what the mother was thinking. In the end, the daughter seized the opportunity of her mother's short absence and left home to seek a life of independence in society. The story fully demonstrates the generational differences between the mother and the daughter and young women's struggle at the time to escape from the shackle of the family.

Bai Wei's "Jumping Through Hoops" reenacts the subject Huang Zhang's narrow escape from family and institutional imprisonment in the early 1920s. In the story, Huang Zhang and her two younger sisters all studied at Hunan First Female Normal School in Changsha. Their father, a wealthy and influential man in their hometown on the border of Hunan and Guangdong, expected to marry off the two younger girls to his local connections and force Huang Zhang back to her abusive husband and mother-in-law. Huang Zhang secretly made arrangements to travel to Changsha, Hankou, Tokyo, and eventually to Paris. However, her plan was discovered. Her father had bribed the school authorities, so they had the whole campus surrounded to keep watch on her. After repeated trials and failures, she eventually got away from a usually closed, unused entrance to an old lavatory with the help of her school friends. They called that little entrance their Arch of Triumph. "Jumping Through Hoops" also strongly critiques sex discrimination in China in the 1940s from an outspoken feminist point of view, which marks Bai's autobiography from many of her contemporaries' writings.

Chu Wenjuan's "Imprints of Life" tells of the subject's childhood misery and career struggle during the war years. The seventh daughter in a late Qing official's family in Zhejiang, the young girl was unwanted, neglected, misunderstood, and often depressed. She found comfort in poetry and history, which continued in her adulthood. As an adult she participated in the May Fourth Movement and later became a teacher, writer, wife, and mother. The narrative offers a detailed description of her frustration with family life and the negative effect it had on her literary career. Particularly interesting is the portrayal of her stress and eventual success as a female editor of a literary journal in the Nationalist army where most officers harbored serious doubts about the competence of women.

Lin Beili's "A Journey of Twenty-Seven Years" offers a positive picture of mother-daughter relationship and shows the direct influence of the mother on the daughter's path to independence. Much of the narrative describes the subject's parents, especially the mother, Xu Yunhua, a unique woman active in her career pursuits. The narrator recounts how the mother transformed into a revolutionary from a young lady in the boudoir of a conventional, wealthy home and the hardship she experienced as a wife, mother, and widow. The mother's inner conflicts anticipated the double burden of career and family of modern Chinese women that was to persist for generations to come. In contrast to other women writers' representations of their mothers as surrogate oppressors on behalf of the patriarchal society, Lin portrays her mother as a role model and source of inspiration. What also gives the story texture is the portrayal of the mother's interference with the daughter's first love, the scar it left on the mother-daughter relationship, and their reconciliation during the war years.

Peng Hui's "A Brief Autobiography" begins with the subject's early life. The little girl's father died, leaving behind four young daughters and their widowed mother. Living with the sexism of the family and society, mother and daughters kept to themselves on their limited financial resources after the father's property was divided among his relatives. The gifted mother gave her daughters a good literary education at home through telling them stories from the rich repertoire of Chinese folk literature. After the mother died, the four orphaned girls paid for their school education with their dowries. Literary preparation at home and at school helped pave the way for the subject's later career as writer and translator. As an adult, the subject married and had children. Her writing career was continually disrupted by childcare and by the war. But she managed to read, write, translate, and publish.

Xie Bingying was an internationally acclaimed writer and feminist. "Midpoint of an Ordinary Life" recalls the young Bingying's fight to resist foot-binding and arranged marriage, her patriotic passion, her experience as a soldier, writer, and editor, and life as a mother determined to bring up her children for China. Her personal story was closely bound up with the history of China during the turbulence of the 1920s and throughout the War of Resistance against Japan. At the conclusion of the narrative she apologizes for her "unworthiness" and resolves to work harder to make herself a more useful person in society.

Ye Zhongyin's "My Autobiography" begins with the heroine's lonesome childhood and the the new self she found in singing, dancing, and acting after entering school. As acting was not open to women and was considered a lowly occupation then, the subject's pursuit of acting as her life's work reveals much about her personality as well as the changing gender norms in her time. As a professional actor, she participated in "drama for national defense" together with eminent dramatists during the War of Resistance against Japan. Performing numerous Chinese and foreign plays on resistance themes around China, she did her part for her country and improved steadily as an actor.

Zhao Qingge's "Can This Also Be Called an Autobiography?" touches the reader's heart with the young girl's love for crickets in her solitude and the tragic loss of her loved ones during the Japanese occupation. The narrative begins with a nostalgic recollection of the North where the subject grew up. Abused by her father and stepmother, she had no one but her grandmother to turn to for love and comfort. Having no companions to spend time with, she found consolation in and fell in love with songs of crickets. When her pet cricket died, she placed it in a match box, buried it under an osmanthus tree she had planted with her own hands, and offered chrysanthemums at its grave. Upon graduation from high school at seventeen, she worked in the same school while preparing for college entrance examinations. She became friends with a young male staff member named Little Mahu who shared her passion for crickets. With the elapse of many years, the end of the story laments the loss of the subject's homeland and lovingly remembers her grandmother and Little Mahu, who were among the countless people who had lost their lives during the war. Through reminiscences of the two people who touched the young girl's life, the narrative gives a glimpse of her inner life and tangentially reflects the historical context of the time.

Zi Gang's "Self-Criticism and Self-Encouragement" presents the challenge faced by a female journalist during the War of Resistance against Japan. Zi Gang wrote this short autobiographical account upon the request of young women interested in pursuing journalism as a career. She reflects on her responsibility and questions her position to speak adequately for the wounded soldiers who fought for their country and female factories workers who toiled long hours to support their families, being aware of how her privileged status set her apart from the people who depended on her for representation. She also calls attention to the evils and corruption of high society that she as a journalist witnessed but lacked the power to expose. Gender issues constitute another area of the Zi Gang's concern in the narrative, particularly the conflict between career and family for women. Uneasy about focusing on herself, she declares at the end that the narrative only serves the purpose of self-motivation and does not provide a role model for other women.

For readers accustomed to book-length autobiographies that narrate lives in a more extended manner, it is crucial to note the scope of these narratives and how they helped construct and define the genre of autobiography in the historical context of the 1940s. As the narratives here demonstrate, any given moment in the writers' life deserves remembering. An autobiographical narrative can begin *in medias res* and capture a critical juncture in a subject's life as exemplified by An E's "How I Left My Mother" and Bai Wei's "Jumping Through Hoops." It can tell one's childhood trauma and give a detailed account of one's career path, such as Chu Wenjuan's "Imprints of Life," Peng Hui's "A Brief Autobiography," and Ye Zhongyin's "My Autobiography." It can focus entirely on reflections of one's professional life as Zi Gang's "Self-Criticism and Self-Encouragement." It can give a chronological account of family genealogy in addition to one's own life in the manner of Lin Beili's "A Journey of Twenty-Seven Years." It can also summarize one's life and career experiences up to the point of writing as does Xie Bingying's "Midpoint of an Ordinary Life." And it can certainly be a heart-warming, nostalgic as well as implicitly tragic tale like Zhao Qingge's "Can This Also Be Called an Autobiography?"

These autobiographical narratives, unique in their own ways, share common themes. They all portray the subjects' efforts to break out of the sex discrimination and oppression in the traditional home from which the only avenue to liberation was the pursuit of education and participation in the revolutionary tides of their time. Written during the War of Resistance against Japan, these stories all reveal the impact of the war on the personal lives and careers of the subjects and the ways in which they tried to help their country. Following the convention of full-length autobiographies by women writers of the 1930s, these stories demonstrate the tendency to focus on the subjects' professional lives, most often their literary endeavors. Written in the early stage of the writers' careers, most of these narratives assume a forward-looking position at the end, moving beyond the integration of the present with the past. The drive to direct their stories toward the future and work harder for greater prospects in life invokes what Elizabeth N. Evasdaughter calls "futuristic women's autobiographies" (1995, p. 131). The narrators in the stories here envision not only a better future for themselves but also equality for all women and prosperity for their country.

Carefully annotated, these stories bring out sparkling points in the rich cultural and literary heritage of China, such as folktales, historical legends, musical drama, poetry, fiction, storytelling, and music. They also showcase a multitude of literary journals and newspapers that promoted the New Literature and contributed to China's modernization. Of these narratives, Ye Zhongyin's self-representation is particularly noteworthy, because it depicts the significant role that spoken drama played in China's struggle for national survival during the War of Resistance against Japan. The notes to her story offer rare information about modern Chinese drama and dramatists, information that cannot be found in any single sourcebook. All of these elements add to the value and usability of this collection as a textbook.

The translation and annotation took long hours of intensive work, but all the effort will be made worthwhile if this book contributes to the corpus of Chinese women's autobiographical narratives in English, fills the gap of women's life stories during the War of Resistance against Japan, and offers new perspectives to the study of women's autobiography in a global context, which are goals that I stated at the opening of these introductory remarks.

Jing M. Wang

How I Left My Mother

An E

Translated by Jing M. Wang

An E (1905–76), *originally named Zhang Shiyuan, also known as Ding Na, was from Huailu, Hebei. She distinguished herself as a song lyric writer, poet, playwright, novelist, translator as well as an outspoken feminist. She graduated from the National School of Fine Arts (*Guoli meishu zhuanmen xuexiao*) in Beijing in 1925 and joined the Communist Party in the same year. She studied at Zhongshan University in Moscow from 1927 to 1929. In the 1930s and throughout the War of Resistance against Japan, An was actively involved in left-wing film in support of China's national survival. "Song of the Fishermen" (*Yu guang qu*) and "Newspaper Selling Song" (*Mai bao ge*) are among her well-known songs. After 1949, she became a professional writer at Beijing People's Art Theater (*Beijing renmin yishu juyuan*), China Experimental Theater (*Zhongguo shiyan jutuan*), and China Association of Dramatists (*Zhongguo juzuojia xiehui*). Her representative works include a collection of poetry* Sons and Daughters of North China *(*Yanzhao ernü*, 1938), poetic drama* The Sorghum Has Turned Red *(*Gaoliang hong le*, 1936), Fiction of An E *(*An E xiaoshuo*, 1950), and reportage literature* The Growth of A Labor Hero *(*Yige laodong yingxiong de chengzhang*, 1951).*

My classmates told me that Mother recently waited for me everyday in the school reception room. When I first heard about it, I did not quite believe it.

"Mother is so highborn in her manners," I thought, "and she puts a lot of stress on 'status.' How could she have waited for me in the reception room with all the servants there? I remember that when I first moved into the school dorm, mother was very upset that I would condescend so much as to share a room with poor girls. Maybe my classmates mistook someone else's mother for mine. But they were very certain that it was my mother that they saw. Perhaps she just asked about me a few times at the reception room, and my classmates were very inaccurate when they said she was sitting there. Well, if she just wanted to ask about me, why bother dropping by personally?" I never understood why, and simply gave up.

Although I did not believe that Mother actually came, I didn't dare go to classes. It wouldn't affect my grades whether I attended classes or not. Especially at a school of fine arts such as the one I attended, a few extra paintings at the end of the semester would guarantee good grades. But today I had to go to school, to attend a meeting. At the meeting we would plan student demonstrations on a broader scale in Beijing to protest against Japanese imperialism and warlordism. Unfortunately, this meeting would be held on campus. Recently, it was in fact rather hard for twenty people to gather except at Beijing University and Chaoyang University. It was easier to find space at BU, and CU didn't attract a lot of attention. But the students of our school had ways to deal with the authorities. The former president had left and the new president was not sworn in yet. The students had maintained a good relationship with the staff of the Dean's office over the past six months or so. The staff members of the Dean's office all supported the Northern Expedition Army,[1] and some of them had once worked in Guangzhou. Therefore, they wouldn't interfere even if they knew about our meeting. Besides, some of my classmates' fathers and brothers were very influential figures, and these students were fearless.

It was now November according to the lunar calendar, but it was very sunny in the North. As long as the sun was out, it felt just like spring. It was as sunny today as the day before, and it was not windy. As soon as the sunshine touched the window panes, I rose from my canvas recliner. I rolled up my bedding as usual and put it on the empty shelf next door. Then I groomed myself and walked ten li^2 to class. I was the earliest riser in the school. Class began at nine o'clock, and I set out around seven. Before, I used to buy two freshly baked sesame biscuits, hide them at one end of my white scarf, and eat them in a quiet corner of the street. I couldn't relish them slowly as I would at home, but took big bites when no one was looking. Then I covered my mouth with my handkerchief as if to keep away the dust and swallowed quickly. Recently, I run out of biscuit money; so I was free from the inconvenience of eating in such a manner. When I saw the peddlers coming, I just walked on without even glancing at them. Today we were supposed to convene at eleven o'clock. I left my room around seven as usual in order to go to some of my classmates' places to find out if Mother had indeed waited for me in the reception room. I got to Lingyu's house quickly. She confirmed that Mother had come for me, and she too, found it surprising.

"I suggest you change into a different outfit! Perhaps that way your mother won't recognize you," Lingyu said.

I walked with Lingyu to her bedroom. She found a black *qipao*³ for me from her wardrobe.

"Here, since you never wear black, this might help a little," saying that she handed me the *qipao*.

I looked at her without taking it. Thinking that I didn't recall, she said, "Don't you remember? Qin, you and I each made a *qipao* like this. You kept yours here. You can have it back now."

How could I forget this *qipao*? Since the three of us had the three dresses made, Qin and I had sadly parted ways! Since that time, I never wanted to set my eyes on that dress again. That was why I asked Lingyu to keep it for me.

Lingyu and I were not classmates. But because she was Qin's best friend, she was also my friend. The three of us hung out for over a year. We visited Hot Spring Hills, Fragrant Hills, Longevity Hills, and every known corner around the Qinghua campus. We also enjoyed good food at many restaurants around Huguo Temple, Heavenly Bridge, and indeed all over the eastern and western parts of the city. We took the city loop train sightseeing in the suburbs. We chatted and sang all night, discussed on the phone the New Testament (Xin yue quan shu) and the Old Testament (Jiu yue quan shu) for hours during the day, and we talked about films or sang arias from traditional operas. We were carefree, and knew nothing about society and life. However, to the question "What is the purpose of life?" the three of us had three different answers. I said, "People begin to die on the day they are born. I hope not to leave any trace of me after death, so that no one can talk about me, as if I had never existed."

Lingyu said, "I don't understand why I should live. It would be best for the world to be rid of people. I'd rather women remain unmarried and enjoy freedom until the end of their days."

"I don't care about the meaning of life. Nor does it matter to me if people talk about me after I die. As long as no one irritates me, no one interferes with my life, my brother still loves me after he gets married, I will die contented at the age of thirty-five. I wouldn't bother to think how heart-broken mother, father, and brother will be. All I know is that I will be free from any responsibilities after death."

Even though we had different opinions, we never imposed our views on one another. Sometimes we argued about trivial things, yet we did that for the sake of argument and never cared who won. We often ended our arguments by saying, "Oh, you're impossible!" We talked endlessly, but never fell out with one another because of our individual ideas.

Lingyu knew my family as much as I did. She understands all the subtle feelings between Mother and me. She knew that I was an obedient daughter to Mother most of the time, and that Mother loved me very much. But the divergent outlooks on life caused a gap between Mother and me. My obedience gradually turned into revolt. She could not avoid my rebellion, just like the rocks by the sea could not escape lashes from the waves. Mother had mixed feelings of love and hatred for me, for I did not grow up to be the kind of person she had expected me to be. Her hatred for me gripped her heart like a chain. Any slight move would cause her pain. But we were mother and daughter! As long as feudal traditions existed, there was no way to resolve our conflicts, although I had once hoped to work it out with her.

"All right! I will bear it out! When I get married, we can get along as friends," I said to myself.

However, I did not really want to marry as a way to end this pain. On the contrary, I did not want to get married at all. My argument with Qin over this issue cost us our friendship. Qin had wanted me to marry her brother and thereby gain independence from my impossible family. But I refused. Our different positions led to our breakup! I admit that parental oppression sometimes made girls want to marry early as an escape. But that was just one way out, and I did not think that I had to resort to that.

Lingyu also knew that Mother considered reconciliation with me. Sometimes Mother was so frustrated that she would rather I died. She could then grieve and give me a decent funeral afterward. It would be easier that way. She hated to see me take a path against her will. She could not bear the thought that her daughter could be thrown into jail or beheaded!

Mother and I never articulated these thoughts, yet we could read each other's minds.

However, I did not want to wear the dress that Lingyu had found for me. Lingyu whispered to me:

"Or, you could wait outside the school for a while. When more people arrive, you could go among them unnoticed."

I nodded and walked out of her house despondently. I did not remember today's event until I reached the school entrance. I entered with much misgiving, without turning to look into the reception room. No one stopped me.

"Mother did not come today? Maybe my friends were mistaken after all," I almost congratulated myself.

I was just thinking these thoughts when I heard my name called from behind.

"Yuan! Yuan!"

I turned calmly to see a forced smile on Mother's face. Of course, Mother did not want to embarrass me. On such an occasion, if she had embarrassed me, she would have embarrassed herself. Suppose she had been rude to me, I would have been rude back and would not have followed her home. Then we would have hurt each other's feelings beyond repair.

"Let's go home!" I suggested, putting on a smile, before Mother had time to say anything.

My classmates looked at me in surprise. Without bidding them goodbye, I left with Mother. Usually I would take the rickshaw behind Mother's, but this time Mother said to me, "You take the front one."

I did not expect that, but did not suspect anything. When the rickshaw started moving, I suddenly felt deeply humiliated! I bit my lower lip and kept back my tears! I felt that I was under surveillance!

"I'm your daughter, not your prisoner!" I said in my mind. "Do I have to obey you just because I'm your daughter? Did you bear and raise me to shame and torture me? Did you produce a machine to vent your anger on?"

Irritation, fear, shame, and anger filled my heart!

"What's Mother going to do with me? ... Fifth Brother and his wife will be ever so triumphant!" I was scared to think of the moment when I would enter their house.

When we got to the railway station, we just missed a train. My rickshaw driver did not quite know where he was going. It was noisy and dusty outside.

"Oh, how annoying! It's so stupid of you!" I took out my frustration on the rickshaw driver, stamping my foot petulantly. Unintentionally, I pressed on the bell and attracted attention from a lot of people. This so irritated me that tears came to my eyes. I did not raise my hand to wipe them away so as not to let Mother see that I was crying. I did not want to show any signs of weakness. I kept my eyes wide open, looked into the horizon, and forced my tears back.

"Take your time. No hurry," Mother's voice carried gently from behind. I knew she was trying to be nice to me — to show me that she did not mean any harm by taking me home. But her effort really made me feel hurt by a loved one.

"But I'm me! I'm a human being! Why do you bother to take me home?" These words kept ringing in my mind.

When we reached Fifth Brother's house and saw him, he just smiled and then turned away. He still held a grudge against me for taking away his microscope and medicines, although I did not regret avenging myself. His attitude now made me wish I had destroyed his entire hospital.

The atmosphere was awfully tense. I did not say a word, nor did Mother and Fifth Brother. I made a phone call to my school friends, asking them to send my belongings to me. Hearing my friends' voices, I choked with tears. Their laughter made me feel lonely, just like a ship that had lost its bearings in the sea, drifting aimlessly with the waves.

As Mother and Fifth Brother were both listening, I could only tell my friends that I wanted my things to be sent to me. In fact, I did not want anything. I was simply trying to make my friends understand my situation, to let them know that I had not missed the meeting for no reason.

When lunch was ready, I did not want to eat with Mother and Fifth Brother at the same table, because I did not want them to know how I felt. So I said I wanted fried rice. When I was served fried rice, I went to another room to eat by myself. Tears fell into the rice, and I had no appetite whatsoever. But I forced the food down my throat, so I could get sick with indigestion and stay in bed without having to talk to anyone.

My school friends sent over what I had left in school: a little imported knife, a fountain pen, a box of painter's supplies, two painting albums, and a silk dress. They gave me some pretty envelopes and writing paper as gifts.

Mother took the dress in her hands and checked the buttons. She said, "Is this the dress you plan to wear at my birthday celebration?"

"Yes."

"I bet you wore it already?" Mother said confrontationally.

"No."

"No? I can tell from the button holes," she said, sounding very hostile. Perhaps Mother felt it was an insult if I had worn the dress before her birthday.

I restrained myself. I thought, I had a right to wear my dress whenever I pleased. As long as I had decent clothes to wear on her birthday, it was all right.

"Maybe it was from trying it on," I answered, holding back my impatience.

"How did the embroidery get rubbed?"

I was about to lose my cool, but I checked myself!

"Maybe I did not keep it well," I said.

"Try it on for me."

My God! How could anyone be so irritating? Oh, merciless God!

"Come on!" Mother demanded.

I would never want to wear this dress — this symbol of injustice! I had to have it made because Third Brother planned to host a public celebration of Mother's birthday at his official post, so he could use the occasion to fleece the local landowners and peasants of their money. He wanted Mother to serve as a bait for him and my sister and me as Mother's company. Mother wrote and told me to have a dress made. Reluctant as I was, I had to be prepared, just in case Mother decided to go.

"Try it on!" Mother urged again.

Mother's words came as a gentle command. I put on the dress to avoid argument. Mother was very critical of the dress.

Mother, Younger Sister, and I would be leaving the next day for Baoding, and then we would go to Shijiazhuang. There, we would join some other families to collect gifts at Third Brother's office.

At night I slept in a very comfortable room. The bedding was first rate, too. Yes, in this family, I enjoyed the most material comfort. I had special privileges among my siblings; but I was also the sole object of Mother's oppression. In other words, I was given priority in both physical and spiritual terms. Because Mother took out all her anger on me, she always tried to reward me in some tangible form. Therefore, I got compensation for my mental suffering. I remember Fifth Brother once trying to ingratiate himself with Mother, "When I was little, I often longed to grow up so Mother wouldn't scold me anymore! Now, when I'm away from home for long, I miss Mother. Yet, I feel scared of Mother in less than three days!" What he said upset me. I said to myself: "If I could be free from being scolded, I wouldn't mind not having a mother! I just don't want anyone to control my life. I'd rather live in poverty and give everything for freedom! Wealth, power, family, and kin combined were not as valuable as freedom!"

My brothers and I received and responded to Mother's scolding differently. To them, it was merely annoying, like the humming of flies and mosquitoes. For me, in addition to that, I had to deal with the anger and frustration caused by differences of opinion with Mother. I could not and dared not argue with her. Nor was it of any use to do so. In her old age, the historical changes that had taken place dampened all her ambitions in life. She had thus become touchy and irritable. I was the one to bear the brunt of it.

At the end of every scolding, Mother and I would have the same conversation. As soon as I heard its beginning, I felt so relieved that I would say to myself: "It's going to be over."

"Don't you think I'm right?" Mother would say.

"Yes, you're right." I would reply.

"Will you respect what I say?"

"Yes, I will."

"Have you learned it by heart?"

"Yes, I have."

"Will you disobey me again?"

"No, I won't."

But she never demanded what I most feared, which is, "Now repeat to me what I've just said." If she had asked that, I would have been undone. Even though I dreaded this and tried to be ready for it, I could never bring myself to pay attention to her instructions in the recent two years. I only heard one sound: "Buzz!" I only noticed one word: "Nag!"

We went to Baoding the next day by train. When we got to Fourth Brother's house, he had already left for his factory. Only Sister-in-law was at home. She was nice to me. Fourth Brother was also a very good person. Although he owned a factory, he liked to socialize and interact with people rather than obsess with his business. Since he was not at home, I was rather quiet. In my family, I basically kept to myself and did not mind anyone else's business. Although Sister-in-law and I were on friendly terms, she did not really understand how I felt. So I did not say much.

Mother did not really want to go to Third Brother's place for her birthday. She knew that it was not only exploitation but also showing off. Third Brother was muddle-headed about financial matters. Father hit him many times because of it. Concerned that he might get reported to the authorities for taking bribes, Mother wanted to cancel the celebration altogether. Although she became bad-tempered in old age, she still had good character. She never fawned over the wealthy and befriended them only if they were virtuous people and if they initiated contact with her. This was because she did not want her children to become vain and badly influenced. I never saw a woman who cared less about money. Mother often said to us: "Wealth is a trivial thing, but face is worth a lifetime's fortune." Whenever she heard us talk about money, she would scold us: "Money! Money! You are forever talking about money! People shouldn't care for nothing but money! People should have character and virtue! Open your eyes and think far! You lowly idiots!" Mother always helped the less fortunate. She gave food, clothing, and other necessities to her poor friends. In return she asked that they should be industrious and thrifty. She often advised us, "Don't always look up. Look down. If all other people live in poverty, you will feel bad wallowing in your riches."

When Third Brother proposed to celebrate Mother's birthday publicly, Mother never agreed. Everyone in the family except Third Brother thought it was a wrong thing to do. But Third Brother insisted that he just wanted to hold a birthday party for Mother. Normally, this was a filial act and a mother's honor. What's wrong with that? But because I was forced to participate, I had a right to express my opinion. I said to Mother, "I'm not going."

Seeing that I quit, Mother felt more reluctant to go. "Why should we make other people spend money on us?" she said. Mother wrote to tell Third Brother her thought. She said if he insisted, he could do it without her presence. Now, what remained was the struggle between Mother and me. I was thinking every minute of the day: "How do I persuade her to go?" Mother was also thinking every minute of the day: "I'll stay for her." Maybe she had planned it all out? She had not scolded me a bit since she found me at school. Instead, she overwhelmed me with three big themes: eating, clothing, and *majiang*! On my part, living in poverty for the past few months, I was at the end of my rope and could do with a break. However, I was not going to live like this forever. I knew full well that it was wrong to lead such a life. Since the money I used was not even honest money, how could the life that I led using that money be anything but immoral? As long as I knew what I was doing, it was all right, I thought. Therefore, I slept until eleven o'clock the next morning. I washed myself, ate breakfast, and for the rest of the day, played cards, watched operatic shows, and occasionally scolded the servants. As New Year was approaching, it was a time for relaxing, and I just enjoyed myself with the rest of the family.

Letters from my school friends reached me. Between the lines I could feel their youthful enthusiasm. They called for me to rejoin them! They tried to persuade me to follow a path of real happiness. I became restless, for I wanted to go back to school. Yet I lacked a reason to present to Mother. After all, school did not start yet. Mother perceived everything, and she was no less restless than I was. I knew I would get out sometime, and I just agitated to leave sooner rather than later. Mother felt very differently. She knew that if I had my way this time, she would never be able to regain control of me! Thus, she figured out a way, which was to make me get married. She said to others: "Marriage will change her way of life, which will in turn change her thought. Gradually she will agree with her mother and her family." Convinced that she was right, she quoted a saying: "All water returns to the sea." That saying really angered me. Lacking the courage to talk back, I said to myself: "OK. Let's wait and see!" Did Mother really want me to marry? Not at all! As her first daughter, I served as the object of her anger. Before that task was transferred to my younger sister, Mother would never let go of me, even though my younger sister was just beginning to get promoted to the status of "target of Mother's anger"! Indeed, Mother felt a secret joy over me, her elder daughter, a joy that no one could share! I remember that every day after I put on makeup and got dressed up, she looked at me with satisfaction as she would a flower, a plaything, an exhibit. If I neglected to do this, she would feel disappointed, as if the exhibit had been removed from the house. But Mother's appreciation rather resembled eating ice cream. The coolness is in the eating, and then it is over. By the same token, her pleasure in my appearance was also a fleeting one.

Recently she indeed talked with people about the issue of my marriage, as if it was really going to happen. Since I knew she did it for self-assurance, I just considered it some plot in a novel.

Father ran a school, which was situated in an old administrative office complex. Behind the complex, there was an unused lot and some dilapidated rooms. As it was rather warm today, my sister and I came to Father's school to look for some fun. We grabbed some newspapers from his office and went to read them outside.

"Bloodshed in front of government office on March 18th.4 Over twenty students died."

These words caught my attention. Tears streamed down my cheeks as my eyes moved through the lines! I did not want anyone to see me cry, so I took the paper behind the office building. I read it again and again, and I could not keep my tears back. I knew that if I cried my eyes out, other people could tell. But I could not help it. The report on the death of my classmate Yao Zongxian saddened me the most. I recalled his looks, his words, his paintings, his drama performance, and his speeches at our meetings … After I grieved over all the details, I read through the entire report another time and wept more. At last, I checked myself and held back my emotions. Through trying to distract myself with many irrelevant things, I managed to regain my poise and put on a normal face.

For days, news of the tragedy and Yao's death stuck in my mind. I could not enjoy life and was bored by what was going on around me. My only wish was to become part of the struggle again.

In addition, something else bothered me. I began to rise early in the morning, wash myself without waiting for warm water to be brought to me, eat breakfast, and then shut myself up in my study reading, mending my books, and putting my books in order without paying attention to anyone. Unexpectedly, this caused Mother to detest me more. She blamed me for reading all day.

"Books! Books! Books can replace your mother!" she said. "Books are dearer to you than your mother! Every time you take up a book, you ignore everyone. What good will it do for a girl to read so much? Can you hope to support yourself by becoming a teacher? Just wait for me to burn all your books, and then you'll stop reading!"

I continued to read. Sometimes Mother would snatch my book from me. Then I would take up another one. One morning I was awakened by a conversation between Mother and Younger Sister. I looked out of the window to see Younger Sister kneeling in front of Mother saying, "I'll quit school and keep Mother company at home."

It was so ridiculous! In the eighteen years of my life, I had never seen Mother reduced to doing this — having another person take an oath on their knees. Maybe Younger Sister was influenced by the manner of family disciplining in A Dream of the Red Chamber (Hong lou meng).5 I never thought Mother could have made her kneel, and I believed Younger Sister did it out of her own will! Although Mother often scolded her children, she never abused us physically. I remember that when I was young, Mother was sometimes at the end of her wits trying to stop Sixth Brother and Seventh Brother from bickering. Then she would entreat them to stop: "I beg you! I kowtow to you! Please stop this!" Now, this was too big a scene for me to go back to sleep. "When a mother is angry, her daughters should stand in waiting," as the saying goes. I got up and walked over to Mother. I stood there, ready for her to begin preaching. But contrary to my expectation, she softened up.

"Yuan!" Mother began. "For all these years, your father is as good as dead. My seven sons all pursue their own careers away from home. I have no one but you two sisters. Because you go to school, I only get to see you a couple of months a year. When I do see you, you don't have anything to say to me. I think I have lived my life for nothing! Now, quit school and stay with me at home. How many more years can I live? You can have whatever we own in this house, and no one will say a word. Or, I will have your father sign a paper and put twenty thousand dollars under your name."

Mother broke down. So did younger sister. I did not have the courage to walk away. After a while, I said I was sleepy and went back to bed. I faintly heard Mother say, "Oh, Heavens! Just look at her temper! Before I even begin to scold her, she already got upset! She wouldn't even let me bring up the subject of quitting school. What sins did I commit in my former lives? Now I only wish for my life to end soon!"

Mother was not simply threatening us. She really didn't enjoy life anymore. She found this world more and more removed from her ideals! She had placed all of her hopes on Father, and yet Father walked out with a second wife. Then Mother invested everything in her seven sons, and yet they all left her to meet the expectations of society. At last she had to depend on her daughters. Things were fine when we were little girls. Now that we grew up, she missed us as much as she did her sons! Mother was most reluctant and yet compelled to give up her demands on her daughters. Therefore, she felt lonely, disappointed, hurt, resentful, and angry. She had failed in all her ambitions. Mother was a brave woman, intelligent, capable, ambitious, enthusiastic, and loving. She did not want to fail. When she saw her life falling apart, she thought of death.

Third Brother telegrammed from Shijiazhuang to inform us that Eldest Brother was critically ill with high blood pressure. Nothing short of a blood transfusion could save his life. Eldest Brother and Third Brother were Mother's most beloved sons because they accompanied her through hard times. They did not enjoy school, so Father punished them a lot physically. During those years, Mother never had a moment's peace worrying about them. It was a long time before Eldest Brother established his enterprise and Third Brother obtained an official post, both in Shijiazhuang. Since they rarely saw Father then, Mother felt very relieved. Mother's distress over these two of my brothers over the years was one cause of her bad temper.

I eagerly waited for Mother to leave for Shijiazhuang, so that I could return to Beijing. But I dared not express this wish openly. Mother hesitated to go because she was afraid that Eldest Sister-in-law would give her a hard time. Mother was also concerned that she might feel uncomfortable to see Sister-in-law and their daughters pick on Eldest Brother. She wanted to bring along Younger Sister and me, yet she didn't like us to get too involved with family affairs. Her biggest dread, though, was my departing for Beijing. She did not have the courage to confront me lest she should lose. If that happened, she would find it hard to go on living.

"Yuan, do you think I should go or not?" Mother asked me.

"I don't know."

"You don't know?"

"No."

"Tell me what you think."

"I'm not in the position to judge for you."

"I'm not asking you to make a decision for me. Just tell me your opinion."

"If I let you go, I'm concerned that the journey will exhaust you. If something happens to you, I wouldn't be able to forgive myself. If I don't let you go, you might miss seeing Eldest Brother for the last time should he not survive. Then, I wouldn't be able to forgive myself, either."

"In that case I probably should go, right?"

"It is up to you. If my brothers ask about this, I can explain it more easily. I hope you will weigh the consequences carefully."

When at last she went, I did not feel joyful like a bird released from its cage. On the contrary, I felt sad and depressed!

"If I walk out now, it will be too cruel!" But I asked myself, "If I don't, where is the next opportunity? Eldest Brother will probably die. Fifth Brother is a good doctor. He said it would be hard for Eldest Brother to recover. If Eldest Brother dies, I walk out on Mother, what will become of her? But I have to go! It is not a question of filial duty. It is society that spoiled our mother-daughter relationship! Even if she gets hurt or commits suicide, I still have to leave! Otherwise, I would commit suicide myself! I have my social obligations, and I shouldn't commit suicide! I tried to repay Mother by wasting myself away (feigning illness and self-destruction). I tried to return to Mother the physical body that she had given me; Mother accepted such gratitude. Unfortunately, we did not succeed. I tried my best to be a dutiful daughter like a traditional woman, and she strove to be a good mother by trying to make me conform to ancient codes of feminine conduct and by teaching me to tell right from wrong. Yet the hammer of the times hit our heads and smashed our dreams! It was traumatic for both of us. I had to make a critical decision right then. It was impossible to perform one's filial duty and serve one's country at the same time! I could serve my country more easily than I could Mother, for even if I stayed with Mother forever without marrying or going to school, she might still be displeased. This is so because the root of her problem was not my course of action. She once said: 'I have a personal problem. Even if you gave me a gold mountain, I would still be unhappy.' That means that my body and soul put together could not redeem my debt to her as daughter (If one cannot please one's parents, one is not filial) … Go! It is my only chance! If I get away, at least one life would be saved."

I suddenly remembered a classmate from middle school. She was actively involved in student movements. I found her address and went to see her. When I entered her room, she was cooking corn meal for herself. Seeing me, she was at once surprised and embarrassed. She hastened to cover the corn meal to greet me. Upon being asked about the student movements in Beijing lately, she hesitated to tell me. When I told her that I was going to work in Beijing, she was shocked, as if not believing what I had said. I asked her to help me find out the train schedule to Beijing, she agreed. After I took leave of her, I was certain about my trip back to Beijing. I felt more cheerful.

One morning in spring, I got up before dawn. I packed a bundle of necessities and went to Younger Sister's room. She could tell that I was leaving and did not say anything until I finished washing my face and combing my hair.

"Are you going to come back?" she asked.

I did not reply. When I was completely done with my hair, I grabbed a handful of money from underneath her bedding, maybe a little more than ten dollars.

"What shall I tell Mother?" she began to cry.

The word "mother" pricked my heart like a needle! I said angrily and painfully, "What are you crying for? I'm not going to die!"

I walked out of her room, trying to hold back my tears. She did not get up to see me off. The reason I went to her room to wash myself was because I wanted to say goodbye. But Mother taught us to be firm, not to show emotions, and not to try to please others. If I had shed tears in front of Younger Sister or revealed any feelings, I would have lost face. Therefore, I scolded her, although I could not bear to leave her.

Carrying my little bundle and holding the money, I walked out of the house. I took a last look at everything in the courtyard, the grass, the flowers, the trees, and the house.

"Farewell, my home for the last ten years!"

I planted, watered, grafted, debugged, and trimmed many of the trees and plants with my own hands. When they were in full bloom, they attracted beautiful butterflies and complemented each other in their colorfulness. Such scenes inspired me in a very poetic way. On summer evenings, cicadas sang in the trees. In the moonlight, my entire family gathered together to share fruits, pastry, and stories. In those days, Father taught me to read literature. When autumn came, we had fragrant fruits and melons to eat that we had grown in our own yard. My siblings and I had various activities to entertain ourselves, such as watching cricket fights, raising long-horned grasshoppers, flying kites, kicking shuttlecocks, chatting, and sharing what we had learned in school. We had a lot of fun. The most beautiful season was winter when snow covered the trees. Everything looked like a richly decorated crystal palace from afar. We made snowmen, threw snowballs, practiced skating, and broke icicles hanging from the roofs. Sometimes the boys offended us girls, and soon we would reconcile. When annoyed, we would tease, embarrass, and say angry words to each other. Once we made up, we would enjoy each other's company again, doing homework together, discussing novels we had read, going to the theater, or cooking in the kitchen. If Mother was in a good mood, she talked and laughed with us; when she was upset, her scolding silenced us all. Father read all day. Sometimes he talked about poetry to me. But with my brothers, he always put on a stern face. When he and I were alone, he might teach me a few lines from a Beijing operatic drama. All of these memories, I had to erase from my mind never to bring up again!

I walked out of the main gate without being discovered. I got to the railway station too early. I waited for an hour and no train was anywhere in sight. Suddenly Fourth Sister-in-law appeared in front of me. Looking very distressed, she said, "Come home with me, all right? Wait until Mother comes back."

"I'm going to school to make up an exam. I'll return when I'm done."

Fourth Sister-in-law knew full well that I would not follow her. But since she had found out about my escape, she considered it her duty to come after me and try to persuade me to come home. Honestly, although Mother quarreled only with me, the tension must surely have affected Sister-in-law, too. My absence would at least restore half the peace. But if I stayed, Sister-in-law would have no objection.

Sister-in-law left. The train came. After I boarded, I learned that the train's destination was Changxindian. All passengers had to stay there for the night before they could go to Beijing the next day. I found that a bit hard, for I had never dealt with a situation like this before. Fortunately, there were two other students in the train who promised to help me out. But somehow, the train kept going from Changxindian and reached Beijing at dusk after some stops along the way. Once I was out of the railway station, I called a rickshaw and bade the driver to take me to my former residence in East District. When I got there, I found the house empty. I called out for a long time, and no one answered. The door of the next house opened. A middle-aged man stuck his head out and told me that the occupant in the house had moved out a month before. I could not but go to Xiao Feng's house. No one answered there, either. I went to a female comrade's place to find an empty house once again. On my way to A Zhang's house, a military police officer stopped me and asked to see my pass. I told him that I had none.

"You cannot go any further without a pass. Marshal law was declared," he said.

I ignored him and told the rickshaw driver to go ahead.

"She just got off the train and did not find any of her friends after several attempts," the driver explained on my behalf.

The military policeman allowed me to go. The neighborhood where A Zhang lived was extremely desolate. I was again stopped by a military police officer. But for the rickshaw driver's negotiation, they would not have let me go. It was very dark, and it took me quite some effort to find A Zhang's house according to the address. But the occupant told me A Zhang did not live there. He suggested that I go to the police station and try to find information through residence registration. I got to the police station, and to my disappointment, I did not spot any name that even resembled A Zhang. But since I was there, I was determined to find him. I returned to the same house and got the same answer. It was getting late at night. The wind was biting cold. It was pitch dark. I tried all the addresses I knew! The driver urged me hurry up, for he had to return the rickshaw. I hesitated for a while and decided to go back to Xiao Feng's place. This time someone answered the door. He said he was a student of Beijing University and did not know anyone named Xiao Feng. Now, I was in despair! I had three solutions: one, go to West District; two, find a hotel; three, go to a friend's house. The driver refused to go to West District. I did not want to stay in a hotel. And I could not go to a friend's house in such a sorry plight at this time of the night. Furthermore, since graduation, I lost touch with many of my friends. I sat in the rickshaw telling the driver to keep going. When I passed Qin's former residence, I remembered that I was an honored guest there only six months before and was almost a host. Now, Lingyu's family had all scattered. I sighed for the unpredictability of life! Now that I thought of Lingyu, I could surely go to her place. After I knocked on the door, I had the misfortune to learn that she and her family had moved to Tianjin three days before. I remembered Lingyu telling me about it in one of her letters, but I did not expect them to leave so soon. There was only a housekeeper there, so I did not feel comfortable staying. Now, my only choice left was to find a hotel, which the driver persuaded me to do. He said he did not want to go much further. All right, I would go to a hotel. I decided to go to Beijing Apartments first, which was a meeting place for students. But when the accountant learned that I was a student, he insisted that they did not have any vacant rooms no matter what I said. Perhaps they got into trouble on March 18th? So they had to be more cautious! I thought I should go to a bigger hotel. It was only then that I realized I did not have much money on me. I could only go where the driver would take me. After trying several places in vain, I found a small hotel. A maid was nice enough to offer me her room. At last I had a place to sleep. I got off the train at eight o'clock in the evening, and now it was three the next morning.

After fighting bed bugs for three hours, it was daybreak. I got up, convinced that I should try Xiao Feng's place again. Of course, Xiao Feng was not there. The same man (I could tell from his voice) recognized me and gave me an address. I asked him, "Why didn't you give it to me last night?"

"How could I have given it to you then? I did not know who you were and where you came from. What if a spy was following you?"

I smiled and left to look for the place. It was the contact point of a student society. They told me that A Zhang came here every day. At that, I decided to go back to my hotel immediately to get my luggage. Walking out of the door, I ran right into A Zhang. Pleasantly surprised, he talked with me. I said, "I'm going to fetch my things. Wait for me here, and I'll be right back."

I came back with my bundle. In A Zhang's company, I burst into tears.

A Zhang tried to comfort me, and it was quite a while before I recomposed myself. He took me to his house and cleaned out a room for me. I stayed.

Jumping Through Hoops

Bai Wei

Translated by Jing M. Wang

Born Huang Zhang (1894–1987) in Zixing, Hunan, she renamed herself Bai Wei. Bai was forced into an abusive marriage at the age of sixteen. She escaped to become a student at Hengyang Third Normal School (Hengyang disan shifan xuexiao). In 1918 she enrolled at Changsha First Women's Normal School (Changsha diyi nüzi shifan xuexiao). Upon graduation Bai ran away to Tokyo and continued her education there in extreme financial strain. She started her writing career in 1922 and wrote poetry, fiction, essays, and drama. Bai is mainly remembered today as a playwright. Her most important plays include Lin Li *(1926) and* Breaking Out of the Ghost's Tower *(Da chu you ling ta, 1928). She also wrote a novel entitled* The Bomb and the Migrating Bird *(Zhadan yu zhengniao, 1929). Often ignored, however, are her autobiographical writings, which include the short piece selected here and* My Tragic Life *(Beiju shengya, 1936), a 900-page text that portrays the subject's prolonged battle to survive sexually transmitted disease and her desire to join the revolutionary tide of her time.*

I

Despair and hope had battled in me for quite some time now. A fire burned in my heart. Hot blood rushed like ocean waves. Although I had an iron will, an overwhelming force pressed me down, almost crushing my mind and body! I always longed to fly, fly, fly — like a bird caged for a long time. I struggled so bitterly to escape that my mind and body were extremely fatigued, like weathered flowers.

Father, my life-giver, teacher, doctor and nurse in sickness, Father who loved me and yet would kill me. From our hometown at the foot of Dayu Mountain right on the border between Hunan province and Guangdong province, he came to Changsha to wait for my two sisters and I to graduate from Changsha First Women's Normal School, so that he could drag us home and present us as gifts to others. Then his worries would come to an end.

When I saw him, I felt love in my heart. I wanted to hug him and kiss him as a little girl would kiss her mother. But I shuddered, as if the sky was going to fall on me, when I thought of the purpose of his visit, especially what it would mean for me. I felt that the monstrous claws of feudalism had snatched me in the midst of a thunderstorm. Endless horror enveloped me, throwing me into a sea of sorrow!

Oh, my beloved father, teacher, and doctor! At that moment, he was the judge to pronounce my death sentence, the god of death to end my life! These are the ways I felt about him. He oppressed me with feudal constraints, too severe to be reasonable. He did the same to my younger sister Xian.

Oh, Xian, the singing bird! She was a healthy and lively girl with a fair complexion. She was known in the entire Hunan province for her singing, dancing, and gymnastic skills. Her vigor, candor, and carefree nature made everyone believe that she was capable of nothing but joy and would never experience sorrow.

She was a singing bird in the clouds, happy as a fairy!

About six months before we graduated, she became depressed and cried a lot. Her tears frequently wet her dress and desk. Her classmates were shocked and wept for her in sympathy.

Only I remained calm. While others tried to comfort her, I did not utter a word. Instead, one quiet evening, I went to see her. Holding her hands, I said firmly: "Don't cry! It's no use crying. Let's escape as soon as we graduate."

She had barely calmed down when my words upset her again.

"How could that be possible?"

"Otherwise, there is no choice for you but to marry that stupid man."

She looked into the distance and cried fitfully. Suddenly, she fell into my arms. I felt heartbroken. But my heart hardened. It vexed me to see her so weak. I said angrily, "You're so useless! Don't be afraid! In our situation, the only way out is to run away."

"Run away … You have the courage, but I … I'm so scared."

"Don't be afraid. I'll be with you. We'll stick together even if we run to the end of the world. We'll work hard for a bright future."

At my words, she became lost and scared. She said after a long silence, "If we did that, Father and Mother would worry to death!"

"Would you rather they push us to the verge of death? Besides, Father and Mother will never worry to death because of this."

"Die! I would rather die than be sent to that man's house!" She mumbled in a dreamy way while tears rushed down in torrents.

The moment she regained balance, I said adamantly, "Would you rather die or live? If you would rather die, then stop crying. If you wish to live, you'll have to figure out a way. Lack of courage will only lead to tragedy, and tragedy is impending."

"I know. That's why I'm so scared … Oh, how terrible!"

She broke down again. She grabbed my shirt to wipe off her tears. I got so frustrated that I seized her by the shoulders and shook her while staring into her eyes. I wanted to wake her up.

"What can you accomplish with your cowardice?"

She stared at nothing and stopped crying. She thought for a minute, sat up, and said, "Sister, just think, Father and Mother have to marry us off as they are bound by their promise. If we escape, can they deal with the pressure from all the relatives? Father came here specially to take us home!"

"You're right. But it doesn't matter what he came here to do. For the sake of a better future, we must run away. Afterward, we can write a letter to the gentlemen in town and explain to them that Father and Mother have nothing to do with our escape and that we take full responsibility for our own desperate actions. If the whole town understood why we did this, our relatives would not give Father and Mother a hard time out of respect for public opinion. You don't need to worry about it!"

Shaking her head slowly, she said sadly, "It's so hard!"

I lost my patience again. I emphasized with vehemence, "Hard? So what? This is life and death for us, especially for me! We simply have to escape. Otherwise, we'll be undone. Be brave. Let's work together and get out of this dire situation. Once in the world out there, we'll always have each other."

I held her in my arms, burning for her to make up her mind.

She looked very pretty, wearing a cold sad smile, "Ha ha ha … escape! Escape like a flying bird … but where to?"

"From Changsha to Hankou! We can teach school in Hankou. Then we can go to Tokyo and Paris."

Her laughter began to sound more gruesome. She mumbled feebly, "Ha ha ha! What a dream! But you haven't thought about the hardship once you're out there."

I was so full of high hopes for her to take heart that my blood was boiling. Her state of mind deeply disappointed me and dampened my enthusiasm. I blamed her crossly, "You fool! You underestimate our abilities! Following Father's instruction, I read many modern books as well as classics outside the curriculum. I also studied some science and have good drawing skills. You've got great talent in singing, dancing, and gymnastics. You're also good at handcrafting. Right now we haven't yet graduated, and we already received job offers from many schools. After graduation, you can teach music, gymnastics, and handcrafting. As for me, I'll draw, and teach geography, mathematics, natural science, and Chinese. We are qualified to teach many subjects. We can easily making a living. Make up your mind and hesitate no more!"

I held her hands tighter and tighter, hoping to squeeze a definite answer out of her. But her hands grew feeble, and her facial expression changed from uncertain to assured: "It's too risky to run away like this ... too risky! You're putting too much at stake!"

Her words stabbed me deeply. I dropped her hands with force.

"Little devil! You wait for your destiny then!"

I left her in the dark and sat on a tree branch in the courtyard. I heaved a heavy sigh while I stared into the vast sky. I sighed again but could not dispel the weight on my chest. In a little while, she came under my feet. Full of love and tenderness, she smiled, "You're always rebellious and brave. But at times like this, if young women like us try to make it on our own, away from home, without family and friends, without money, we could end up in the streets. How can we endure it?"

Although I felt a bit uneasy at her words, I had already made up my mind. Nothing short of physical destruction could bend my iron will. I jumped down from the tree and told her patiently, "If we decide to take this route, we have to stop fretting too much about the hardship awaiting us. I'm prepared to endure anything. Now, are you?"

Unable to bear with her prolonged silence any more, I sighed and walked away.

II

Time flew and we were going to graduate very soon. Xian cried even more. Perhaps she thought of her fiancé who failed every exam and always ended up the last in the class. He had attended primary school for six years and still could not pass second-graders' exams. He could read and write no more than one hundred characters. He was an impossible son and hit his own mother for no reason. His kind mother did not know what to do. He ate nothing but delicacies. At the slightest displeasure, he would break the rice bowl, overturn the table, yell vile words, seize his mother, and beat her. Such was his temperament. Now, my husband was well fed (so he was fair-complexioned and his lips red), spoiled, shy, and physically weak. He was not strong enough to compete with a woman, much less a man. Xian must have thought that her situation was worse than mine. Woe and sorrow gnawed at her heart.

Although she felt acute pain deep down inside, Father's arrival in Changsha did not affect her the way I had expected. She was too young after all. Father was a man of character, handsome, smooth, strict with us and yet very loving. With him, we felt nothing but joy and happiness. Xian liked to socialize, and he supported her with his money. The simple-minded Xian wallowed in Father's love and generosity, but did not fully realize the threat Father posed to our future by coming to Changsha.

I knew that Father treated the president, the faculty, and residence managers to several feasts. I saw immediately that he used fine foods to strike a deal with them to have them keep an eye on me, so that they could cast an iron net to prevent the poor bird in me from flying.

Looking around at the net, I felt desperate!

Before the final exams, Father had loaded most of our clothes, books, and daily necessities on a boat, leaving me only two garments and the books needed for the exams. He also returned the fare I had borrowed indirectly from Mr Zhao Hengti. Knowing that I was very pressed for time, my good friend Zhao Yuhua, Mr Zhao's niece, offered me the gold bracelet and gold ring her uncle had given her as engagement gifts so I could sell them for travel fare.

I did not have the heart to use her engagement gifts to facilitate my escape, so I declined her offer. With six dollars in the world, which I had saved out of my seventy-dollar annual allowance, I sighed, "Heavens! What can I do with six dollars?"

I worried about travel expenses, boat schedule, and getting a ticket. None of my friends had money. I had never traveled out of Hunan and had no idea about raising money and getting tickets at the wharf. Besides, I was under surveillance and could not step out of the school gate without permission. Graduation was in sight. What should I do?

I agonized for seven days almost without food and sleep. Surviving on water and gruel in the summer heat, I was emaciated and my stomach ached. Under such circumstances, I could not focus on studying for the final examinations. I got straight A's in previous years, but this time I did not know if I could pass at all. I remember that the topic of the essay for the Chinese exam was "Describe Your Plan after Graduation." I wrote: "In order to realize my ambition, I am determined to break out of the iron cage of my environment. Just in case I fail, I will drown myself in the Xiangjiang River." I turned in the essay in three minutes, caring nothing about the grades. All I wanted was to speak my mind. If I ended up being a ghost in the Xiangjiang River, at least I would be one with her wish expressed.

Quite unlike most parents, Father did things the smart way. He came to his daughters' graduation. The day after commencement, he took us out, showed us around the city, and treated us to good food and drinks, as he would important guests. He also took us to his friends' houses to visit, as if to show off his daughters. Even his two younger daughters graduated with excellent grades.

At sunset, the heat had dissipated. As we had had all the fun we could think of for the day, I took leave of my father to see the mother of good friends Yang Rongzhen and her sister Yang Runyu. Their mother was most loving, kind, and respectable. She was a widow and worked very hard to raise her children. Plain living did not keep them from spiritual aspiration. They lived by the principles of cleanliness, beauty, morality, and self-respect. I adored this family. I admired the sisters' continued effort toward self-improvement and respected the mother's kindness even more.

The love I felt for their mother sometimes surpassed that for my own. Their mother was caring and compassionate; mine was understanding, open-minded, and full of rational thoughts.

When I bowed and bid Father farewell, I was heartbroken. I thought, "Goodbye, Father! I don't know when I will see you again, maybe not for seven or eight years, maybe not ever!" I swallowed my hot tears and managed to put a faint smile on my face. My feelings for him made me want to get closer to him. I wanted time to slow down, so I could be with him a while longer. But the three of them, Father and his two other daughters, had already hopped onto their respective rickshaws and headed for their destination. Tears trickled down my face as I watched the flowing traffic, the long street, and the stores on both sides. When I mounted a rickshaw to go to Mother Yang's house, I felt such emotional pain that I almost sobbed. "Goodbye, Father!"

Like a racing horse, I visited several people, including Mother Yang and some good friends. I also went to see the teachers at Luoxingtian Primary School where I did my teaching practice. I spent with them what little time I could afford with sincerity, enthusiasm, and slight sadness. Every time I felt sad, I would try to force a smile, so I could hide my true feelings. After all it was not a graduation farewell. It might turn out to be our last meeting.

III

The ancient rice field roared, silently. Every heart was beating for its roar. Everybody worked diligently for the victory of this roar.

This was all because at our ancient rice field of a college, which people called an abbey, a nun was about to rebel. She was not returning to the world, but waging war against the age-old cannibalistic feudal ethics!

Yesterday, I said goodbye to Father, who loved me but would kill me. Today at daybreak, I woke up Xian and took her to a remote classroom to confide my pressing matter in her.

"I'm leaving today. Now, are you coming with me or not?"

Her mouth and eyes wide open with surprise, she muttered in tears, "Leaving? ... Really?"

"Right. I'm taking off today! Are you coming with me?"

"Heavens! You're leaving like this, unprepared and penniless? It's too risky!"

She held me in her arms and sobbed. I lost my patience.

"Stop invoking the heavens! Are you coming with me or not?"

"I can't. Father bought us so many gifts. We must return home."

It was only then that I realized Father took them shopping yesterday after we had parted company. Very disappointed, I said with displeasure, "All right. You go back home, and I'm leaving by myself."

Not fully understanding the weight of my words, she did not quite believe me.

"Are you really running away?"

"Yes. My boat sets sail at ten o'clock this morning."

She broke down again and held me tight, "Oh, you'll have no place to live. You'll starve to death."

"Why jinx me?"

"You have no money, no company … You're too unscrupulous! It's just too risky!"

She sobbed so hard that she choked.

"Keep quiet, so others don't hear us. Otherwise, I'll be undone."

She controlled herself.

"All right. Tell me how you could possibly escape?"

"Promise to keep it secret, and I'll tell you everything."

"I promise."

"I'm travelling with two students returning to their hometown in Jiujiang. They've purchased a boat ticket for me."

"Oh? What about money? Where did you get the money?"

"I've saved six dollars this year. That's enough for a ticket to Hankou. Several of my classmates are willing to help. Their donations will add up to more than ten dollars, which will get me to Shanghai.

"Once I'm in Shanghai, I'll contact Professor Chen Zuwei. She promised to assist me with eighty dollars so I can go to Japan."

Having heard me out, she let go of me and sat down, looking a bit more assured.

"Since you are so resolved, maybe I can give you some money. Father gave me a hundred dollars yesterday. We bought some clothes and several suitcases. I still have money left."

"Really? Why didn't you tell me sooner?"

"Father wouldn't allow us to give you any of it. It's all in Yaoyao's hands. I'll go get it from her."

She got up instantly to go, but I stopped her.

"Don't go yet! When you try to get money from her, she'll ask you why. If you tell her, that would be the end of me. But you won't get a cent from her otherwise."

She paused a little, and then stood up again. She really wanted to help me. She said with a giggle, "Haha … I'll cheat the money out of her."

"Oh, you silly girl. You think you can outwit her?"

Realizing the impossibility of the task, she stood there and sighed dejectedly, "Right. She's just too wily."

We fell into silence, as if in a deep sleep.

"That's why I beg you to keep it confidential. Never tell her. Never ever."

"All right. I swear not to tell her. I swear to keep it to myself."

Xian also promised to give me a small suitcase that she had just bought. Then, the bell rang for all students to get up. We took leave of one another.

After breakfast, I noticed that everyone seemed nervous and alert. Strangely, some looked into each other's eyes knowingly. Others acted sneakily like spies. For some reason, the entire campus was restless and tense, as if under marshal law. Such an atmosphere got on my nerves. I hurried to the school gate to see what was happening. The president, wearing a white silk robe, paced back and forth in the spacious garden. The dean stood tall and straight at the gate, very much like a steel pole. The residence managers and the professors spread out everywhere within and without the gate. When they saw me, they told me to stay on campus. "What's wrong? Is there going to be a police inspection?" I thought. Strangely, Mother Jiang and Mother Chen, the servants who fetched wash water for us, also gave me funny looks. All of my classmates, both the arrogant and the timid, stared at me in a strange way. They walked about uneasily and occasionally whispered something to each other. "What's going on?" I tried to figure it out.

I dragged the water woman into an empty dorm room, put a dollar in her hand, and said, "Mother Jiang, buy yourself some peanuts with this money. When I return from home, I'll give you more."

"Miss, aren't you going to run away today?"

"Oh, nothing like that!"

"Look, the president and the dean are keeping watch at the school gate. The entire campus is surrounded by people."

"Oh, I thought there was a police inspection."

I understood everything. When she left, I saw a student in the next room. She and several other students were talking there secretly a while before, and now she was alone. I entered the room.

"Hu Xianying, what am I supposed to do? My plan has been discovered."

"Right, we were just discussing it. The faculty and staff have surrounded the entire school."

"It must be my sister who leaked it."

"You mean Huang Xian?"

"Right."

"That stupid girl!"

"I'll go find her. Please get everybody here, He Qin, Zhao Yuhua, the Yang sisters, everyone trying to help me. We'll have to work out something for me! The boat sails at ten o'clock in the morning."

"I know. I'll do everything within my power to help you."

At saying that, she looked like a grown woman to me, instead of a school girl. She was about to take leave when I stopped her and said, "Please tell Shen Zhuiyue and Yin Yunqi to wait for me on the boat."

"Sure."

Feeling totally lost and bewildered, I found Xian and dragged her into the classroom where we had talked earlier this morning. I said to her sternly, "Now the school is completely encircled. You betrayed me!"

She hung her head, not uttering a word. I jumped up.

"Why did you wreck my plan? Now, I'll die for your blunder."

My despair shocked her. She looked up at me in tears but still could not squeeze out a word. I grabbed her by the shoulders and stared into her eyes.

"Do you love me? Or do you want to kill me? You promised to keep my secret, but now, they have blockaded the whole school!"

Turning deathly pale, she stammered nervously, "This ... this is not ... not my work. Yaoyao did it."

This made me furious. I screamed, "What? Yaoyao did it?"

"Yes."

She wept, shaking with remorse. I felt dizzy with rage. She told Yaoyao! How could we outwit her? It was time I left, if I wanted to catch the boat. I was so exasperated that I had no tears, only fury.

"You scoundrel! Yaoyao couldn't have known if you hadn't told her."

"I barely said anything, but she was crafty and extracted it all out of me. Then she persuaded the president not to let you out of the school under any conditions."

"Shut up! I cannot believe how unreliable you are! Didn't you swear to keep my secret?"

My blood boiled with wrath. I pushed her aside. Suddenly, I collapsed and sobbed in despair, "Now I'm a caged bird that can never get out! You know, if I cannot run away, I'll drown myself in Xiangjiang River."

My words and my ripping sadness touched her kind heart. She looked at me with eyes like twinkling stars, shocked and sorrowful.

"Oh ...! You ... you're determined?"

"Yes, I have no choice!"

I stood up straight to show my resolve. She grabbed my shirt, and said with concern, "Even if you fail to run away, you don't have to die!"

"You know my situation. I would be tortured to death if I stayed."

"You're right. Your life at home is miserable. Another person would have been pushed to the limit long ago."

"Then, speak from your heart. Do you think I should live this hell of a life until the end of my days? If you stand in my way, I'll kill you!"

I grabbed her and throttled her throat. We fought silently between the tables. Of course I was just trying to give her a piece of my mind, without really meaning to strangle her. But the boat's scheduled hour of sailing urged me to hurry up. I was blazing with rage.

"Let go of me! Let go of me! Of course it hurts me to see you live such an inhuman and miserable life."

I let go of her, still very upset.

"Then why did you tell Yaoyao?"

"I was afraid that your escape would kill our parents."

"You fool! I love our parents not any less than you do. Do you know how Mother hurt for me every time I was battered?"

"Yes, I do. She got sick and coughed up blood. Your mother-in-law bit and severed your Achilles tendon. You were bleeding badly. Your clothes were all shredded. Mother fainted the moment she saw you. Mother hurt only too much for the ways that you were abused."

"Right. Mother has quarreled with Father numerous times on my account. Mother wanted him to get me out of there, but Father refused to help me because the problems that he had."

She was quick to come to Father's defense: "It's not that Father doesn't want to save you, but that your mother-in-law is all too impossible!"

She had much to say on his behalf. Then, holding my hands, she went on, "Once, Uncle came over and suggested that Father file a lawsuit to get you out of that situation. You know what Father did? He drank a lot and cried his heart out. Father never cries! But he cried that day for you. Can you say he doesn't love you? Of course he does. But your mother-in-law is uncompromising. There's really nothing he can do. Later Uncle said: 'What if she cannot take it any more and kill herself?' Father just kept drinking and sighing: 'It's all too complicated. I'm at the end of my wits! In any case, I have six daughters. If she's tortured to death, I still have five more."

I lost patience with her for wasting so much time talking. I simply confronted her, "Since you knew all of this, would it be better for me to be tortured to death? Or would it be better for me to run away and seek out life elsewhere? If I escape and live, it would make our parents much happier than if I return to my old suffering. What's more, after I get away, my mother-in-law and her son would have no one to vent their anger on. Maybe that would be the end of things."

By this time, she had thoroughly understood my position. She said at once, "You're right. All right. Go! I'll help you."

She held me and smiled. Then, she got up and left hastily. At this moment, a female servant came running and told me, "The president wants to see you."

The president had now changed into a well-laundered white cotton robe, looking very respectable and kind. He received me with courtesy. He first explained that Father had asked him to keep me here. He told me that Father had left for Zhuzhou and would be back to Changsha the next day. This piece of information cheered me up a little. I thought to myself: "This is an excellent opportunity. I might find a way to escape within the next hour or so. After all, it is much easier without Father's immediate interference!"

The president went on to say that it was not his intention to go to such lengths to keep me here and that he had planned six months before to send me abroad to continue my education. This was because he found me to be a good student in many ways, especially the way that I read extracurricular books every day at daybreak in the woods. Therefore, he was going to arrange for me go abroad along with a couple of other students after graduation in the summer.

Now that was news to me. As I had always wanted more education, I was overjoyed! It felt like a cool current running into my seared heart. Excitement temporarily eased my anxiety.

But he returned to my father's wish. Just like a priest, he vividly preached the Three Followings (*san cong*)[1] and other gender restrictions on women in the feudal tradition. He went on and on for almost an hour. It was not until well past the boat's scheduled sailing time that he released me from his office. By then I felt that I was in a trance, as if both my hope and strength had gone with the departed boat. I fell into extreme despair.

IV

I walked along the road beside the playground with willows on both sides. I looked around to find that there were few people in the vicinity, and spying eyes had disappeared, as though marshal law had been lifted. As I entered the school gate, a lively figure came fleeting from the left. It was Yang Runyu. She gave me a pat on the shoulder and said, "Do you know? The boat has been rescheduled for three o'clock in the afternoon."

I almost jubilated with excitement. Yang Runyu went on to say, "Your luggage bears my name. I've had it taken to the wharf."

I was suddenly uplifted from my lethargy, overjoyed and extremely grateful, "Thank you! That's wonderful! But what luggage do I have?"

"Huang Xian has prepared a small suitcase and packed your blanket, sheets, a few pieces of clothing, a towel, a toothbrush, and so forth. Since we couldn't possibly get it out of the school with your name on it, we put down mine. Please prepare to leave. Some classmates are trying to figure out a way to get you out."

How could I describe my joy with words! I got up immediately to join the fighters who were helping me.

After lunch, we started working in the heat of summer — finding bamboo ladders, ropes, and rags. We gathered in the shade of a tree close to the wall and bound two ladders together to form a longer one. With combined efforts, we got down to work, some keeping watch, and others searching for a spot where I could climb up the ladder and get to the other side of the wall. Xian acted as leader and coordinator. They looked all over campus to locate the best place for me to get out without being discovered.

I climbed to the top of the ladder. I was just about to mount the wall, put the ladder on the other side, and get down. At that moment, my glad heart felt like a blooming white lotus at dawn! Jump! Jump! Jump out of hell! My heart was laughing. I could realize my ambitions. My heart could pursue its goals. Jump! Jump! My happy heart felt like a white lotus in full bloom at dawn.

On the wall, however, I saw my enemies hiding on the other side. They shouted out together, frightening me out of my wits. I almost fell from the wall. When I stepped back down from the ladder, my heart was pounding wildly. With extreme wariness, we took the ladder to a different point. Many hands put up the ladder; many eyes kept watch; many mouths wished to say something; many faces tensed with nervousness. All hoped that I could make it this time around.

I reached the top of the ladder once more and was again about to get onto the wall. I looked down first. The people on the outside yelled. I came down to the ground with despair. But my friends quickly put up the ladder at another location. One person ascended the ladder to peep outside. Shaking her head, she descended with disappointment. Our eyes all met in despondency, at the end of our rope. We did not give up. We took the ladder to yet another site, and it was the same.

I hated their plot! How could they take such a measure against a young girl who only wished to seek liberation and education? They blocked my way wherever I turned, as if at war against some enemy!

Our wall plan caused much commotion, so that a real battle started. All the people on campus were busy with something. In one camp spies kept watch over me. In the other camp my vivacious, brave, and enthusiastic supporters worked tirelessly and alertly for me. These were obviously two different fronts opposing each other in chaos.

Xian led the battle on our side. In this battle, every one's position was crystal clear. I knew who were the progressives and who the conservatives, who were my allies and who my enemies. The camps formed unequivocally. Sadly, some good friends and even flesh and blood in days of peace now turned out to be spies and opponents! Yet, encouragingly, people whom I had not befriended much were now ready to assist me. Hu Xianying was one of the latter. Because of this, the entire school seethed, and every heart palpitated with excitement. We all worked for the victory of our respective camps. Our eyes spoke and recognized one another either as allies or adversaries. The school became a battlefield, where we supported some while fighting against others.

V

They wanted to capture me before we had a chance to fight it out. The president, the other side's commander-in-chief, summoned me to his office again. This time his respectability turned into crossness, kindness displeasure, and courtesy high-handedness. He was obviously the victorious general, and I the traitor in captivity. Under such pressure, I cringed. I felt lost, dizzy, tired, and hungry. As I had much stress in the last ten days or so, and had eaten little, my body felt light and feeble. The president paced the floor. All my supporters and enemies, including those on their way home for the summer with their luggage, crowded outside his office to watch this prosecution — prosecution of a traitor.

The president turned around and said to me calmly, "Didn't you hear what I said to you earlier this morning?"

I stood there and held my head high without answering. He sat in front of his desk and went on: "Would you like me to repeat everything to you?"

"You've said enough."

"Then why did you still try to escape?"

"I wished to escape, therefore I tried to escape."

The president was outraged. The onlookers burst into laughter.

Slowly he took a deep breath and became very austere, trying to suppress my rebellious spirit with his severity. The students outside became even more intrigued. The president told me to sit down and then continued, "If you don't want to listen, I wouldn't impose upon you. However, if you leave, you must wait until your father comes back. When I hand you over to him, I'll wash my hands of it. Then you can do whatever you want."

He said a lot more, but I was so depressed about the whole situation that I missed the rest. I was thinking only of the boat that would sail for Hankou three o'clock in the afternoon. But trying to drag it out, he went on and on. He had also invited our stern class teacher and had him preach to me. The class teacher cited the example from Ban Zhao's *Admonitions to Women* (Nü jie)[2] and repeated many outdated ideas. He also dwelled upon the Three Followings[3] and Four Virtues (si de).[4] On top of it all, he basically said that women were not human. I became completely fed up with his long-winded speech! Obviously he had planned to stall for time until after the boat set sail! I had never heard anything so tedious! Uncontrollably, I got up and tried to break out of the room. The president stood up and stopped me: "Now listen ... Obey your father and be a filial daughter."

I hung my head and wept. I said bitterly, "You see, I have to be a human being before I can be a filial daughter. But I'm not allowed to be a human being. I'm reduced to being an animal and a slave."

He seemed to understand my painful situation and tried to comfort me, "Then, you'll be better off if you accept your destiny."

Deeply saddened, I tried to force a smile and ended up crying. I wanted to say, "It's easier for you to say than for me to endure. You want me to accept my destiny while I'm cruelly abused in this hell! Oh, that's killing me!"

Again pacing to and fro, the president looked at his watch. I saw the reading. It was about a quarter to three. I said to myself anxiously: "Good Heavens! I can't catch the boat unless I grew wings and flew!" So I screamed, "You want me to accept my destiny?"

As if someone was killing me, I tried to force my way out of the room in desperation. The president stepped in front of me. Neither of us said anything. At that moment, a book of tragic history turned page by page in front of my eyes. My heart smarted. I trembled, tears streaming down my face. They spoiled my plan to escape! This hurt me more than death. I screamed again as if I were crazy, "You want me to accept my destiny?"

The class teacher got very impatient with me. He said coldly, "What else do you want to do? Break the rules?"

At this, I could not hold it back any longer! All painful memories rushed to my mind, so they began to speak for themselves: "I was often severely beaten, beaten black and blue …

"I was also often denied food for three or four days on end. I ran to the village. Some elderly people fed me, but they were rudely cursed.

"Sometimes I worked like a horse so others could have a good time. But I was still not allowed to eat. Once I took the liberty of giving myself food. They grabbed two dishes full of food and threw them right at me. They battered me so badly that my eyes bled. Bumped and bruised, I fainted …

"Night time was more hellish …"

I choked with tears and was torn with grief at the thought of the unspeakable humiliation my body had suffered! The president listened sympathetically and silently to my catharsis. Xian shed tears for me outside. I continued: "My mother-in-law cursed me outside my bedroom through the night …

"One winter night, my husband took my bedding away and kicked me out of bed to freeze on the cold floor … ."

The class teacher questioned me sternly, obviously convinced that I had done something to deserve it: "Why?"

Xian chipped in outside, "Because she liked to read, and …"

The president gestured her to stop. I picked up from the point where she was cut off, "And on another occasion, he jumped on me like a monkey and threw me on the floor to beat me. He banged my head against the wall so many times that I passed out. Later I felt two hands hitting me, and then four. They bruised and wounded me all over my body. My mother-in-law bit and severed my Achilles tendon, so it bled badly. They tore my clothes into shreds and, with a pickax, forced me completely naked into the streets and to a river. Not daring to go very far without cover, I walked into the river and sought refuge there. The water was reddened by the blood flowing from my torn Achilles tendon, my chest, and my arms."

The president listened in silence to this stretch of words. He heaved a heavy sigh as if to express his sympathy. The crowd outside the president's office began to talk to each other in shock, causing a commotion. In order to resume order, the president drove them away. But I got so agitated that I could not calm down. My throat hurt. This was all because my imagination ran wild over the worse but unarticulated torture that my body had endured.

My mind raced in recollection of the past. Still a young girl, I was forced to live a hellish life in my husband's house. A fight would break out for no reason, and would last for two weeks or even a month. The wives of the local gentry made repeated futile attempts to mediate. Everybody agreed that such abuse was enough to kill me. They worried about me. I endured it all, in agony and in tears. In one of the desperate situations, my abusers gave me a sharp knife and a coil of rope and ordered: "To die quickly, use the knife. To die slowly, use the rope."

In distress I let my train of thought continue to this point. Then I said solemnly to the president, "You want me to accept such a destiny! How do you think I can do that? How can I be a filial daughter?"

I felt that I was going crazy. The thought of how I lived through hell and how my undeveloped, girl's body was forced to do impossible things broke my heart. My body felt the pain of destruction. At the present moment, my mind fixated on escape and the boat's departure. I was still hoping to make it. Go quickly! Go catch the boat! I bounced up to get out, to cross the ocean and leave the fiendish oppression behind me forever.

My desperation affected the president so that he became restless and began again to walk back and forth. Seeing that I was walking out, he stepped in front of me again and said with courtesy, "I hope you can stay and be a filial daughter. I heard that if you run away, your only brother may be killed by your father's foe."

"What!? Why!?" I exclaimed in dismay. On the one hand, I was surprised that the president had learned about this. On the other hand, I loved my brother and felt grieved by what the president had said. The president reiterated the ancient teaching that "of the three kinds of unfilialness, not having an heir is the worst." He urged me to think from my father's perspective on this account and be a dutiful daughter.

I nodded, very moved and very sad at the same time. "Right."

The president smiled with satisfaction. But I declared my idea, "I doubt that my father's foe would really do that. If that were to happen, my father should be the one to resolve the problem. If he is capable of helping others with lawsuits, he should be able to protect his son. Isn't there any way of saving my brother other than sacrificing my life? What did I do wrong? Actually, my stay would probably cause such a tragedy to happen. I'm determined to go to Japan. I want to get my brother to go there, too, in the future. That would be the best way to save him."

After a long silence, the president repeated his intention to send me abroad, and then turned me over to the residence managers. Like jailers, the three unsympathetic residence managers escorted me back to my room. I heard the clock in the hallway strike three. Oh, it was a bell that tolled for me! The boat was setting sail any minute now. That was the end of my hope! Steaming and bathing in my own sweat, I followed them listlessly.

Although I walked with my head down, I was fully aware that crowds were following me along the way. The residence management office and the hallway were packed with people watching me as if I were a prisoner. I looked around and found that Xian was not there. Nor were the other fighters on my side. Where were they?

Seeing that I was so upset that I could scarcely stand, the residence managers comforted me, made me tea, and fanned me as they would pity a person in defeat. I thought to myself: Father's feasts induced them to shed crocodile tears.

They tried to persuade me to take off my skirt to cool off and lie in bed to rest a little. After I took off my skirt, they told me to sleep in the back room. When they tried to push me in, I saw the older residence manager holding a lock in her hand. My heart sank at the sight of it. I did not know how else they would conspire against me. I stood firm and refused to budge. Looking around, I wondered: "Where's my sister Xian? Where are my comrades?"

I hastened to look for my skirt. It was gone. I tried to break out of the room in vain. I was desperate and lost. My empty stomach and my grief made me feel like passing out.

Xian came running in. Everybody looked at her as they would a champion. She called out to me, "Sister, I've just made you a bowl of lotus meal. Go eat!"

The residence managers would not let me go. Xian said, "She hasn't eaten for days. She's going to starve to death!"

Vibrant and energetic like a gust of wind, she pulled me away.

VI

Several classmates were waiting for me in the dorm while others kept watch outside at several spots. Everyone tried to be the first one to tell me, "The boat has been further delayed. Shen Zhuiyue and Yin Yunqi have boarded."

"You're really lucky! You still have time to catch the boat!"

"Hurry up and eat, so you have energy to travel afterward."

"We've found an exit for you where no one is watching. We're certain you can get out from there."

This volley of words filled me with a thrill beyond words! Their sincere friendship and defiance revived my dying heart! Under Xian's urging, I ate the lotus meal heartily. The sentries told us to spread out. So we did. Very quickly, Xian took me to a remote and dirty corner. I knew of no outlet there. How was I going to make my way out? Xian told me, "We made a big hole at the sewage outlet of some old, abandoned latrine pits." Dying as I was to escape, I was a little reluctant to squeeze through a hole in a toilet!

When we got there, I saw a crowd standing in the small courtyard where there was a row of deserted latrine pits. They smiled and waved to me, and jumped with silent joy. I thanked them. A line of partitioned dried-up latrine pits met my eyes. At the back of one of them, a hole was hollowed out, yet too small for passage. My classmates pointed toward a small door at the end of the line. That door was normally locked. A brick wall of sorts was built there to keep it from sight. Now they suddenly opened this door. The door was slightly ajar. At the sight of it, I was so filled with delight I could not utter a word. They did not want me to say anything. Many pairs of hands hurriedly and carefully pushed me out of the door. Even though I was out, they still did not dare talk aloud. They were completely thrilled but contained their joy. It was only after I hopped onto a rickshaw that they exclaimed in unison, "Hurray!" They said, "This is Osmanthus Well Street. After you make it in the world, we'll rename it after you. And this exit will be your Arch of Triumph."

Full of gratitude for their encouragement, I was on the brink of tears.

We did not have time to shake hands one by one. Many hands waved goodbye to me. I heard their laughter of victory. Like ebbing waves, they quickly withdrew from the same door, closed it tight, and locked it from within.

Oh, no! I just realized that I was wearing nothing more than a white cotton shirt. In Changsha at that time, a female student could not go out without wearing a skirt. Should I get off the rickshaw and knock on the door? I was afraid that I might get caught and taken back. But I could not go without a skirt. What should I do? Suddenly, a soft black silk skirt was thrown out from within the wall. I heard Xian's voice: "Skirt! Skirt!" She wore about the same size skirt as I did, only slightly shorter. I slipped into the skirt hastily, asked the driver to let down the rickshaw, and mounted it. Goodbye, my dear friends! Goodbye, Alma Mater!

Suddenly, I remembered: "Oh, where's my other sister? We love each other so much. Where's my dear, smart, beautiful, and elegant sister Yao? She ... oh she cannot come and see me off!"

A runaway naturally feels that the driver's feet were not moving fast enough. I pressed him to speed up. He was probably running as quickly as possible, but I still thought he was too slow, apprehensive that people might come after me. I said silently: "Why don't you run faster? What if the police knew that I ran away and chased after me? What if the school sent people to hunt me down?"

I reached the wharf at about four o'clock. I found my luggage, quickly boarded the boat, and saw my two fellow travellers. It was only then that I breathed a deep sigh of relief. The sense of security allowed me to relish the joy of victory for myself and for my comrades. I congratulated myself: "Oh, I escaped from hell! Never to return! Father, all your schemes failed!" At that moment I could not wait for the boat to set sail, out to the river, to Dongting Lake, to Hankou.

It was five o'clock. It was almost six. There was no sign of departure. "What's the matter? If we keep delaying like this, I'm sure some people would come after me! If the school sends people after me, if Father gets Yao's telegram or telephone call and rushes back from Zhuzhou to get me, then I'll have no other choice than jump into the river and drown." The thought made me nervous and my heart was pounding. I was very fearful that they would hunt me down, ruin my initial success, and nip my will to further my education. I said silently: "Why doesn't the boat set sail?"

It grew dark, and the moon rose. Yet no news of departure came. A cool breeze dispelled the steaming heat. The moon mirrored in the water. The reflections of the masts danced like snakes among the silver waves. Yuelu Mountain kept its silence. The woods slumbered in sweet dreams under the clear white clouds. Songs of nightingales carried over from the other side of the river. The willows along the green banks swayed in the wind and saw themselves in the water. The lightning bugs that flew in the grass were clearly visible in the distance. Such a beautiful sight at this hour in the evening normally would intoxicate me. But now, I only wanted the boat to leave, so I could get out of the hands of my chasers.

"Oh, there comes a group of girls!"

Hearing a passenger utter this, I dashed out in a panic to find out what was happening. Some female students, wearing their hair high in Japanese style, rushed down the wharf toward the boat. I felt both joy and fear, wondering whether they came to see me off or take me back! Should I hide or should I receive them? Heavens, all my success or doom hung on this critical moment!

Lo and behold! On the deck, like a colony of ants trooping out of their hole, like a school of crucian carps swimming forward in the ocean, rushed over the fighters who engineered this battle of my escape! I was surprised that the high-spirited Xian was not among them. Hand in hand, the quiet He Qin and the enthusiastic Zhao Yuhua led the group. All the classmates from Hengshan came, including Li Gui, Li Wan, Liao Dan, the Tan sisters, and the Yang sisters, over twenty of them. I was so overjoyed that I wanted to hug them all at once. I said with extreme gratitude, "Thank you all for coming! Where's Huang Xian? Why isn't she here?"

"The president has learned about your escape. If she comes, they will follow her and track you down."

"Oh …!"

I felt very sad that I could not say goodbye to the person who had helped me the most.

"Then how could you all come without a problem?"

"We asked separately for permission to go out. Some pretended to go home for a visit, and others said they had relatives and friends in town. We agreed to meet somewhere and headed over together."

Completely relaxed, we chatted with abandon for a while. Then they each searched their wallets and contributed however much money they could. Their donation added up to about thirty dollars that I could use for travel fare. With my own money, I now had just a little short of thirty-four dollars. Although this was not a huge sum, it was an indication of true friendship. It was more than enough to get me to Shanghai. Before long, the gong struck for the boat to set sail. We all shook hands and felt regretful to part company. Having no time to linger any more, I bid them farewell from the boat, with sadness and joy, especially with gratitude for their friendship and their support.

My two fellow travelers and I in the boat and the crowd on the bank lacked the words to articulate our feelings. We could only use our eyes to communicate how we felt. The boat began to move. We said goodbye to one another with our hands, handkerchiefs, or tears. The bright moon shone on the wharf and the river. Goodbye, my friends! Goodbye, Changsha! And goodbye, Xian who wasn't there!

"Oh, where's Yaoyao? I haven't seen her all day. She had been scheming against me, but didn't succeed! I can't even see her before I leave!" As I was thinking these thoughts, the boat left the bank far behind. The people seeing me off on the bank became increasingly distant, blurred, and unrecognizable. My thought focused on Yao. I missed her very much: I remembered that we often slept in the same bed at school. In the quiet of the night, we often spoke our minds and disclosed our worries to one another. The more we shared, the closer we felt. Our intimacy surpassed that of ordinary sisters. A couple of months ago, Yao was sick in bed. Xian and I nursed her in turn and spared no effort in every little detail, one on duty the first half of night and the other the second half. We got very tired and missed classes so that Yao could recover from illness and restore to health. But now, she became my chief adversary! I couldn't even say farewell to her when I left! Oh, human affairs are unpredictable! Change can be so sudden!

My reminiscing thoughts slackened, and the moonlight dimmed. The world quieted down. I could hear nothing but the boat pressing forward through the water.

VII

Like a bird that flew out of its cage, I felt calm and relaxed like never before. As much as I missed my parents, my whole body felt relieved. I enjoyed the natural scenery and relished the coarse food on the boat. Unfortunately, I fell ill.

In Hankou, I had dysentery. From Jiujiang to Shanghai, my condition grew worse. As my two fellow travelers both reached their destination in Jiujiang, I did not know anyone on the boat. I had a twisting pain in my stomach and a fever. Occasionally I threw up. I suspected it was dysentery and cholera, an awful combination. Not only was there no remedy, I could die without anyone's knowledge. I had not drowned myself in the Xiangjiang River for oppression. But now my dead body might be thrown into the Changjiang River if I died from dysentery. My parents at home, the tragic life awaiting Xian, my own miserable past and unknown future, and impending death … these thoughts upset me.

Tears welled up in my eyes. To dispel these sad thoughts, I walked out of my stifling cabin to the deck to appreciate the vast waters of the Changjiang River, its green banks, and the hills in the distance. A few clouds disappeared from sight in the horizon.

Suddenly, someone called out, "Miss Huang!"

This familiar term of address came from a few yards away. Totally startled, I thought, "People came after me!" Looking around, I found that it was Mother Chen who worked for our school. She approached me smilingly and said, "Miss Huang, fancy seeing you here!"

"Oh, Mother Chen! How come you're on the boat, too?"

"I'm baby-sitting for a lady traveling to Shanghai."

I was delighted to have found an acquaintance.

She told me that the school turned upside down after my escape. She said very sympathetically, "Miss, it must be hard for you to leave home like this! You three sisters brought maids with you to school. Now you're on your own, with no money, no clothing, and no support from relatives and friends. How can you endure it?"

Then she held me close to her bosom and wept. She was older than my mother, and at this time, we felt like mother and daughter. We let ourselves cry in each other's arms. A young woman roving away from home was bound to be moved by such affection. I felt deeply grateful and cried even more intensely. Seeing that I looked pale and sick, she asked me if I was ill. I told her that I was indeed. She promptly produced two silver dollars from her pocket and placed them in my hand, saying, "I'd like you to take these two dollars. I don't have more than this right now. Once I get to Shanghai, I can give you four or five more."

Her sincerity and generosity completely overwhelmed me! She scarcely earned two dollars a month, and she offered me an entire month's salary.

How generous she was! And she said she wanted to give me four or five more! What deep and special sympathy! This woman, a servant, had never been close to me before. Yet today, she was obviously a devoted nanny! I felt so consoled. Seeing that there was no way to turn her down, I accepted her money very gratefully. My heart softened, softened by the true sympathy and support from this poor woman! I asked myself, "How am I going to return her kindness? Maybe I could pay her back once I made money in Shanghai?"

She gladly introduced me to the lady she was accompanying to Shanghai. In the Western style cafeteria I met this proud and fashionable lady. She was a woman of little over thirty with two children. One she was still nursing, and the other was three years old. Her husband taught high school in Hunan.

After Mother Chen's detailed introduction, this lady readily received me. Besides chatting enthusiastically, she treated me to coffee and pastry. Upon learning that I was sick, she offered me some medication. When I took leave, she insisted that I come again.

I was very grateful for the medication she gave me! I took it, and my fever was gone that very night. I also stopped feeling nausea. I visited her the next day. The moment I entered the cafeteria, however, I was met with a cold face and dirty looks. I spoke her name with much embarrassment, but she refused to respond. I stepped out at once, and she slammed the door and called me names: "Pooh! You're so despicable!" I rushed back to my cabin like a gust of wind. She insulted me without rhyme or reason. I had never had anything like this happen to me in my life. Shortly afterward, Mother Chen came, very concerned. Holding my hands lovingly, she said, "I'm so sorry, Miss! Last night, I told my lady about your escape from school. I was hoping that she would be even more friendly to you, but contrary to my expectation, she condemned your act and said, 'If a woman refuses to listen to her father and her school president, she has to be a bad woman!' That's why she was rude to you just now. Miss, I really meant well, but I ended up embarrassing you."

"That's all right."

I knew that this was the sort of insult that a woman would suffer if she struggled to make it on her own in society. Although I tried hard to control myself, I could not help crying.

"Miss, don't worry. I'll take care of you on your way to Shanghai and help you settle in at a hotel. Then I'll come see you often."

Being without family on the boat and having endured such insult, I cannot describe in words how much I appreciated Mother Chen's effort to comfort me. I could never forget her kindness. I asked, "Mother Chen, where are you going to stay in Shanghai? Please let me have your address. I'd like to come to see you or write to you."

"I'll stay with this lady for a while. I'll ask her to write down her address for you."

However, that was the last time I talked with her. She never came again! Mother Chen, who was paid by the lady, could not come again. When we were getting off the boat, she was nowhere to be found. Mother Chen, I would miss seeing you again! Mother Chen, Mother Chen, how kind you were to me!

I had no choice but to take a brochure of Jiangyi Hotel. As it was my first time away from home all by myself, I wanted to make sure that the owner's wife was there to receive me, just to take extra precaution. A young and pretty woman, who spoke Changsha dialect, approached me with a kind smile. She introduced her handsome and well-mannered husband. His last name was Liu, from Xiangtan, Hunan. His genteel appearance made one think he was a scholar. He was generous and open, too, unlike ordinary hotel owners. They were happy to find out that I was from the same region as they were and treated me exceptionally well. They took me to Big World (Da shi jie)[5] and the theater. I said to myself, "There are so many nice people out here!"

Professor Chen Zuwei just gave birth to a baby in Jiaxing. I did not feel well enough yet to visit her.

A friend's mother, Madam Wei came and took me over to her house.

Speaking of Madam Wei, she deserves an eulogistic poem to be written about her. She was a unique woman from a prominent family in Guiyangzhou, Hunan. She was well-versed in Chinese poetry at an early age and had a passion for ink painting, of bamboo in particular. She cherished ink paintings of bamboo by Madam Guan.[6] All the adornments in her room consisted of bamboo paintings. She also read many classics. She was outgoing and talented. Because as a child she had followed her father to such big cities as Beijing, Shanghai, Suzhou, and Yangzhou where he held official posts, she was well traveled. She was gracious, elegant like an artist, and free from the vulgarity of a wealthy lady, but she had seen much of the world. Three of her daughters were schoolmates with my sisters and me. Mr Chen Wanfu, her brother, was a highly talented scholar. He was once our Chinese professor. Madam Wei and her brother were very fond of my sisters and me, especially Yao, the cleverest of us all. They praised Yao's writing and natural gifts whenever they had an opportunity. When we were attending school in Hengyang together with her daughters, she often sent for us in a pearl-decorated sedan chair, which only officials could enjoy, to go to her house across the river. We ate in her elegantly furnished and brilliantly lit living room, looked at her rare antiques, and listened to highbrow conversations. Then she had us taken back to school in the same pearl-decorated sedan chair that seated three people. She also brought us along when she visited her relatives the Yangs and showed us around their gorgeous garden. This was all because she loved us so much. At that time, the Yangs were the wealthiest clan in Hengyang. From them we learned the manners and ways of the elite. She often came across the river to our school to visit her brother, her daughters, and us sisters, and to socialize with the female professors from Jiangsu and Zhejiang areas. We welcomed her on every one of her visits as we would a fairy. We all loved her, but not for being a wealthy lady. I loved her because she was to me a combination of Venus and the Virgin Mary. I loved her for her nobility, her grace, her generosity, and her artistic gifts. Above all, I loved her aspiration to freedom! Oh, Madam Wei, you are such a wonderful mother figure and a role model. I will remember you forever.

Now her husband's family, the Weis, ranked the third in Hengyang in terms of wealth. Madam Wei had never got along with her dissipating and good-for-nothing husband who had several concubines. When he squandered all his family fortune in a few years, she moved out with her children. At this moment, she lived from hand to mouth and supported herself and her children by working as a servant in a female school and by selling paintings by herself and her daughters. To me, she was a loving mother and a teacher. I felt closer to her in many ways than to my own mother. She appreciated talent in others, loved freedom and art, and was a gifted although unaccomplished artist herself; my mother was illiterate, but was wise and virtuous.

Madam Wei truly cared for me. Even though she was in a tight financial situation, she paid for me to see a doctor of traditional Chinese medicine and a doctor of Western medicine, so that my dysentery was cured. Every morning she went out to buy rice porridge just for me (they ate the coarsely cooked meals at school). She had her daughters keep me company in turn.

In the end, she bought me a third-class boat ticket. My dream came true to cross the ocean to Japan.

It was a brisk morning under white clouds and a blue sky. The autumn sun shone on the waters of the Huangpu River. The waves lapped against the anchored boats. On the crowded wharf, the Yangs waited to see me off with boxes of pastries. They introduced to me a woman from Ningpo whose husband did business in Japan, so that we could keep each other company during the trip. The Wei sisters, Wenxuan and Wenhe, and Yingbo, currently director of Plum Flower Singing and Dancing Troupe, all came hand in hand to see me off.

The siren sounded, and the boat began to move. At this moment, I could not bear to say: "Goodbye, Shanghai! Goodbye, China! Goodbye, my dear friends and family!" My heart was thankfully filled with the tender feelings and friendship they all had shown to me, which were empowering, inspiring, and particularly comforting to a young girl who was out in the world to paddle her own canoe.

We crossed the vast ocean and at last saw islands wooded with pine trees. The clear ocean water was blue and pleasing. It added to my delight! I landed in Yokohama with twenty cents left on me. I remembered what Xian had said: "Risky! You're putting too much at stake!"

Epilogue: .

Two years later, I, a person who jumped through hoops, tried to eke out an existence in Japan by doing menial labor. However, I was attending a fully equipped science college, studying and doing experiments with Japanese female students. Everyone worked with one big microscope, several small ones, and some anatomy tools. In the classroom and the lab, we dissected and studied all kinds of living things and non-living things such as crystal ore. Sometimes our professors would take the class to the mountains and oceans to gather samples. Later we also made time to read masterpieces of world literature.

Xian lacked the courage to run away. She taught music and gymnastics away from home for two years like a refugee. Then she was forced to marry a man rough as a bull and ferocious as a tiger. They tried several times to coerce her to get married. Every time, she was depressed until she became sick so she could not go home. When they tried the last time, she was at home and she got critically ill. But they carried her over in a sedan chair anyway. I heard that they did not allow the bride to have a belt for her trousers in order to prevent her from hanging herself in the sedan chair. Concerned, too, that she might die of illness soon after the wedding, Father, a well-known doctor who cured patients without accepting payment, went with her. The person at the bride's bedside around the clock was not the rude and ignorant groom, nor the rowdy guests making merry in the bridal chamber, but Father the doctor. Acting as both doctor and nurse, Father constantly felt her pulse, watched her breathing, listened to her uneven heart rate, and observed her changing complexion. With gentle attentiveness, he saw to it that she took her medication and drank enough fluid. After such intensive care for several days and nights, Xian became a bride when she was barely out of danger.

Normally, one's wedding should be a grand occasion, the best opportunity for a young woman to exhibit her beauty and to experience the joy of life. But what did the wedding mean to Xian?

From Japan, I sent Father a letter of twenty thousand words to reason with him from my viewpoint and on equal footing. I condemned him for marrying off Xian in such a manner, for obstinately adhering to his pointless promise to the family of Xian's husband, and for incurring upon Xian this endless tragedy. I also strongly opposed him with regard to a list of other things. He arranged my twelve-year-old brother's marriage; he made for my even younger nephew a mismatch with a much older wife; he promised Yao in marriage to a good-for-nothing from wealthy family nicknamed "Stupid Lord" whom she had never set her eyes on. I also protested against his wasting much money on those harmful marriages and not using the same money to help me with my tuition. After all, I was the only person in my family studying abroad. While sending me letter after letter to press me to return home, he tried to pull the strings with Hunan Education Department to terminate my financial support from the government. He wanted me to submit and return to the cage of oppression for lack of a livelihood. That made me furious! Therefore, in my long letter, I stated my opinions and declared war with him. The impassioned words from me, his daughter, really hurt his pride.

In my declaration of war, I fully described what I had suffered, so that others could be saved from the same ordeal. What had been done could not be undone. But I wanted Father to understand that he should not add fuel to the lethal fires of feudalism. I particularly wanted to help Yao get out of her engagement. I would hate to see her young and tender heart endure the infinite pain of her arranged marriage.

Father wrote me back. He berated me for my involvement in "family revolution, patricidal practice, and other immoral acts!" Our relationship as father and daughter ended right there! My illiterate mother could not pick up the pen and write to me. For a long time, I became sort of an orphan wandering abroad without any parental love!

If I registered for classes, I could not work, and livelihood became a serious problem. If I worked, it was impossible to register for classes. I found work as a servant and had often to kneel on the floor to shine shoes for an American lady. I put up with various slights and insults. Late at night, when I reflected on my dilemma, I wondered why Father called my actions "immoral." I simply could not understand what path he was following as a former revolutionary himself. As a revolutionary, he sacrificed his children's personal happiness to give in to feudal vices! He was so intimidated by feudal forces that he became merciless to his daughter who was striving to succeed in the world! How sad! I could not stop my tears from flowing.

I came to the conclusion that the revolutionaries of Father's generation aimed at the political corruption and diplomatic failures of the Manchu government, not injustices of the whole society, and still less the oppression of women.

Since she was married, Xian became the object of her husband's rage. Like a demon, he hit her and kicked her in fits of anger. He often beat her, battered her, and tore her ears apart so they bled. For ten years, twenty years, such atrocities were enacted repeatedly.

Xian, who flew around and sang like a lovely bird, became a bag of bones. She often coughed blood. Physical violence caused her numerous miscarriages. Several of the infants carried to term died at birth because of the mother's poor health. Xian's lively spirits of the past simply evaporated!

The bird could no longer sing!

Now, even if Father and Mother hurt to see her suffer and encouraged her to break out of it to seek out a new life, she did not have the ambition any more, so numbed had she grown of her pains. She was constantly beaten, the eternal object of her husband's temper!

Xian did not have the courage to jump through hoops. Today, after twenty years had passed, such was her life. I jumped through hoops, and how is my life today? It turned out to be more tragic than hers. I am lonely and friendless! A tragedy of ten years! I want to be involved in society, but can not find my niche. Still less can I express myself. There is no way I could nurture and feed my ambitions, much less could I help them bloom and bear fruit. I can only bury them deep in my heart. Without strong stems, sunlight, air, how can a beautiful bud become a healthy flower? Recollection of the past so fills my heart with sorrow I feel like bursting into tears! Yet on second thought, this is in the middle of the war against Japan. Even though I miss the opportunity to do my part and serve my country, I am not so reduced to poverty as to become a beggar in the streets. I should feel lucky.

Recently I settled in somewhere, but I make less money than a clerk or a girl freshly graduated from children's theatrical troops. Such treatment makes me feel frustrated beyond words! Poor and sick, I feel that life could end at any time!

I jumped through hoop after hoop, but what did I get out of all this?

In this society, except the privileged, most women live in a world like fish in a tank or a pool, unlike men who could be compared to fish swimming freely in vast waters.

Fish in the tank or pool, if you are discontented about the constraints, you can jump out! But once you are out in the world, you will wind up on dry land, hard shores, seared grass, or even thorns. There could even be cats and beavers waiting to swallow you.

But jump if you wish. Jump out of that tank, jump out of the confining pool! Jump into the rivers and oceans and swim at your will like men … Otherwise, how is it possible to end the tragedy between the two sexes? How is it possible to wipe out old ideas and feudal shackles? How could it be possible to promote the progress and glory of the nation?

Jump! For progress and glory, jump, girls! A thousand hurdles lie in front of you, but just jump!

At Laijiaqiao in the suburb of Chongqing,
September 1, 1944.

Postscript:

In this piece, the facts [are so extraordinary that they] much resemble fiction. I recorded them here. I wish to use this piece to commemorate my friends, Xian, and Mother Chen, and to pay respects to the souls of Madam Wei and Ms Zhao Yuhua.

In the meantime, I wrote this as my autobiography at the invitation of the editor. Drawing on my life experience during that period of time, I also included Xian. Strictly speaking, I probably should not have written so much about her in my autobiography. But I could not separate that period of my life from Xian, nor could I bear the thought of cutting her out and focusing on myself. Besides, since I had her in the beginning of the story, I wanted her in my conclusion, too. I might have bent the rules of autobiography, but I don't care. I could not bring the piece to a conclusion without mentioning her situation, because there are many women like her in China whose sufferings deserve articulation just as much as those of a female writer. I have never felt that I am a writer. I play but a tragic role.

Imprints of Life

Chu Wenjuan
Translated by Jing M. Wang

Chu Wenjuan (1907–?), also known under the pen name Xiao Yu, was a native of Zhejiang, China. She moved to Taiwan before 1949. Collections of her writings include Female Juror *(Nü pei shen yuan, 1929),* Filial Gratitude *(Cun cao xin, 1947), and* Spring Remains When Petals Have Fallen *(Hua luo chun you zai, 1977).*

Lost times have gradually evaporated from my memory like a thin cloud and a light fog. Yet the sadness and joy remain. The leftover traces weave into the fabric of my current thoughts like delicate threads, making a blurred and misty picture. If I spread out this picture and take a look at it, I may not necessarily find it beautiful. On the contrary, part of it still bleeds.

I. I Was Unwanted

In the northeast of Zhejiang province, there was a misty lake named Mandarin Duck Lake. By the lake lived an extended family of literary and official renown. One clear autumn evening in the late Qing dynasty, the seventh daughter was born into this family. The father held her little head and asked angrily: "Why did you come here?" The little head could not answer him. The infant was not received with love but with disappointment and disgust. The mother could barely tolerate the infant at her breast.

As people teased me with the story of my birth much later in life, I always remember it. It planted the root of skepticism in my young mind.

When I grew older, my elders were not pleased with my speech and manners. I was often alone, silent and lost in thought all day long. If I happened to say anything at all, it usually made the rest of the family shake their heads. I remember when I was seven years old, and Mother decided to pierce my ears. I asked: "Why don't you pierce Elder Brother's ears?"

"He's a boy, and you're a girl. Can you do what he does?" Mother answered with impatience.

"Why can't a girl do what a boy does?"

"Why? Why do you ask so many questions about everything?" She put away the needle angrily and said, "All right. Now I won't pierce your ears. You can just be an ill-bred child!"

I never had my ears pierced, but I still asked a lot of questions. Sometimes I got to spend a little time with my uncles and asked them: "Why are there people in the world? Why am I in the world?" They all laughed and said: "Oh, what a silly child!"

At school, I had few friends. Books were almost my sole company. Gradually I learned to talk with books. I got tired of the textbooks used at school and felt that they could not tell me very much, so I sneaked into Father's study and secretly found big books to read. I understood some and not others, but they were much more interesting than my textbooks.

II. The Heroines in *The Fungus Shrines*

When I was thirteen, an uncle on my mother's side gave me a copy of *Peach Blossom Fan* (Tao hua shan)[1] as a gift and said: "Its lyrics and music are both excellent."

Learning to fill out *xiaoling*[2] lyrics and reciting poems from *Song Lyrics of Ming Ke* (Mingke ci)[3] were my favorite intellectual activities. I turned the pages of *Peach Blossom Fan* and wanted to finish it at one sitting, caring nothing about formal regulations and the musical tunes. All that mattered to me was that I took delight in the lyrics. I felt as though I was in the mountains sharing my secret concerns with Zhang Yaoxing and other characters like him (Zhang Yaoxing leaves his official position for a life in seclusion).

I enjoyed reading history as fiction, but did not know how to engage in scholarship. I relied solely on my intuition, and judged and analyzed historical events from my personal viewpoint. I shed tears for the subjugation of the Song and Ming dynasties, especially for the fall of Southern Ming.[4] In our house we had a copy of *The Fungus Shrines* (Zhi kan ji),[5] a huge work of some forty to fifty volumes in block printing. In its elegant literary style, it depicts the defeats of Emperor Hongguang[6] in Nanjing and Emperor Yongli[7] in southern Yunnan, strewn with the deeds of women such as Qin Liangyu and and Shen Yunying[8] who fought valiantly for the sovereignty. I did not bother to distinguish history from fiction. All I knew was that these narratives of loyalty and heroism were extremely touching. Fictional as they were, I was willing to accept them as facts. I sympathized with the two heroines' misfortune. Sometimes certain lines extoling their heroism would grip my heart, and I would stop reading and try to live vicariously through their bravery. I would write them down in regular script and post them on the upper right hand corner of my desk, feeling as though I had become the female protagonist. Unexpectedly, some of those lines turned out to be a prophecy fulfilled later in my life.

III. Girlhood Without Rouge and Powder — a Romantic Dream

At seventeen or eighteen girls are in their golden age. Who wouldn't want to put on their best looks? But I did not feel that way at all. I did not understand why a person should dress up for other people's visual pleasure. To my mind, aesthetic appreciation was a self-centered act. For example, I could go out and relish nature's glory or I could decorate my room. I would do these things to please my own sense of beauty. Otherwise, I did not see why I should bother to do them at all. "She has no interest in rouge and powder, nor in silk and satin." My mother often looked at me with concern and said that I would either grow up to be poor or I would have a short life.

Actually, my plain lifestyle partly stemmed from my personality and partly from lack of leisure. Although our family owned some land, it was all mortgaged on my father's officialdom. As I grew up, our financial circumstances plummeted. I could not bear to burden my parents with my tuition, so I began to teach at private homes in my spare time while attending school. Sometimes I was too busy to do my hair properly, not to mention dressing up. Thus, there is not much to remember about my girlhood.

On a sad Double Nine Festival,[9] my mother passed away. Within less than a hundred days, my father also died of illness. In severe shock, I felt extreme grief. I had always been quiet, and now I simply became a puppet without speech and laughter. No one tried to induce me to talk or laugh anyway during my mourning period, and it suited me just fine. I read more, hoping by doing so to lessen my grief over the loss of my parents. I learned a little about Chinese history during this time.

As soon as mourning was over, a matchmaker came with a marriage proposal. Unfortunately for her, I already had my heart set on the kind of man I would marry. In character this person should be a complex mixture of all the fictional heroes I had admired since childhood. I called him my ideal "knight." I wanted him to follow me in pursuit of adventures. If we could not realize our ambitions, we would retreat into nature and resign to a life of seclusion far from the madding crowd, literally putting into practice my motto: "Bury one's bones in nature and leave one's name in history." A man not meeting these criteria was not fit to be my partner no matter what he amounted to.

To escape from arranged marriage, I ran away to Beijing, where I tried to heal my pain through learning. I read on philosophy and literature of various countries, so that the scope of my vision broadened. I wished to explore the depths of the universe and human life, yet I lacked a sound methodology: I could not research a problem soberly, seriously, and systematically; nor was I capable of literary research and data sorting. Whenever I tried to read some hard and solid theory, my mind would wander to Percy Bysshe Shelley's odes or Eroshenko's[10] animal characters, and literary works of different historical periods and genres. As a result, I never produced good scholarship.

As for English poetry, apart from Shelley, I also enjoyed reading John Keats. As far as fiction was concerned, I liked Thomas Hardy's short stories best. At the same time, I longed to hear nightingales sing. It was a pity that there were no nightingales in Beijing. Fortunately, other birds chirped in the willow trees along the banks of the West City Moat. I could also hear gurgles of the water and whispers of the wind. These sounds from nature consoled my empty and lonesome heart. In the evenings when the new moon hung high up in the sky, I always went for strolls with some like-minded friends in less frequented spots, such as among the willows in Sizhiku and in the pine woods in Kenongtai, and along the banks of the lotus pond in Sanbeizi Garden. We left our footprints all over these places. The clear water reflected my tears and my smiles. My heart opened up and my life burst into song only when I was in this place. Oh, Beijing, you were life's transient epiphyllum, the brightest petal. If it had feelings, this petal must have withered by now for having no opportunity to bloom again. Indeed, there was no need for it to leave any trace behind when no one was there to appreciate it.

IV. The Bubbles of the Time

The tides of the May Fourth Movement[11] shattered my beautiful yet not completely formed dreams. It awakened my sense of responsibility towards society. I left Beijing, a place of poetry and romance, for Yanggao County in Shanxi province to run a school. The northern and southern parts of Shanxi were literally two worlds. People accustomed to the mores of the Taiyuan area could hardly imagine the culture in the ancient town of Yanggao situated outside the Swan Gate Pass at the foot of Mount Yin. Yanggao was a small town less than two miles all around with only three city gates. The gate to the north faced the Great Wall, and it was considered inauspicious to leave that gate open. Thus, the awesome Temple of the Emperor Wu of Han[12] replaced the city gate to the north. Right in front of the temple, there was a piece of rock from the ocean, believed in folklore to be a treasure that Su Wu had brought upon returning to his official post in the Han court.[13] In Yanggao where one found dirt and sand more than anything else, it was only natural that people would see such a beautiful rock as a marvel and attribute it to an ancient hero. As this was the oldest folklore, why should anyone debunk its myth and disappoint its believers?

On autumn mornings, I always had the pleasure of standing by the stone in front of the temple and looking at the distant views outside the city. Oftentimes I saw teams of camels slowly crossing the vast stretch of yellow dessert. The reddish morning sunlight veiled the top of the mountain. The Great Wall was colored in such a way by the early frost in the north that it looked like a delicate jade green sash lightly floating around the waist of the mountains. And, whenever a flock of honking geese was flying to the south for the winter, the whole sight would fill me with such awe that I would stand there transfixed for a long time, forgetting to return to my place.

Apart from appreciating such natural beauty of the north, my most important business was to redress the classroom situation in the school, which was set up in the ancient temple. There was not enough space for students to sit, and yet many usable rooms were taken up by the clay sculptures of deities. To turn those rooms into classrooms, I suggested that we remove those sculptures. Unexpectedly, my idea offended the local gentry, who attacked me in unison. I, a person from another province, had no connections here. Just as I could hardly withstand it any more, some progressive youths in the local area came to my assistance and turned the tables. Mr Ji Liang, who passed away not long ago, had been one of them.

I began to fight feudal forces. In terms of political belief, my interest gradually turned away from traditional loyalty to sovereignty to a path that can be called revolutionary.

Some friends lent me books and newspapers and encouraged me to write for publication.

At that time, there was a weekly publication in Tianjin called *Women's Star Weekly* (Nü xing)[14] that covered a variety of topics. The editor-in-chief, Li Zhishan[15], was a woman with liberal thoughts. Deeply touched by her ideas, I submitted some of my writings. In the course of our correspondence, we became friends cherishing the same ideals and sharing common goals.

I became more and more involved with writing. I contributed not only to *Women's Star Weekly*, but later also to *Minguo Daily*'s (Minguo ribao)[16] supplement.[17] People from all walks of life wrote me letters, with whom I became pen-friends. One of them was a philosopher whose learning inspired me particularly. He also rebelled against feudalistic ideas and confronted severe attacks from society. Our common experience rekindled my long repressed longing for a "knight." At last I fell in love with him.

I was naturally inclined to have idealized notions about love. I wove a romanticized fabric and veiled my loved one underneath it. I appreciated him with the detachment of a stranger, until I came back to reality. Then the flower withered, and the moon waned. We ended up in an ugly quarrel, which shattered my dreams.

Being a housewife for three years wasted my learning and decreased my ability to function in society. When my child was two years old, I became more preoccupied than ever with housework. But the trivial details of family life bored me. I was constantly seeking to work outside the home.

By that time, we had already moved from Beijing to Shanghai. My husband was a very intelligent and capable man. He had spent too much time abroad, however, to fully understand and come to grips with domestic realities in spite of his learning. As a result, he easily became the target of attacks from ill-intending people. His thought and speech became more and more incompatible with the world around him. I hurt for him and tried to bring him around, but to no avail. Although traditional gender norms made me stay home for three years, the tide of the time urged me to strive for independence. Besides, I already discovered that stretching right in front of us was a rugged road. I had to rescue my husband and myself.

In Beijing, I joined the Nationalist Party and worked on women's issues. During this time, my comrades within the party wanted me to continue with my service. Therefore, I took on some educational and literary work.

China was already at war with Japan. Yet another kind of storm destroyed my family. I had no choice but to seek a life on my own. I looked around and saw a lighthouse at the upper reaches of the Yangtze River that beckoned to me.[18] My husband and I decided that he would have custody of our child, as he was concerned that I could not take care of the child properly. He said, "The child is my life. I can't live without him." I knew very well his love and care for the child. Although the child would be sad to live away from me, his mother, I believed that staying with his father was better than wandering around with me without a comfortable home.

On a gloomy day in late spring, I boarded a westbound boat. Leaning on the boat side, I realized that good days were over.

V. The Pain of Being Marginalized

Once in Wuhan, I found myself in a totally different world. I saw Japanese flags everywhere. The people's nationalist fervor raged like ocean waves. Like a reed leaf, I could not help but plunge into the waves to share their excitement and misfortune. I, a person with no learning or experience whatsoever, had both new and old ideas. I looked timid and inadequate in the revolutionary force. Everyone could tell that I was incapable of any heroic acts, so I was assigned to write propaganda articles and teach school. I was used to teaching, but my writing did not quite measure up to the standard. I realized that I had to learn to do propaganda work from a teacher. I had never had anyone teach me before, and of course I would meet with rebuff.

Later, without an explanation, I was asked to quit writing propaganda articles. I then traveled every day back and forth between Wuchang and

Hankou to teach. Whenever I had spare time, I wrote fiction of sorts to send to the supplement of *The Central Daily News* (Zhongyang ribao)[19] for publication. The editor was Mr Sun Fuyuan[20], whom I knew quite well. In addition, I was sometimes invited to write on women's movement. Needlessly to say, these writings were all rather superficial.

If one's family breaks up, one can try to put on a happy face in public, but one will shed bitter tears alone. As there was no way for me to share my feelings with anyone, I imagined that it was quite all right to write them down. When people discovered my writing, however, I was criticized as "sentimental and demoralizing ..." "No stragglers are allowed in the revolutionary camp." I was faced with a serious problem. But in my veins flows the blood of an old-fashioned scholar, which made it difficult for me to submit to other people's will.

My revolutionary career failed.

I found this experience very perplexing. When I destroyed idols in Yanggao County, people called me "radical." Now, I played but a modest role here, and became "a straggler." I felt very disheartened. Who straggled behind anyway? Who pressed forward? I asked, but no one knew. I tried in vain to figure it out. Conformity was an age-old wall used to restrict people with a personality like mine. What else could I say?

VI. Selling My Writing for a Living

Returning to Shanghai, I found my husband on the brink of bankruptcy. He felt more rejected by society than ever. Always sympathetic to the less fortunate, I did not want to make him suffer more than he already did. Without a murmur, I took it upon myself to support the family. After he departed for France with a friend's financial support, I moved into an attic room to cut my budget. But no matter how hard I tried to save, I could not make ends meet, for it took a substantial amount of money every month to provide food, clothing, and daily necessities for my son and myself. I had to find a job; and yet if I worked, childcare would be a problem. No school would hire a teacher with a child tagging along. There was no one to take care of him at home. I had to look for more flexible work. Several times I had to quit whatever job I happened to be doing because the child got sick. As he grew up on formulas while living with his father abroad, he was tall for his age. His immune system, however, could not compare to that of ordinary Chinese children, so he fell ill very easily. I had a hard time juggling the double burden of work and childcare. After quite some time, I eventually saw that the only way out was to make a living by writing, that is, if I wanted to make money and look after the child at the same time.

However, my present situation was nothing like the days when I worked in the literary circle. Back then, whenever I was in the mood of writing up something for publication, editors all jumped at it, as I did not ask for royalties. Now that I was out of the circle and needed to make a living by writing, it was not that easy any more. Fearing rejection, I submitted to some less well-known newspapers a few carefully wrought essays. Luckily they were accepted, which encouraged me to write more. I expanded my scope and contributed to daily newspapers and journals both in Shanghai and in Wuhan. I made a good impression in Wuhan, my second hometown. After a while, I tried my hand at the short story, which proved to be a difficult form. When I finished my first attempt at this genre, I found that the writing was not good. I tore this story up and went to the library to search for instruction. There, I located a book on the art of writing short stories published by the Commercial Press, and took it home and studied it carefully. It was only then that I learned a little about the technicalities. I began with a story about a female juror based on my own experience in Wuhan. It was published in a journal. Then I wrote another one, about a female woodcutter, which also came out. Later, I gathered several short narratives in a collection titled A Female Juror (Nü peishen yuan) and sold it to Guanghua Book Company for ninety dollars. After its publication, Mr Wang Tiran reviewed it in Shanghai Journal.[21] When I opened the book a few years later, however, I blushed. How unscrupulous of me to have shown the world such crude and naïve work!

I realize that my stories in A Female Juror are not well crafted. Yet for all my inadequacy, I had high standards and disliked well-plotted, skillfully wrought stories with mediocre characterization and little substance. From my personal point of view, I think the mission of literature is to promote human progress, not simply to reflect social realities. In other words, literature makes an epoch, it is definitely not the dregs of an epoch. I do not wish to be confined by the theory of art for art's sake. Cut off from life, how should literature justify its own existence?

As long as one strives towards a set goal, one feels happy even though one may not reach that goal in the end.

I had ideas and raw material in abundance, but I lacked ways to express my ideas and process the raw materials to produce good stories. I wanted to emulate the closely-knit structure and detailed description of the short stories by Guy de Maupassant. I thought his exposure of social realities in France in his time testifies to his love for life and his aspiration to a better future. His ironies, full of blood and tears, always touch his readers deeply. Reading the story "Boule de Suif" I heard his angry outcry against social evil. Who says this master of short stories was an unfeeling onlooker?

Diverse ideas influenced my reading of literature. I liked romantic writer Victor Hugo's novels and poetic drama. I enjoyed Alfonse Daudet's works, for they are full of flesh and blood. But Maxim Gorky's *Mother* was my favorite, which I considered a first-rate novel in characterization. In such a long narrative, I did not find one unnecessary word from start to finish. Unfortunately, I had no knowledge of Russian, so I could only relish the work by comparing Japanese and Chinese translations. Thanks to the excellent translations, much of the original flavor was preserved. With minimal literary training, I just followed my instinct in selecting reading materials. I did not dare touch books beyond my ken, and never read what I did not enjoy, lest I should be discouraged. If I liked certain books, I usually perused them several times, jotting down what particularly appealed to me and adding my own comments. When my friends saw what I did, they said, "These are nice book reviews. You should have them published." As a result, my "book reviews" often appeared in *Reading* (Dushu),[22] a monthly journal published by Guanghua Book Company. I, one with little knowledge of literature and foreign languages, actually expressed my opinions about Western literary works. Ignorance is the first reason behind bravery. I still believe this.

In order to make a living, I could not afford just to read without writing. Besides, I did not have a strict mentor like Gustave Flaubert to stop me from publishing my immature work. Of course, I am not so arrogant as to compare myself to Maupassant, and I was just trying to give an example. I wrote in a wide variety of genres at that time, except drama and long novels.

VII. Maternal Love Found Outlet

Four years had passed. During this time, like a quiet stream, I tried to flow toward the sea of literature. Although I did not know when I could reach that broad and profound state, I aspired at heart and persevered in effort. But something unexpected occurred to distract me from my goal.

In the winter of 1931, my husband returned from France to his native place in Guangdong and declared that he would establish a business there. In early December, he came to Shanghai and asked me to take the child and go to Guangdong with him. Memories of the past came back to me: our difficulty getting along, our different outlooks on life, our arguments … I saw nothing but grimness awaiting me. I remembered what I had heard once: "It is better for a child to live with one parent in peace than to suffer with both in argument."

He simply would not let me have custody of the child. Sadly I saw the two of them embark on the boat. When I returned home, the place suddenly seemed unbearable, as if I had lost something. I went out and walked aimlessly. I visited friends, but was unable to appreciate their friendship. Everything had changed. Before I knew it, I found myself at 16 Riverside again, the wharf where the boat had sailed the day before. The yellow waves churned and seemed to laugh at me, "You're so silly! You allow the conflict between reason and emotion to ruin your life. Why do you come to me?" I turned away, feeling very upset, and entered the gate of the steamboat company. I walked straight to the accountant's office and asked, "Nothing happened to the boat to Shantou, is that right?" The clerk stared at me. It was quite a while before he answered, smiling, "No, of course not. The weather is very peaceful here in winter." I left, feeling as though people sneered and looked at me coldly.

It was not until I received a letter from my child that my life gradually returned to normal. But I still suffered from insomnia and had no appetite for food, for I missed my child all the time and tried to imagine what his new environment was like. I often had sleepless nights or survived on two biscuits a day. However, I refused to give in to depression. My unyielding nature urged me to overcome these ailments and triumph over the external, oppressive circumstances. I was determined to live, and live well, because I had my life's mission to accomplish. I would not want to waste away like this! So, I made strong efforts to seek medical treatment. Xie Bingying introduced to me a doctor trained in Western medicine, who was willing to treat me without charge. He diagnosed that I had serious neurasthenia and chronic gastritis, and put me on medication for a long time. At last my health improved, but I lost sleep at the slightest stimulus. Insomnia greatly hindered my intellectual activity; I could no longer read and write.

On January 7th, 1932, I received a letter by the express mail from a friend in Hankou inviting me to teach in a private middle school there. I was hesitating whether or not I should accept this position when the January 28 Incident[23] broke out.

In a frantic escape from this disaster, I lost my home. As the old joys and sorrows of my life no longer existed, I wanted to look for alternatives and start life anew. Furthermore, it was not healthy for me to continue to indulge in grief and solitude. The upbeat life of a school might cheer me up. I decided to go to Hankou.

This was a revisit to Hankou, and sadness seemed unavoidable. But my outlook on life had grown different from what it had been four years before. Age and wisdom empowered me so I did not feel all that sentimental. I quickly got over what little sorrow had left in me. I wanted to look deeper into myself and at the psychological reasons behind my actions. Before I really understood any issue, I did not want to jump to conclusions.

Hankou Private Middle School was a boy's school with quite a large student population. I taught Chinese to two classes with a total of sixteen hours per week. I had the mornings to myself for writing. I devoted my time to teaching after ten o'clock. Keeping busy was a good cure for insomnia. I felt better and became increasingly involved in my work. The students' love and respect especially gratified me. Apart from teaching in the classroom, I also tried to share with them my experience in life. Such bonding with the students enabled me to transfer my maternal love onto them. I even concerned myself with their health. A heart that embraced all humankind, no, all children, compelled me to be more than a teacher to these students. I mothered these grown children. My colleagues all laughed at me for this; with good intentions though. As for me, I just did what I felt was right. I could not care less about what people thought.

During this period, I was not productive. Whatever I wrote at this time of my life was so full of sorrow that even I myself could not stand it, and I just repeated myself. I was displeased with my writing. Maybe my life was too monotonous? Or maybe I did not have enough experience?

VIII. Joining the Army

I had been good friends with Mr Chen Danyuan for years. By the time I became a soldier, he had already transferred to the army from civil administration and served as chief in the information section in the Eighteenth Route army of the ground force. He was from Hanyang, Hubei.

On his way back home at the end of the year, he came in passing to Hankou to see me. Noticing my writing spread out on the desk, he read it carefully. I was afraid that he was going to critique it, but he made no comments. He only asked after my health and my life in general. Then, he said with assurance, "If you go on like this, you can't write, nor can you restore your health."

I suddenly felt that someone had just poured cold water over my head. I was very disheartened.

"What am I supposed to do then?" I retorted mechanically, having nothing else to say.

"How about a change of environment?" he suggested.

"Of course I'd like that, but …" I hesitated to go on. He understood what I did not utter. So he said, "Of course, we have to be careful before making any real move." He paused a little and then added: "Let's wait and see."

Then, we turned our conversation to something else.

After Danyuan had left, I became preoccupied with this issue. Life was multifaceted, and I had been confined in the same environment for a long time. The pain caused by the disintegration of my marriage gnawed at my heart like a poisonous snake. I hurt so much inside that my writing suffered severely. In order to experience more of life, gather material for writing, and become a happier person, I decided to go elsewhere.

As soon as school broke for winter vacation, Danyuan sent me a telegram. He said that Commander Chen, Mr Chen Cixiu, invited me to edit a journal in the Eighteenth Route army.

I knew all along that Danyuan was planning to find me a new job. But I did not at all expect that he would get me into the army. By that time, the political and other sectors in the army had dismissed all women. And I, a woman … Didn't Commander Chen know that I was a woman? To take extra precaution, I wrote to Danyuan and shared these thoughts. Danyuan wrote back: "Commander Chen said that women and men are equal and have the same capacity." He tried to help me dispel my doubts and persuaded me to join them as soon as possible.

The Eighteenth Route army was stationed in Nanchang. To get there from Hankou, one had to transit in Jiujiang and head south from there. I took leave of many people who were close to me. The day before I left, my students all came to say goodbye. As they had been in my classes for several years, I felt sad to leave them. But they all controlled their feelings and tried to console me with positive words. They encouraged me to work hard for a brighter future. I was deeply touched by their thoughtfulness. Dear young friends, each of you had a heart of gold! Your understanding of life was more perceptive than mine was. I did not deserve to be your teacher. Rather, I had a lot to learn from you. Although we had to part now, we would work together in the academic field in the future.

I arrived in Nanchang after traveling first by boat and then by train. It was the New Year's eve of 1933. I met Mr Chen Cixiu the next day. He told me the history of the Eighteenth Route army and the reason why they decided to start their own journal. In the end he also informed me of the editorial plan. He was extremely sincere and perceptive. Attention to details was a major characteristic of contemporary soldiers, but he surpassed most in this respect, which I did not know until later. Right after my first meeting with him, I still thought: "The real success of an ambitious young man is above military affairs."

The journal that I edited was named *Cooperation Monthly* (Xiexing Yuekan) because this journal was jointly published by the Eighteenth Route and the Fifth Route armies, and it was intended for their officers. Mr Luo Zhuoying, commander of the Fifth Route army, was a literary talent. He wrote excellent poetry and prose. His learning was quite extraordinary among the military. He was particularly courteous to people of letters. At our first meeting, he raised many questions to me regarding politics and economics. Modern military affairs were closely related to politics and economics. He clearly perceived this connection.

Despite the fact that the two commanders had confidence in me, the junior officers, especially those high-ranking aides and staff who had once been officers, were quite shocked by the presence of a woman. They said, "Why should a woman deserve the position of a lieutenant colonel? Is a woman capable of editing a journal? A woman ..." They made such remarks. I was rather discouraged by their attitude and wished to quit this job. But Danyuan said, "If you leave without having accomplished anything, that would really make women look incapable." He knew the kind of person I was and challenged me with these words.

"A woman ... I must prove a woman's worth, for all women if not for myself." I decided to take the challenge and put my best foot forward.

After the first issue of the journal came out, I no longer heard people's dubious voices. But I soon discovered that a hidden arrow was aiming at me.

I could have managed the journal's funds myself, but I asked the wife of a military supplies officer to be the accountant and to take charge of the budget and end-of-month reimbursement. Actually she was but a nominal accountant, as her husband handled the real work.

I also set up three don'ts in daily life: Don't go to the movie theater; don't go for a walk; and don't discuss anything other than work-related issues with male colleagues.

The hidden arrow I just mentioned focused, as it usually does, on financial matters and traditional ethical codes. However, because I had built strong enough defenses, they had to acknowledge their defeat and stop their attack. Unexpectedly, they began to assault me openly. They declared: "The commander is not that easy to please. Someone edited a pamphlet and got severely scolded for but one wrong character. Now it is her turn." I heard what they said and decided to take proofreading upon myself. I usually checked the important articles four or five times. Whenever I woke up in the middle of the night and remembered a sentence or a word that sounded awkward, I would go right to the typesetting room of the printing factory and make sure that proper changes were made. If the text was in English, I would set the types personally. The owner of the printing factory shook his head and said that the workers complained and asked to recruit more staff.

After working with such intensity for an entire year, colleagues on all sides began to befriend me and accepted me as a "comrade in gown." (Nonmilitary personnel were referred to as "comrades in gown.")

I now felt more comfortable. In order to fit in better, I began to translate short narratives or write theoretical articles depending on availability of material. The constricted work environment stiffened my thinking.

Now, my husband and I had not exchanged a word since he had taken our child to Shantou. In the autumn of 1934, all of a sudden, he wrote me a letter from Hong Kong, asking me to go there to get the child. He explained that he went to Hong Kong because many people in his hometown could not tolerate him and it was no longer possible for him to make a living there. I did not even have time to think twice about it before I obtained permission and set out in great haste. One week later, I saw my child whom I had missed day and night. He was very thin. Nothing seemed to have changed about my husband. As he was having a hard time, I did not want to say anything. I just took the child, and we traveled back by the same route. We spent a few days in Shanghai. I had several garments made for him. I did these things to compensate for the pain of separation for the past one and a half years. In the westbound boat, we stood on the deck watching the scenery along the banks of the Yangtze River. I began to notice all the clouds and the trees that seemed to be filled with life. The sun smiled down on us. All of this warmed the hearts of mother and son after so much hardship.

The year 1934 passed peacefully.

Early in 1935, I was transferred to the general headquarters based in Nancheng to be a secretary. Since then, I have had to relocate with the general headquarters. As my son was but nine years old and had to follow me wherever I went, he did not have a good elementary education. I played the roles of mother, father, and teacher. When I absolutely could not have him with me, he boarded at school. Once I received orders to accomplish a task in the southern Jiangxi on short notice. I had to send him that very night to the primary school section of Yuzhang Middle School. After everything was properly arranged, I left. When at last I had finished the job and was on my way home, I looked into the gray sky and thought of our wandering, homeless life, and I was heartbroken. Fortunately, my son was very understanding, and he was conscientious in his studies. Because he often traveled with me, he developed a keen perception of people and the world. He had more common sense than children of his age. I took it as a reward for our ordeal.

By then, I had joined the rank of aides and staff. As the only woman there, my life was rather boring. Meanwhile, it was hard to budget my time, because life in the army did not go according to schedule. We could work overnight when pressed for time or did not have to lift the pen for an entire day when relaxed, but we had to be on call day and night. The nature of my job prevented me from engaging in creative writing. The strict hierarchy had completely clogged my literary inspiration.

Why then did I stay with this job? To make ends meet and support my son? It was a fact, but not a purpose. To serve my country? It was rather ridiculous, for what could an insignificant aide and staff do for the country?

When the War of Resistance against Japan broke out, we devoted ourselves enthusiastically to the nationalist cause for quite a while. Even though we could not directly engage in combat, we did our share. The thought of it made me feel better.

Now, it has been exactly ten years since I joined the Eighteenth Route army in 1933. During this period, I did not publish anything, yet I witnessed the dark side of society as well as the bright. I was painfully burdened by the ideas that accrued in me but found no articulation. Now, my son is in college. As I transferred from the army to civil administration, I have more control over my time. I very much want to resume writing, but with so much amassed and entangled in my mind, I do not know where to begin. When I have a chance to sort things out, I will write for the reader's pleasure.

A Journey of Twenty-Seven Years

Lin Beili

Translated by Shirley Chang

Lin Beili (1916–?), originally named Lin Yin, was a poet from Minhou, Fujian.

I. My Motive for Writing

I will write down here the story of a twenty-seven-year-old woman. Readers will probably consider it strange, for the collection which includes this narrative already indicates its nature. But why do I not directly say: "I will write down my own story here"? Let me now explain the reason, which is my motive for writing.

It must have been late June that I received a letter from my friend L! Attached to it was a letter from Ms Huang, an editor with Plowing Publishing Company (Gengyun chubanshe). She asked me to write my life to be published in a collection of women writers' autobiographies. I instinctively thought, "Say no! How can I write my autobiography? I've never written anything and if my story were included in the collection, it would be completely out of place." But another thought entered my mind with even stronger force: my refusal would greatly disappoint L. He had been so kind to me that I could not bear the thought of letting him down. Indeed, I should not let him down.

Before then I had read many autobiographies and had found most of them unsatisfying. The writers (either men or women) often loved to write about how they struggled, how they conquered difficulties, and how they had made sacrifices to benefit others. What meaningful and practical lives they had led! All the talk of their endeavors and sacrifices were nothing but a beautiful and splendid curtain. My life concerns no struggle, conquering, or sacrifice. I will definitely not brag about myself. I will simply write down my journey of the past twenty-seven years, realistically and objectively. It will be as if I were writing about somebody else.

As everybody knows, a grain of seed will grow according to the soil, climate, and planting methods. All species are the same, their nature stems from their habitat. Human beings are no exception. Therefore, I must write down my background, my family and my education as follows, so that you can understand how I became who I am. At the same time, one might have a glimpse of my parents' generation, their world, as compared to mine.

II. My Birth in 1916

The Second Year of the First World War

It could be said that war never left me. I was born in the second year of the First World War, and now it is the fourth year of the Second World War.

When capitalism progressed to imperialism, powerful nations became aware of the cruelty and terror of war and tried to avoid an unprecedented slaughter. But vying ever more heatedly for economic benefits in colonized countries, the tension accelerated in imperialist countries. Not long after fierce international competition, the First World War broke out in the autumn of 1914. At the second anniversary of the First World War — July 27, 1916, at dawn, when the sky was overcast with red clouds and the sun gradually rose above the horizon, overshadowing the glare of gunfire, I was born in a corner in Shanghai.

The Downfall of Li Yuanhong's Constitution, Yuan Shikai's Loss of Power, and the Wars Among Northern Warlords

Although the honorable Mr Zhongshan[1] succeeded in 1911 with his revolution in overthrowing the Manchu dictator government, the lingering feudal powers in China were not eliminated. Even five years after the founding of the Republic, China did not become a liberated nation as the honorable Mr Zhongshan had envisioned. After I was born, Li Yuanhong's fall from power was followed by that of Yuan Shikai. After that came the chaotic wars among northern warlords.[2] I was born and raised in such a tumultuous time.

III. The Family I Was Born Into

Father and His Family

My father's surname was Lin, his given name Jingxing, styled Hanbi. Later he used Hanbi as his name. Father was grandfather's eldest son. He was handsome and tall, with fine features, which won him the nickname "Handsome Man." He had large, bluish eyes shadowed with long and thick lashes. His fine, black hair had a brown tint to it. These were the most apparent features that I inherited from him. His temperament was mild and graceful, and he treated people politely. He was pure and dignified by nature, and his thought was progressive. He treated grandfather with piety and his brothers with love. Father acted like a lamb when dealing with kind people, but was like a tiger when fighting against the evil, yielding to none.

I heard that he was very smart as a child. Once, when Great Grandfather was celebrating his birthday, Grandfather asked a newly elected *zhuang yuan*[3] to compose a birthday eulogy. The day before the occasion, the eulogy was written and delivered to the house. It was indeed a great honor and the entire family was passing it around in excitement. Father also joined in rushing to read it. He was only seven years old, but was already able to write short essays, so grandfather handed him the composition. After he finished reading it, he suddenly crumpled it and tore it into pieces, yelling, "The content does not fit the title, completely meaningless." This happened so unexpectedly that nobody was able to stop him in time. In the feudal society of patriarchal dictatorship, such behavior was outrageous. Great Grandfather was shaking with rage, and Grandfather was gnashing his teeth in anger. As for Grandmother, she was shivering with terror. The people surrounding them were all scared, looking at one another in dead silence. This was truly too much. Even though Father was Great Grandfather's eldest grandson, Grandfather's eldest son, and the most adored child in the family, he committed a grave crime this time. Destroying an essay by the new *zhuang yuan* of the imperial court not only humiliated that official, it amounted to the crime of "deceiving the emperor." How horrible! With such a charge, even Grandfather with his official title could not take the consequences, not to mention the retired Great Grandfather. The family decided to give him a thorough beating and use his bruised little body to redeem his mistake with the *zhuang yuan* the next day. That might mend his crime somewhat and alleviate official punishment. A ruler was produced, and Father was forced to lie down on his stomach. Who could bear to afflict the soft and white skin of a child with such violence? But who could rescue him? Grandfather, the executor as a matter of course, picked up the ruler with shaking hands. Father did not cry, only defiantly awaiting the beating. Great maternal love conquering fear, Grandmother threw herself on her beloved darling and shielded him with her own body. She begged Great Grandfather, Grandfather and everybody else there, hoping that someone would stand up and prevent such cruelty, a disaster in the Lin household. Grandfather softened, but then tried to muster his courage again to carry on this punishment in order to rid the family of potential disaster from the emperor. He sighed, saying to Grandmother: "You get up! This is a show to win sympathy from the imperial court. What other choice do we have? Unless somebody knows the original essay and manages to copy it all down, nothing less could redress the situation. But Heaven knows! Who would know the original wording?" At this, Father suddenly started laughing and jumped up, yelling, "The disaster is over! The disaster is over! Ha! Father, why didn't you say so earlier? You broke my heart! I don't fear that the emperor would cut my head off, but I am really afraid that you would beat me to death. Because I love you so much, if I die this way, I would certainly become a wronged ghost. As for retrieving the essay, that's easy. Give me a pen and ink quickly. When I'm done, I have to hurry and go horse riding!" Though the entire family knew he was smart, this was an exaggeration! Having no better solution, they could only let him try. After Father finished writing, he ran out of the door in the wink of an eye. Grandmother was sweating, worrying whether Father got it right. Then everybody passed around and read out loud the essay Father recalled from memory. Nobody dared say that it was completely correct, they merely felt it was about right. A severe beating was thus avoided.

On Great Grandfather's birthday, every room in the house was decorated with lanterns and colored streamers. A great number of guests came, all in a jolly mood. Great Grandfather was a little beside himself with joy. Grandfather and Grandmother were constantly worried, and anxious about the essay the child had reproduced. Grandfather feared that if that essay turned out to be incorrect, and the *zhuang yuan* started pressing charges, what could he do? Even if it was reproduced correctly, the handwriting was obviously different and he might get offended, and then what? Soon it was noon and the *zhuang yuan* swung in, riding in a sedan carried by eight men. Upon entering the front gate, he saw Great Grandfather and the the rest of the family kneeling down to show respect. He immediately got out of the sedan, saying, "I don't deserve this! I don't deserve this! I should bow to Great Grandpa. Get up, get up quickly!" But instead of getting up, everybody kowtowed to him. This indeed startled him, since this kind of ceremony was carried too far. He said to himself, "What is this? Why is this happening?" Only then did Grandfather dare raise his head and said in a trembling voice, "Your lowly servant deserves to die, to have such an unfilial son who violated your imperial writing. If you could kindly forgive the seven-year-old child, your lowly servant will report the whole thing to you." The *zhuang yuan* said: "No harm, no harm, what major crime could a child commit? Get up and tell me!" Grandfather assisted Great Grandfather to his feet, and with his voice still trembling, started telling the *zhuang yuan* how his essay was destroyed by the child and how that child had tried to retrieve it from memory. He asked the *zhuang yuan* to correct the essay and kindly forgive the child. Upon hearing this, the *zhuang yuan* frowned, but then said, "Forget it. Since the child could write it out from memory, why not let him recite it to me?" So Father was dragged in, and he calmly recited the whole essay from start to finish. After he heard Father's recitation, the *zhuang yuan* thumped the table. Everybody started shaking again, thinking something horrendous was going to happen. But to everyone's surprise, he cried, "He is an infant prodigy!" He asked for a writing brush and ink and wrote "prodigy" on a horizontal inscription board. Putting down the pen, he quickly held Father in his arms and set him on his knees, holding Father's little hand and asking him this and that. He also gave Father a silk robe and two cakes of precious ink as presents. Only then was the entire family relieved. From then on Father's name as prodigy spread out all over the county.

Father's was an official family from the old feudal society. They lived for generations in Minhou, Fujian. They owned houses, land, and other property. After Great Grandfather died, Grandfather carried on as an official, and thus kept up the appearance of a prominent family. Unfortunately, however, when Father was nine years old, my virtuous and capable Grandmother died of illness. After losing his domestic assistant, who showed authority and humility on appropriate occasions, Grandfather soon revealed his true nature. In just a few years, he obtained concubine after concubine and started drinking and philandering. Father was very filial to Grandfather, but his dignified nature did not allow him to hide his discontent with such a family, nor could he treat those concubines with due respect. Pretty soon the entire family considered him "a nail in the eyes." At the end of that year, with the excuse of "quiet study," Grandfather packed Father off to a nearby scenic spot — Mount Gu, where he hired a teacher for him. Father then started his monk-like life, without actually becoming a monk. Thanks to this experience, he laid a solid foundation in literature. While Father was engaged in learning, Grandfather's family was failing steadily, either this concubine walking out or that one running away, which disheartened Grandfather completely. Later he ended his official career on the pretext of retirement. He already knew by then that his two younger sons — my second uncle and third uncle — did not have the potential that Father did, so he summoned Father back from Mount Gu and sent him to school. After that he would often stroke Father's head and say: "You are very good, you can study hard. You should study diligently and make something of yourself. The Lins have no one but you to depend on. I am too old. In recent years we've truly had bad fortune. Don't forget that you are Grandfather's eldest grandson!" After entering school, Father indeed put great effort into his studies. He resented his conservative family but accepted the mission to restore it. He also intended to reform it. As for exactly how, I do not think that he had a clear idea.

Upon graduation, Father immediately went to Japan where he enrolled in the Imperial University to study law and government. He was only twenty then. He returned to China the following year and met Mother in Shanghai. At that time, Mother was a member of the Revolutionary Alliance (Tong meng hui),[4] and an immediate assistant to Qiu Jin, Female Knight of Jianhu.[5] Mother had by then devoted herself for five or six years to the revolution to overthrow the Manchu government. Father's uncle was a local government official in Mother's hometown, so that Father and Mother were connected by this relationship between the families. They started out being friends and then fell in love. Mother's condition of marriage was: "Never serve under the Qing government and never be an official." At the age of twenty-two, he accepted this condition and married her. That was a grave blow to Grandfather. He felt that not only did Mother rob him of his son, she also destroyed a candidate who was to carry on the family career of officialdom. Because Father had given up the mission he had promised to accomplish, Grandfather resented Mother from the beginning.

After getting married, Father returned to the Imperial University to continue his education. But because of Grandfather's bitterness, Mother had to provide for Father financially. Later Father went to study in Germany and did not come back until he was twenty-eight years old, the third year of the Republic. By then he had joined the Revolutionary Alliance and later the Nationalist Party. Returning to China, Father was appointed the Secretary of the Congress. He had his own political ideals, but as politics in China never moved along in any stable fashion, he was frustrated all the time. He only associated with a few people, among them Song Jiaoren.[6] Song and Father depended on each other and Father had become Song's indispensable assistant. I heard that Father drafted all of Song's political addresses and papers. Unfortunately Song was assassinated. Afterwards, Yuan Shikai appeared on the political scene eager to be an emperor. During his presidency, he dismissed the congress and ordered any anti-Yuan activists to be arrested. Father had to move his family to Benxi Lake in Shenyang.

Father's appointment was too short, and his political expenditures high. Besides, he had to provide for Grandfather. As a result, in a few years Mother's financial condition got worse. Within Father's family, he had Mother, my three-year-old sister, two cousins also in politics, a male servant and a maid. I was at the same time growing in Mother's womb. Mother had serious pregnancy symptoms and could not work, so the family lived on her savings. Because of our financial strain, Mother dismissed the male servant. Still, the six-person household was hard to manage. Fortunately she sustained the family with incredible strength, we got by all right. Father never learned how to run a family, but with Mother's constant love, he lived an easy life, except for worries about his career.

Nine months later, Father received a telegram from Grandfather. He was bound by filial duty to leave the north for the south. I've mentioned earlier that I had two uncles. My second uncle was not particularly intelligent, but was very kind and straightforward. He worked in the business field all along, which suited him very well as a lifetime occupation. My third uncle was not a bit less intelligent than Father. His expertise was rapid reading and his credentials in literature, science as well as politics were very strong. He knew exactly how to curry favor, and I heard that he did not make good use of his talent. He was a politician, a businessman, later a newspaperman, and an educator. But he always changed his name and moved from one occupation to another. While Father was at Benxi Lake, Third Uncle was the manager of a bank, but because he could not account for certain expenses, the government wanted to confiscate our family property. Father received a telegram that read: "Quickly raise funds, rescue Third Brother, and save our family reputation." Father wanted to gather funds to save face for Grandfather, but worried that his acquaintances in the north would talk about the embarrassing event about his younger brother. Left with no alternative, he decided to go to Shanghai alone first. The night before he left, Mother said to him in an unusually loving tone: "Bi, you go on first, and be sure to find a job, as long as it is not against our agreement. We have many old friends in Shanghai and my sister is there. You could gather some loan money from them and send it to your father for now. But don't forget to keep some for our return to the south. We don't have to, nor can we, live in the north any longer. Besides, I am about to give birth, which is another factor." Father promised to do what she had said, consoled her for the whole night, and left for Shanghai the next morning. Upon arrival in Shanghai, he became the chief writer for *The China Times* (Shishi xin bao),[7] writing editorials to attack Yuan and the warlords. His editorials were both accurate and powerful, winning him the reputation as a leader in the Shanghai press circle. But Father never sent Mother money to facilitate the entire family's journey to the south. Not that he forgot Mother's bidding, but that he was not good at borrowing money and he did not want to tell my aunt about it. He might have gathered some money from his limited resources and have sent it to Grandfather. It was nine months later, thanks to my aunt's assistance and Mother's own effort, that Mother took us to Shanghai.

It was midnight, the seventeenth day of my infancy. On his way home from his newspaper office, Father was knocked down by a car on Mahuo Road. The driver was a British man named Keming in Chinese. Some said that Keming was assigned secretly by Yuan Shikai to assassinate father, and some said that he was drunk and careless while driving. What we knew for certain was that he was a running dog of the warlords and later died on the battlefield in the Jiangzhe area. Father's life was thus sacrificed for no good reason. Mother refused to accept Keming's offer of a generous compensation fee, and took the case to court. But the consular jurisdiction was in the hands of the imperialists, leaving us the oppressed with no hope of winning. I have virtually no impression of Father, other than these scattered accounts I heard from Mother.

Mother and Her Family

Mother played a major role in my life. She raised me single-handedly and influenced me the most. Naturally I know more about her than about Father. Her surname was Xu, a prominent family in Chonghua, Zhejiang. Her given name was Yunhua, styled Xiaoshu, but later she used her *hao*[8] for official documents. She was an extremely strong person. Her strength of mind outshone her tenderness, as her emotions did her rationality. She was full of sympathy but at the same time would not tolerate wrongdoings. She would soften on her attitude but would never give in. She liked to follow her own will, but never deviated from justice. She had an independent mind, and she taught me to be the same through love and tenderness. A progressive activist of her time, she carried out her mission, risked her life, and devoted forty years of her blood and sweat. What did she get in return? The Japanese invaded her hometown, destroyed her land and property, and now she led a life of wandering and poverty. Was this her fault? Did she fail the epoch? Or was it the epoch that sacrificed her?

The house in which Mother lived as a child was just like the Garden of Grand Vision (Da guan yuan).[9] Growing up in her prosperous family, she enjoyed all kinds of luxury and comfort. Great Grandfather was a high official in the Manchu government, and Eldest Uncle also reached the official position of *dao tai*.[10] Grandfather, living among these high officials, naturally lived a carefree life. People said that Grandfather was very much like Jia Baoyu,[11] with high literary talent but never desiring any official post. He liked to have many beautiful maids in the household and also enjoyed associating with courtesans. But his wife, of serious nature, hardly ever joked, so that for all her talent, beauty, and the children she bore, she and Grandfather never developed a loving relationship. Half of the time Grandfather stayed in courtesans' houses. After she died, Grandfather married a cousin on his mother's side, and his second wife was my grandmother who gave birth to Mother.

This grandmother was over twenty years younger than Grandfather, very beautiful, but illiterate. Early on, everybody tried to persuade Grandmother's mother to turn down the proposal, telling her that the former wife was bullied to death. This old lady, however, said with assurance, "I thank you for your good intentions, but it's only because you don't understand my nephew that you think this way. I am quite certain, if my daughter marries him, the two of them will be very happy. His former wife did not understand my nephew a bit, so of course her talent and beauty was of no use. My daughter shares his taste and they will make a loving couple." Her prophecy fulfilled itself. After my grandparents got married they indeed loved each other very much. Born generous and agreeable, she was precisely what her mother had said, most suited to be Grandfather's wife. Very peculiarly, illiterate as she was, she showed excellent comprehension whenever he discussed poetry and literary allusions with her, which made her the perfect companion for Grandfather. She not only bought Grandfather many beautiful maids, but also ordered them to practice playing music and singing. Courtesan acquaintances would all address my grandmother as "adopted mother" and by now Grandfather stopped visiting at courtesans' houses altogether. Later on Grandmother bore two daughters and several sons.

My aunt was the second among all Grandfather's children while Mother was the youngest one. Aunt was plump, and Mother was slim. Although they were born of the same mother, Aunt's personality exactly resembled that of Grandfather's former wife. And for that reason my grandfather especially doted on my mother. Grandfather had stunning musical talent. He played all different kinds of Chinese musical instruments and was a peerless singer of *kun qu*.[12] He built himself two boats and had them decorated with comfortable interiors and luxurious exteriors. In spring and autumn, he often took my mother along in the boat for sightseeing. He often said, "Yunguan" — my mother's nickname — "is very considerate of me. Without her, what do I have to live for?" One could tell from this what Mother meant to Grandfather. Besides Mother and a band of maids who played music, there was a girl called "Daiyu in the Xu household."[13] Her surname was Lu, a study companion for Aunt. She was the Daiyu in grandparents' house. She was known for her ravishing beauty, and her poetic talent equaled that of Mother and Aunt, but her wit surpassed them both. She was particularly good at painting plum flowers. Grandfather just adored her. While Mother traveled with Grandfather, she also studied hard. Thanks to her intelligence and the favorable influence from nature, she gradually built a solid foundation for literature.

In those days marriage was arranged by parents and match-makers. That was how Aunt married the only son of the rich gentry Mei family as she just turned twenty. But because the bride had all the beauty in the world and the bridegroom had zero talent, Aunt regretted marrying him the rest of her life. A few years later, her husband died, so Aunt came back with her daughter to live with her parents. Regret and sadness somehow inspired strength in my aunt. She stopped meaningless self-destruction and did not allow herself to fade away. She decided to devote herself to social affairs. At this time, Dr Sun Zhongshan's revolution was like the light at dawn after a long night, and the Revolutionary Alliance was just recruiting new members to strengthen itself. Aunt again left her maternal home. But this time, she took a route to transform herself. In Jiangsu she met Qiu Jin, the knight of Jianhu, and became sworn friends with her. As a result, the Revolutionary Alliance gained another important member — Xu Zihua.[14]

Having witnessed Aunt's unhappiness after marriage and her misery as a daughter-in-law in the old feudal society, Grandfather decided that he would not let Mother suffer the same fate. He announced that he would find someone after Mother's own heart and have him marry into the Xu family. He said furthermore that people from rich families had too many bad habits, so he would pick someone from a modest background. It was all right if the future son-in-law was poor, for the Xus had plenty of money. Because there were so many children and daughters-in-law living in the same compound, Grandfather was concerned that Mother might have difficulty living there after she got married. So Grandfather had a new house built for her, an extremely beautiful and stately house with exquisite sculpture and carving. Everybody in the village was impressed and wondered which talented man would have the good fortune to be Grandfather's son-in-law. Upon completion of the house, Grandfather assigned land ownership among his offspring. He ordered special redwood furniture and elegant decorating pieces to be installed in the house in order to welcome the new couple. Mother's female cousins were all jealous of her privilege. But Mother was not happy over this. On the contrary, she felt frustrated and stifled. Of course, she loved her father and appreciated what he had done for her. She also had a strong attachment to the happy home that she grew up in. Yet on the other hand, she knew that times were changing fast and she sensed the imminent storm and the fate of a family like hers. She foresaw its inevitable fall. She was not going to build her ivory tower over what would be ruins the next day. She envied her sister's social activities. Every time her sister came home, Mother would drag her aside and ask her about the secret work she was doing. If her sister said that secret work was not to be revealed, she would make solemn vows to keep it confidential, writing out her oath with blood. She would often tremble with excitement listening to her sister's descriptions.

As Mother could not quite decide what she wanted to do in life, even to the day she turned twenty-one, Grandfather still did not succeed in getting her married. In that very year, Grandfather died. Mother grieved deeply. After that she asked Grandmother to let her go to Shanghai to study. Naturally Grandmother would not allow it, but she could not resist Mother's coaxing. Aunt used her influence on the side, so finally Grandmother gave in. Nevertheless, Grandmother had difficulty raising Mother's tuition. Mother proposed that she use her dowry that Grandfather had prepared for her. She offered to give up her new house and assign the land as gifts to my uncles. Grandmother could no longer find any more excuses, so she let Mother leave for Shanghai after the mourning period for Grandfather was over. Mother entered the Patriotic Women's School (Aiguo nüxue) founded by Mr Cai Juemin.[15] From then on she joined Mr Juemin, Qiu Jin, known as the knight from Jianhu, Aunt, and many other revolutionaries in their work to liberate the Chinese nation.

Extremely bright, Mother spoke eloquently and excelled in writing. With her resolve and courage, she soon became a major woman warrior in the Revolutionary Alliance. She helped Qiu Jin edit women's newspapers and also secretly made bombs. Once a bomb unexpectedly exploded, almost causing a major tragedy. Fortunately Mother avoided disaster by cleverly negotiating with the policemen. Seeing that she was young and cute, they did not believe that she could be up to anything dangerous. After Knight Qiu died, both Mother and Aunt became wanted suspects. They feigned sickness to be admitted into a Japanese hospital, but shortly after that they risked their lives going to Hangzhou for Knight Qiu's funeral and burial. However, they did not succeed. The grave they dug was leveled up by the Qing court. The government tried to arrest the people involved in her burial. Mother and Aunt again struggled secretly with this evil power, and finally at a stormy dawn they succeeded in burying Knight Qiu's remains at the inner West Lake (Xi hu), near Xileng Bridge (Xileng qiao), which is today's Wind and Rain Pavilion (Feng yu ting) built in memory of Knight Qiu. Her knightly bones were at last laid to rest. After that, Mother continued her underground work.

The party once held a meeting and passed a resolution, requesting Mother to marry a certain diplomat in the Qing Court. The reason was that this capable diplomat played a crucial role in the political scene. To win him over from the Manchus, the Revolutionary Alliance decided that Mother should play the star role in the sex-trap. Mother refused, on the grounds that she was not certain she could change such a person who had long immersed in the official circles. She did not want to risk the freedom of her body and mind on such an adventure. She was willing to accept any other assignment, no matter how dangerous, for the sake of the party, the country, and her beliefs. Her appeal was accepted by the party. She did not play Xishi,[16] but continued her combat life.

When she met Father at twenty-three, she guessed that this young man would contribute his talent, sweat, and toil to society and the country. They planned to walk together on the real road of life by marriage. But unfortunately when they got married, Father had not finished his education. The first blow came from Grandfather's discontinuation of financial support to Father. To show her defiance, Mother persuaded Father to continue studying abroad. As a result, she shouldered the heavy responsibility of the family finances. One year later, added to that burden was the birth of my sister. By then, the Revolution of 1911 had succeeded. Seeing Yuan's signing of the traitorous "Twenty-one Demands,"[17] his ambition to be the emperor, and the battles among the northern warlords, she was heartbroken at the thought how the real revolutionaries over the years had sacrificed their lives. She decided to shift focus from revolution to education. On the one hand she devoted herself to educating the younger generation, on the other hand she used the payment from her work to support her family. Her expectations of her husband, children and students were just like her earlier expectations of the success of revolution. It was only until Father came back from abroad and she was eight months pregnant with me that she stopped teaching temporarily.

Fate never loosened its harsh grip on Mother. As I mentioned earlier, since Father failed to succeed in politics and was forced to lead a secluded life, Mother had to continue to support the family. Father left her for the south to perform filial duty to his parents. Knowing that the baby she was carrying could not wait for its father to send them money to be born, she decided to go south herself. First, she pawned her jewelry and clothing, using the proceeds for travel fare to Shanghai for one of my cousins. The latter then in Shanghai gathered a sum of money and remitted it to Shenyang. With that money, another cousin went to Shanghai. At the same time, she redeemed some other items to be brought to Shanghai for further consignment. She thus managed to send the entire family to Shanghai. But finally it was Mother herself who was left behind, because they had a short-term loan in Shanghai. The jewelry and money they had brought there barely covered their fare and paid back the loan. She sold all the furniture in Shenyang, and that money went to the redemption of the items pawned earlier, things Grandfather had given her as tokens of remembrance, not to be given away. After weighing the situation she decided to send Father an express mail in care of Aunt, asking him to think up some solution. Coincidentally, when the letter reached Aunt, it had a burnt circle in one corner. According to the customs of Mother's hometown, a letter with a burnt mark meant either an emergency or bad news. So Aunt took the liberty of opening the letter. Knowing that her brother-in-law was not good at financial and family affairs, Aunt simply kept quiet about that letter. Meanwhile, she immediately sent Mother money for traveling, and that was why I was conceived in Shenyang but born in Shanghai. Father named me Beili, Northern Beauty, in memory of Shenyang.

My Family Life and Its Influences

This was indeed an unfortunate start. Although Father cherished me, everybody rejected me, because he suddenly met with disaster while Mother was still in bed less than a month after my birth. Being regarded as a jinx was a major burden I could not avoid. Other than Mother's occasional caress and insufficient nursing, I lay in the little bed by the door all day. What a pitiful little creature I was, and yet who had the spare time to care for me? When Father died, our family finances fell into hopeless straits. Fortunately, due to Uncle Li Bake and a few friends' help, as well as Mother's own struggle, Mother, Sister and I managed to have a roof above our heads. Father's remains were buried next to Xileng Bridge at West Lake, following his wishes. I heard that during the first few days after his death when people were busy arranging the funeral, Mother was so heart-broken that she fainted once. So I was forgotten in that little bed, crying for hunger almost the whole day. By pure luck Mr and Mrs Hu came to offer condolences. Mrs Hu was still nursing her baby and she gave me a share of a meal. This embrace and milk from another's mother warmed up the pathetic half-frozen body of an orphan. Although I had a hard time, I surprisingly survived. After all, a mother never fails to love her child, and a loving mother never blames her child. My mother saw my miserable condition and sensed my innocence through her own grief. She could not bear to see me suffer like this, so she thought of Grandmother, who would definitely love me, due to her love for Mother herself. After

I was a full month old, she sent someone to take me to Chongde, where I spent my childhood in my grandmother's house. There, I suffered from everyone's snobbery and neglect. Grandmother loved to play *majiang* and enjoy herself in peace, ignoring all household matters. Although she loved me, she did not bother much with me, and naturally I was not very happy in those days.

My first wet nurse loved me very much, but she was too weak and sickly, so I almost died for malnutrition. My second wet nurse was plump, but she cared for nothing but money. She colluded with the maids in the house to sell her milk, and often smeared hot pepper sauce on her nipples so that I would become scared of nursing. Whenever I cried, I would receive severe mistreatment. No one paid any attention to how I felt. Although Mother also came back to Chongde to make a living, she used Grandparents' old house at West Gate to found Chongde County Women's Normal University and its affiliated elementary school. As a result, she seldom had time to come to Grandmother's place to see me. I gradually understood my wet nurse was abusing me, and later whenever I saw Mother I would not let my wet nurse hold me. Every time I was taken to see Mother in her school, I would wail about not wanting to go back to Grandparents' house. Mother was very touched by my attachment to her, and later she heard from my own words about how my wet nurse treated me. She took me with her and raised me herself. From then on her school was my home.

When I left my wet nurse, I was not yet one and a half years old, but because I had been under nourished and neglected, I was very fragile and my digestion equaled only to that of an infant. After she dismissed my wet nurse, Mother managed to simmer thick gruel and longan soup as a substitute to feed me. Mother often said to herself, "This child has suffered so much. She was half destroyed by this wet nurse this past year! I mustn't forget that she is her father's favorite. Her father often said after her birth, 'You take care of the elder child (meaning my elder sister), I'll look after my little daughter.' Now that her father died, I must bring her up properly." Although I was five years younger than my sister, and could not yet toddle, I started talking unusually early (when I was eight months old). Exceedingly sensitive, I already knew how to determine other people's moods. Whenever I woke up hungry at night and wanted to cry, I would always hold back my tears and say to Mother, "Mom, I shouldn't cry, right? The teachers are next door, they'll think I am annoying, right?" Sometimes I would suddenly tell mother, "Mom, I am so sad that I don't have a daddy and a home. Living in school is not good, annoying to others, right?" Mother was ever so proud of my perception.

My sister's name was Hui, and her infant name was He'er. Ever since childhood, she was peerless in her looks and intelligence. When we were in Shenyang, she was only five, but she could recite many Tang poems and a dozen Song poems. Growing up in Shenyang, she became fluent in Japanese. During Mother's stay in Benxi Lake, Sister took charge of all our transactions and negotiations about transportation, so she won Mother's special favor. After Father died, Sister did not realize that she had lost her privileges. She still said whatever she wanted to say and did whatever she wanted to do. Besides, she was mischievous in nature and caused a lot of trouble for Mother, creating fodder for gossip of people living in Grandparents' house. Because of this, I was favored over her and Mother concentrated her love on me. The more Mother loved me, the more my little cleverness showed its full capacity in understanding people and the world. Inevitably, Mother often spanked and scolded my sister. Sister was born kind and generous, very broad-minded. She loved Mother and me even though I had to have the upper hand in everything and sometimes reported things to Mother that caused her physical punishment. She often said, "Sister is Mother's comfort and I'm Mother's vent. Comforting is indeed necessary, but venting is equally indispensable." Who said that Sister was not sensitive about the way of the world? What she said contained profound philosophy.

In those years, Mother was exhausted by my constant illness. Talk of my sister's lack of perception in worldly matters bothered her. At the same time, she had to deal with the intrigues and conflicts of interest in society, so that everyday she worked hard. Fortunately for her tenacity, Mother slowly but surely regained balance. The fear harbored by Grandparents' family that she was coming back to claim her share of family property after her husband's death now automatically dissolved. The attack on her from adversaries in the community also subsided. Because of her skillful management and diplomacy, the year when I was five, Chongde County Normal University and the affiliated elementary school had their own campus built at South Gate, thanks to financial assistance from a gentleman. The school no longer needed to rent Grandparents' house, nor did the students have to suffer the bad influence from a declining family. I gradually grew stronger, but tragically, my sister contracted a stomach disease and died when Mother was busy supervising the construction of

County Women's Normal dormitory. With limited material resources and assistance, Mother could not take care of both her public and private concerns. For the benefit of thousands of other children, Mother ultimately sacrificed her ten-year-old daughter. My sister could not come back to life, and Mother blamed herself for her negligence. At the same time, she contained her grief and continued to supervise the construction of the new campus.

After the dormitory was completed, we moved along with the Women's Normal University into our new home and started my new family life in school, which influenced me in many ways. For instance, I was sometimes very strong-willed, but I respected truth and never had any resentment. This, of course, partly derived from Mother's influence, but partly from my environment. I observed good discipline, I treated workers equally, I was honest, and had no interest in gambling. I was giving, thoughtful, and sensitive. When I met with frustration, difficulty, or mistreatment, I would always keep calm no matter how I felt inside. But for all appearances, I could be quite depressed deep down inside.

IV. My School Life

Elementary School

It is not too far from the truth to say that I am very afraid of my mother. Even to this day, I can argue with her about right and wrong in writing, but not face to face. I will always remember one event, the biggest humiliation I have ever endured in my whole life. At about seven years of age, Mother for some reason scolded me harshly. I must have "eaten a tiger's brain or swallowed a lion's gall" that day and I retorted to her from the next room. To my amazement, Mother ran over, picked me up as if I were a chick, and took me to her study. She threatened to beat me and scolded me for bad behavior, for purposefully irritating her. She said I was hopeless. Gnashing her teeth she cursed me, and forced me to admit my mistake and beg for forgiveness. Her eyes were filled with tears. I was full of regrets too, and in my little heart I deeply felt Mother's love. But pride dominated my entire consciousness. I did not think that I did anything so wrong, surely not deserving such severe punishment. I could not accept it. Finally, I got a good beating. Mother even pushed me down so that I fell on my knees.

In spite of that Uncle Zhen who really loved me came in several times to persuade me to say sorry, I simply ignored him. I knelt there for about one hour, and then I suddenly realized that Mother had already gone out of the room and there I was, still kneeling. What a fool I was! So I jumped up, dashed into the bedroom, and got into bed. I skipped dinner that night, thinking, "Is it because Mother feeds me that I have to endure her scolding and beating? If not, why don't I get to beat her and scold her when she makes mistakes?" As Mother and I shared the same bed, there was no avoiding her at night. When she came to bed, she was still nagging me. I was as resolved as ever to ignore her. The next morning I refused to get up for breakfast. She said in anger, "Very well. Don't get up for the rest of your life if you insist." I already felt a bit dizzy from hunger, but I did not budge. Uncle Zhen was afraid that this deadlock would go on and cause a crisis, so he continued to mediate between us. All the teachers in the school knew what happened. Knowing that I was eager to save face, they kept silent and simply pretended that I was sick. They offered all kinds of consolation. But I held my ground. Later I felt more and more dizzy, but I thought, in the worst scenario I would die, and what was the big deal? Finally Mother relented, probably thinking that she should not contend with a child. She became quiet and did not rouse my anger. Uncle used the excuse that Grandmother wanted to see me and took me to her home. Now, wishing to compensate for her neglect of me in my early childhood, she treated me with special kindness and affection. I loved her in return. When I arrived that day, Grandmother had already prepared many of my favorite foods. She persuaded me not to be stubborn and break Mother's heart. She also promised me that she would scold Mother for overdoing it. That made me jump with delight. That night, I ate dinner heartily and afterward was taken back home by A Wu, our long-term hired hand. This wound healed between mother and daughter, and we loved each other as ever. But through my various small acts, Mother discovered my uncompromising nature. She knew clearly that I could not make something of myself by being spoiled. As there was no way I could be comfortably contained in the Women's Normal University Affiliated Elementary School, she sent me to Shanghai's C. S. Affiliated Elementary School the following year. From then on, I was completely on my own.

C. S. Affiliated Elementary School was a typical missionary school. Thanks to the flourishing world economy during that era, the school was well-equipped. Educated in that environment, I became increasingly accustomed to privilege. At C. S. I learned to speak fluent English and acquired European manners and an eye for beauty. I also learned how to receive people with courtesy and genteelness. At the same time, that environment inspired in me a love for music. I began to take singing lessons and then piano lessons. Shortly after I entered C. S., the civil war in Jiangsu and Zhejiang broke out. Defeated soldiers ransacked the interior of those two provinces and plundered my hometown (Chongde). Early that winter, Mother traveled all the way to Shanghai to see me.

When I was eleven, I graduated from elementary school. That summer, a terrible scarlet fever, an epidemic, affected my whole hometown. Like many other children, I also contracted it. The death rate reached as high as eighty percent. However, due to Mother's careful attention and my doctor's special treatment, I narrowly escaped death. I still remember my doctor Mr Chen Yuancan, a native of Haining, Zhejiang. He was of small build and mild temperament. Later he became our family friend and long-term medical consultant.

The Nationalist Party reorganized itself in the thirteenth year of the Republic. It launched its purge within the party in the sixteenth year of the Republic.[18] Some of the conservative forces in Chongde wanted to take advantage of this chaotic time to gain ground. They besieged the County Women's Normal, examined all the documents in our house, and threatened to arrest Mother on the pretext that she was a leftist in the party. Some even accused her of being a Communist. Naturally it was beneath Mother to fight directly with them. As the saying goes: "A brave man does not make instant confrontations."[19] Mother took a night train to Hangzhou. Soon after, she assumed the position of Minister of the Women's County Party Division of Hangzhou. The hard facts gave those rascals a great blow and they no longer dared harass us. Even their coveting of the position of President of Women's Normal was shattered. Under Mother's leadership, Women's Normal was very well organized, so that while she acted as Minister, she was concurrently the president of Women's Normal. After Mother completed her service at the Party Division, she resigned from her official position and returned to her hometown to continue her educational enterprise.

That year I was just twelve years old and had recuperated my health. Mother felt that I should no longer receive the elite education at C. S., so she took me to Hangzhou to sit in the entrance examination to Provincial G High School's Affiliated Elementary School. I entered that school in late

July. G High School's Affiliated Elementary School was a sizable school with a long history. It had academic first-rate facilities, except that the school buildings were very old. It was to C. S. as an ancient temple to heaven. In terms of the cultures and customs of these two schools, they were significantly opposite. I changed from the highly aristocratic privilege to the lifestyle of commoners that required me to take care of myself. I had a hard time adjusting. Some daily necessities and toys, which I considered worthless, were treated as treasures and valued by my classmates. That made me laugh in secret. Fortunately my aunt Lu lived in Hangzhou and delivered snacks and pickled vegetables to me several times a week. Mother from time to time would also send me food by boat, so in terms of eating I did not have any difficulty. I was by nature a bit aloof and quiet, and did not socialize much with others. When I first went to G High School's Affiliated Elementary, my classmates all said that I was gloomy. Later on, my teachers discovered my talent in writing, speaking, and learning dialects, so they often asked me to do public speeches at assemblies. During those events my performance was very good each time, which earned me more opportunities to speak and to socialize. As time went on, I grew used to doing such things, and my personality changed completely. Mother was very satisfied about my education there. I had earlier disliked greeting people, and now I was able to mix with many easily and smoothly. During a rally in Chongde, I gave a very lively speech in Mandarin. In addition, my introspective and neurotic personality gradually took an outward turn. My love for competition and argument also formed at this time.

My Middle School Days

During the two years at in G High School's Affiliated Elementary, my grades were steady, but I rarely scored ninety or one hundred on my report cards. The school judged students according to their grades and I, too, did not hesitate to estimate myself by my grades. Therefore, that year — the eighteenth year of the Republic — facing G High School's entrance examination, I was extremely frightened. Because I did not know where to start to prepare for the test, I went back to Chongde Women's Normal to enjoy my happy life. I chatted cheerfully with the resident teachers at Women's Normal and we played and sang together. After the summer vacation, Women's Normal University's Affiliated Elementary combined with other public and private elementary schools to form the First Central

Elementary School of Chongde. Mother assumed the position of principal. She was soon preoccupied with planning the construction of their new campus. This time Mother's had enough money of her own to finance the construction. The school was located at the old site of the revolutionary martyr Mr Lü Wancun's ancestral temple. For that reason the First Central Elementary School was also named Wancun Elementary School. From then on I lodged at Wancun during school breaks. After I passed the entrance examination to G Junior Middle School, I moved into yet another new environment in early September.

G Junior Middle School's demanded that all students do their own laundry, and yet there was no facility for running water. So we all had to draw water from a well. Even an empty bucket was heavy to me, and when it was filled with water, it was even more difficult. It so happened that I loved to be clean and changed clothes everyday. Originally I thought about bringing laundry home as the local students did. I could take it to to Aunt Lu's home and do it there. But I was embarrassed to do so. So I forced myself to try doing it myself. The first time, I slowly lowered the bucket into the well but could not make it sink in the water and fill up. Later I remembered the principle of gravity in physics. I lifted up the bucket, turned it upside down, and threw it in. Only then did it gather some water. But as I had many failed attempts, each time I did laundry I had to draw water countless times and often made a complete mess. That semester I was assigned to live in a campus dormitory and our assigned laundry site off campus across from the river. Ever since the beginning of school, just doing laundry kept me constantly on the run. After one month of school, Mother sent Mr S from Chongde to see me. That afternoon I was drawing water to do my laundry, and my cloth shoes were all soaked. When S saw me, he was first surprised at the awkward appearance of my shoes. I was both embarrassed and irritated, and could not keep my tears back. After S found out why, the next time he came, he brought a female student from the G High School Teachers' Section along with him, and my laundry problem was easily solved. I soon learned that, as long as I was willing to pay, female students from G High School would help me.

Regarding my English, I started learning the spoken language when I entered C. S. Affiliated Elementary School, and by the time I graduated, my English was already quite fluent. When I came to G High School Affiliated Elementary School later, my first impression of the English teacher was her funny and stiff pronunciation. So I took the elective English just to recite English to my teacher. After I entered G Junior Middle School, we started from ABC again. Since I did not feel interested, I continued neglecting my English.

At C. S. Affiliated Elementary my mathematics teacher often said that I had talent and would definitely excel in the subject. But I dreaded mathematics and had no interest in it. When I entered G High, I still felt that way. I remember trying to solve a problem about "chickens and rabbits in the same cage" in an intermediate mathematics class. I was quite vexed by those homework assignments. It was not until the second year when we started algebra that I discovered we had to use many hypotheses and the four fundamental operations. And with those, values of unknown numbers such as x, y, z would be easily solved. That gave me great satisfaction, so during our reading hours I would often flip through the algebra book and do the algebra exercises. The popular saying is quite true, "practice makes perfect." From then on I no longer worried about mathematics tests. In the last year of my junior middle school, my grades soared in mathematics, and I had an even better grasp of geometry.

Sitting in Mother's lap, I had as a child heard many stories of history and learned quite a bit of poetry, so that I had a relatively good foundation in reading and writing. Our Chinese teacher, Mr W. W., taught a combination of both old style and new style Chinese. As I had gone through the subtle molding of Mother's old style literary training, and loved reading fiction, my writing was right to my teacher's taste. He often praised my work for its terseness, depth, and vividness. He also often encouraged me to write for wall newspapers and literary supplements. As a result I loved literature more and more. During that time, I kept a diary which I wrote in *belle lettre* style. Those who shared my literary experience included my classmate Miss Xingzi, the deceased poet Mr Liu Dabai's[20] second daughter. Her handwriting was very beautiful which often made me feel quite ashamed of my own. I decided to imitate Liu Gongquan's[21] calligraphic style. Looking at the model, I could imitate it very well, but once closing the book my handwriting would be completely out of shape. I got so furious that never did I try copying the calligraphy styles again.

After three years of junior middle school, I took another entrance examination and by luck entered the highest institute in Hangzhou — H High School. More than seven hundred students enrolled, and except for athletic training, all classes were coeducational. In those days, very few schools operated that way, and as a result the female and male students related to one another rather awkwardly. Some people, due to lack of contact with the opposite sex, would easily fall in love. In summary, the students fell into several kinds. Some did their utmost to engage in unscrupulous political attempts under the cover of studying. Due to the social and economic crisis of the time and their own lack of conscience, they accepted subsidies to work for certain political organizations. Some just got by with their exams, indulging all day long in their sentimental, romantic dreams. Still others were the so-called scholars who aimed to score one hundred points in all tests and buried themselves in books day and night. At that time, to be frank, I completely ignored all of them, considering them too simple-minded. So I never developed a relationship with any male student. To political and social issues, I paid very little attention. Mother was disheartened and weary of politics. As for Father, when he took up politics it happened to be the low tide in the political realm. So when I was born, he immediately named me Yin, meaning "to live in obscurity." Perhaps he wanted me to be a hermit. Because of Mother's opinion and Father's wish, as a child I already knew a lot about the dark side of politics. All along, Mother wanted me to become a famous doctor when I grew up. In her book being a doctor would allow one to stay away from politics, and medicine was really the most noble, pure, and free occupation. Due to these influences, I had always separated myself from political and social matters. I almost never wanted or even thought about getting involved. I was just then developing a stronger and stronger interest in mathematics, and I even started dreaming about becoming a scientist someday.

As the crisis in global capitalism deepened each day, many countries started fascist practices. The frantic Japanese imperialists fired the first cannon on China, with the September 18 Incident[22] and the January 28 Incident[23] happening in succession. This unprecedented raid pounded hard in the hearts of all patriotic Chinese and awakened many Chinese from their illusions. I realized that I could no longer continue my daydream about being a scientist in my little universe. Without political awakening, without solution to China's social problems, and without liberation of the Chinese nation, each and every single one of China's sons and daughters would have no freedom to dream of. I started collecting all kinds of materials about these incidents, writing for wall newspapers and contributing to periodicals. I wanted to use my pen to summon all Chinese with a conscience to "hold their heads high and straighten their backs." Since then I participated in all kinds of student activities, including rallies and petitions, hoping to use my conscious effort to push the giant wheel of anti-Fascism. But to what avail? I almost cracked my throat from screaming and my hands were sore from writing. I was willing to give my life, which earned me nothing but cold satire and fiery rebuke. "Save the country while studying" had already pacified all the hearts of the youths. I understood deeply then how this ancient, great nation had long been numbed by the evil power of old traditions. And how difficult it was to try to make it rebound and retaliate upon its enemy right now! We could only prepare, prepare for the arrival of a great storm. Convinced that I myself needed to be prepared first, I used my spare time to research all kinds of basic problems in society. In the few years that followed, I indeed put a lot of effort into reading books on many politics, economy, and philosophy to find therein a remedy for China's problems, hoping to do my limited part for our national liberation. At the same time, I gradually differed from Mother in political opinion. She often criticized and interfered with my reading to keep me from unwanted influence. But like other rules, these were useless. I had already built up my own ideals and knew which road China should take and how we should exert ourselves if we wanted real liberation of the Chinese nation.

My College Days

With my high school diploma I graduated from H High School. It was like standing at crossroads not knowing where to go. Mother hoped that I would sign up for the entrance examination to medical school. But not only was I not interested, I did not hold as much respect for that occupation as others did. I found that doctors had neither freedom nor independence, just like monks who could not take part in the world.

The summer after graduation, I read all the enrollment requirements from various universities in the country. There were many different subjects, but I could not find a school that I liked. I originally wanted to take the examination for science and engineering, but before I graduated from H High School I had had severe neurasthenia for half a year, and the doctor said that I was not to study science and engineering in the near future. I wanted very much to study journalism and diplomacy, but only one or two universities offered such majors. And among those schools either campus life was too aristocratic, or the academic thought did not agree with mine. Having no choice, I signed up for the examination for the economics department at C University and the literature department at G University in Nanjing. I did not pass the examination to C University, so I had to go to G University.

During the two years in Nanjing, the capital of Republican China, the world economy reached its worst state of panic. When I saw the rampant corruption my heart became heavier and heavier with growing bitterness and disappointment. Every day I thought: "What is the use of studying all this? I can not learn anything." So in the spring 1937, I left the capital determined to go abroad to the Cherry Blossom Island.[24] I wanted to go there to see how our enemies were preparing to slaughter us. The procedures for going abroad were not completed until early May. But just before I set out, I was hospitalized for more than one month because of tonsillitis. Then the July 7 Incident[25] broke out, and because of this reality, I parted ways with school life from then on.

V. Love and Me

Falling and Out of Love the First Time

I investigated issues and read books that I was interested in. Frankly, I dreaded loneliness, as I had been used to a very active social life. I had frequent associations with boys but was never intimate with any. I enjoyed their company, but always avoided spending time with just one person. I had long believed that "love affairs" would turn out more sour than sweet in the end. A plain smooth sailing kind of happy drama could not possibly have a rich content, and I certainly did not find it worth my while to play a tragic role simply for an individualistic love affair. Besides, I was biased and conflicted about love. To me, a middle-aged man's "first love" was the only real and stable kind, but then how rare it was for a man to wait until then to taste their first love. I did not want to have anything to do with the people around me, for I needed a man who could dominate me. Paradoxically, I was afraid to meet such a man, for I knew I was not willing to be controlled in any aspect.

For all my bias and conflict, I failed to resist love. Yet the moment I found myself falling in love and was warmly loved back, the loss of love had already arrived. My first love was just like spring blossoms not able to withstand the force of wind and rain.

It was like this. When I was only thirteen years old, I met Yin[26] through Mother. He was the eldest son of a declining family, and had already lost his mother. Being thin and tall with a fair complexion, he had an almost feminine kind of beauty. But his steadfastness and unreserved manner gave him a special masculine force. Yin was usually well-groomed, soft-spoken, and elegant in his movements. But he could be stubborn when disagreeing with someone, either in opinion or in plan of action. Mother had known him much longer than I had, and she often said behind his back that he had an indomitable fiery temper. But precisely because of these special characteristics, he gained my appreciation. With his ordinary occupation, he might have difficulty making ends meet. He was seven years older than I was, and about three years before we met he was already struggling to survive on his own.

At that time I was a great enthusiast for the wild countryside, and loved all wonderful things in nature. I often wanted to capture all those things I loved onto paper, but each time I failed. I never painted a picture to my satisfaction. Mother asked Yin to teach me how to paint, which was how we became acquainted. To my amazement, the moment he put or erased a few strokes on my painting, he would bring it to life. Besides applying finishing touches on my work, he often showed me skills in sketching, finding subjects, and brush application. After he instructed me thus for a while, my painting obviously improved. I surprised my art teacher in school who once even said to me, "Your recent paintings are like works by another hand. If you did not paint them in the classroom, I would think you had brought in someone else's paintings." Mother was also very happy about this, as she was very fond of art and sometimes painted. Mother at this time dearly loved Yin for his intelligence, grace, and his reticence.

Yin was particularly talented in music. In spite of the lack of formal training, he played both Chinese and Western instruments with superb skill. Whether he was singing or playing wind or string instruments, his performance was just like his facial expression: smiling, with a touch of desolation. He put his soul into his music. I already liked music when I was at C. S. and now I had gone from the appreciation stage to the learning stage. Yin and I often spent winter and summer vacations together, and I studied from him then. I loved to sing western songs and he often played music to accompany me. What made me most happy was that I learned from a master how to play the ancient Chinese seven-string zither. My teacher was Mr Xu, a nationally acclaimed musician who hardly ever took a student. Once I went with Mother and a few friends to visit Southern Peak. On the mountain we met Mr Xu. That day he was sitting with an elderly monk, carrying a zither and sampling tea. Our fellow traveler D, an intimate friend of Mr Xu's, introduced us. It turned out that Mr Xu also wrote poetry and painted orchids. He had a quite agreeable talk with Mother. Right then, I casually plucked a few strings on his zither. Hearing it, he jumped up and said, "Rare, rare, this girl has extraordinary talent." He then listed many good points of the seven-string zither. He also said, "The zither is ancient and profound, but rather difficult to learn. It is not comparable with other musical instruments. Usually, playing one instrument makes it easier to learn another, but skills in all other instruments does not guarantee mastery of the zither. It takes an expert to play the zither, and only an expert's performance is worth hearing. Not everyone can make an expert. The following types of people could never reach that level: one, feeble-minded people were not qualified, two, the vulgar were not qualified ... three ... four ... . And yet this youngster does have some innate talent." I was curious by nature and upon hearing this I said: "In that case, Uncle Xu, I'll bow to you as my teacher now." He agreed with great joy. Mother wanted to make it official, so she picked a date for me to meet him formally as a teacher and prepared red invitations for that event. He would not accept tuition. We found out that he was very fond of antiques, and presented him with twelve gold wine cups passed down for generations in my grandparents' house as well as some curiosities which Father bought from beyond the Great Wall. We agreed that I would have my lessons at his house that summer. As he lived in Hangzhou, I went to Hangzhou during the summer vacation after spending a few days in Chongde.

Before I started my lessons, I told Yin about it. He was extremely happy, hoping that I could teach him after I mastered the skills. Two days before I left, he wrote out a sheet of ancient style music in gong, shang[27] symbols and tried to teach me how to read it. He said, his guess was that the musical score of the seven-string zither could not be "doh, ray, me, fah ... ." Instead, it must be in "gongchi ... ." This was the first time since we knew each other that we could not spend summer vacation together. But we were both happy and kept up our hopes. In Hangzhou, I lived with Aunt in Autumn Society (Qiu she)[28] at West Lake. Every evening I went to the Xus' to take my music lesson. As Yin had predicted, my teacher asked me to get a copy of *Rudiments of Music* (Qin xue rumen)[29] in which gongchi was used. I did not have to start with the musical symbols, but started right from the skill of the fingers. My teacher was a true master and Mrs Xu was very amiable. As for me, I took it very seriously, not as entertainment, the way I had treated other things before. I felt from the start that I was on a mission. I practiced very diligently. So my accomplishment of that summer's studying was astonishing, causing many people to admire my intelligence. After the summer, I still went to study on Sundays until Teacher Xu left Hangzhou. During that winter vacation, Yin asked Mother to buy an ancient zither for him, and I presented him with a copy of *Rudiments of Music*. Because of his talent, he learned how to play it in just a few days. I still remember the first song I taught him to play. It was "Three Repetitions of the Yangguan Tune" (Yangguan san die).[30] Part of the lyric goes: "I urge you, Sir, to have another glass of wine. After you exit the Yangguang Pass headed toward west, there will be no old acquaintances ..."[31] and "Alas! Once we part here, we will be yearning for and dreaming frequently of each other. Wild geese will be my only visitors."[32] The way he played made it particularly woeful and touching.

Yin and I had spent summers and winters together for the past six or seven years. The nature of our friendship was always close but not intimate, sincere but not romantic. I sympathized very much with his fate, but never offered him any consoling words. I liked his easy grace, and at the same time felt that he had a hidden strength. For that reason I never dared act strong-headed or play rough the way I did with other boys. I would bring him good food and put exquisite toys or stationery on his desk. I often said to myself: "God! Please do not torture him anymore!" I hoped that Mother would love him, and was not a bit jealous. Sometimes I also thought that he should have a kind, loving mother to care for him and that he should have a beautiful, vivacious, and tender lover to console him, and to inspire his talent. But why was it that God had long ago taken away his mother? Why did he still not find a lover to face life with him hand in hand?

My life was very comfortable then. Due to Mother's effective budgeting and saving, we had long ago got out of poverty after Father's death and built ourselves a comfortable home. I had enough money, and I naturally loved material comfort, but still, I never felt that hardship and poverty were too deplorable a condition. I was not particularly sensitive to the physical aspects of life. I never hoped for luxuries, nor did I ever think that I had to live in luxury.

Yin was also very good at literature. The spring when I was eighteen years old, I had neurasthenia and rested at home for half a year. Yin and I often visited each other. That fall, when I recovered and was going back to school, Yin wrote a farewell poem to me. The last line was: "By the south window I am now too lazy to avail myself to the fragrant flower." That poem was about the most sentimental moment of our friendship. Too bad I do not remember clearly all the lines. As friends, we often made botanical specimens, and discussed various social and philosophical issues, as well as art. I respected his opinions, but he lacked diligence and tenacity, which I thought was his fatal weakness.

In the years that followed, everything went on as usual, except that Mother's attitude toward Yin changed. She no longer liked him as before and from time to time even betrayed her dissatisfaction about our friendship. Often during our conversations she would, perhaps without intention, say, "Yin is content with his current circumstances. Looks like he is not planning to move on … ." Sometimes she would say, "Art stands between him and what he should do in life. Everything in his life is about art, he has virtually forgotten all about reality." Once she said: "Yin is a good youth in fantasy. If somebody marries him, she will have to starve to death … ." Another time she said: "I, too, am for unconditional love, but extreme financial difficulty would be a fatal blow to the love between husband and wife." I felt that what she said might have been true for her generation, but why did she tell me? What did it have to do with me?

Mother was indeed quite capable and experienced. On the one hand, she expressed her dissatisfaction of him to me, and on the other hand, she did her best to praise Yin's virtues and still acted very warmly toward Yin. She constantly tried to persuade him to find himself a suitable companion. She further suggested to Yin that he should find a daughter from a rich family. As long as the girl's family did not care about family status, then Yin could marry into the family as a son-in-law. Making use of his future wife's financial resources, he could pursue further studies. Besides that, Mother often volunteered to be the matchmaker and sought out quite a few girls for him. At that time I was eagerly assisting Mother with this, but I felt the girls mother had found for Yin may not bring Yin happiness. As for Yin himself, he never refused Mother's kindness. To those young ladies Mother introduced him to, he would normally make one or two perfunctory dates, always ending with a letter addressed to Mother. They all read like this: "Your great kindness moved me to tears, yet this match will not go anywhere. It is all right. I have to attribute it all to my ill luck. But I feel very uneasy to have wasted so much of your effort! Alas! I can only pray to Heaven so you can forget about me and not worry in vain for me." These letters were always full of gratitude.

When indirection failed, Mother started to work on me. It was the last two years she and I lived together, and I was seventeen or eighteen years old. She often came forward to interfere with our relationship. When the two of us chatted or played music together, she would often come for me under some lame excuse. Sometimes she would send me on an irrelevant errand, and sometimes she would call me to eat snacks or fruits. I resented this, but I did not want to protest openly, as I feared her and loved her even more. But I felt that she was about to snatch my freedom away. I knew well that nothing but my own will guaranteed my freedom. Only my own will would give me power and that power was even more valuable than freedom. If one knew how to exercise one's will, one also knew how to use one's freedom. In the days that followed, I did not stop seeing Yin, but each time we saw each other, we sensed an indescribable melancholy. Time flew. Mother won. I learned that a few days before I boarded the bus from Chongde to Hangzhou at the beginning of the summer vacation, Mother and Yin had an intimate and polite talk. And after that Yin decided to leave us. He did not linger a bit. The day I returned to Chongde, I found him packing with determination. That was a rainy midsummer night. Like a flash of lightning, I lost my childhood companion. He only left me with a few incomplete pages of his diary as follows:

January 5, 1929, sunny
 … I finally discovered my angel in a desert, and she is so alive and innocent. She is more adorable than beautiful …

January 7, 1929
 The weather is bad. It is rainy and cold, depressing my lonely heart even more. Today I started to long for my deceased mother again. Alas! My unfortunate fate! …
 Thank God, this afternoon my angel came. She wiped away all the haze before my eyes and I felt that my sun has already come out. She was so lively, the silver bell of her voice again made me forget about everything. She is God's favorite child. Loneliness is not her lot, as she has a mother who loves her doubly. She has

not suffered hardship in life, and yet she seems quite capable of understanding other people's pain … .

July 5, 1930, cloudy

My angel is back for the summer vacation today. Oh, thank Heaven! Happiness is with me again! …

August 9, 1931, sunny

… Today her light green mandarin dress made her apple-like face look even more beautiful. She did not wear any make up, but seemed holy like a little angel. In front of her, I often detest my own vulgarity. Oh God! Will she love me? …

February 3, 1932, snowy

… Today I almost begged for her love, but her innocence stopped me from voicing it. I lacked the courage to ask …

January 17, 1933, sunny

She is a good person, and I cannot blame her. How can I make her sacrifice her ideal for the love of me? Whether she is right or wrong, she really loves her daughter, and that is a fact. I sympathized with her, so much so that I would rather sacrifice my own happiness. Oh, this dilemma … this dilemma … .

January 21, 1933, snowy

The whole morning I was immersed in musing. I looked back into the past, from the first day I met her, yes, it is true, she has all along been very nice to me. But does she love me? There are more and more people pursuing her each year and their qualifications are better than mine. Why should she love me?

January 24, 1933, sunny

… I've been thinking about this for days, still I have no confidence. Does she really love with me? Heaven knows that her mother recently detests me, and if it was not because she loves me, what else could it be? …

April 6, 1933, sunny

… I would much rather look for my angel in my dreams than embrace a daughter from a rich family in my waking hours … To be a son-in-law at the in-laws' house? What a joke!

January 1, 1934, sunny

It is the beginning of the new year, a bright sunny day. Everybody is joyous. Everybody has a new year resolution. They all resolve to try to make their wishes come true. But what is my wish? It was pitch dark all around me. I cannot see a single ray of light. Recently I have often been scared, scared that I am going to lose my angel. If I lose her, what else do I have? I want to do everything in my power to fight for a better future for myself and to strive for freedom and equality for oppressed people. But if I lose her, I will have no support. Worse than that, I will lose all my motivations …

June 15, 1934, sunny

… Yin! Let me call you by your name for the first and also the last time. Yin, the angel of my dreams! I will lose the happiness of my life and die forever in your heart. Farewell my dream lover … .

Oh, he was gone, never to return. After that it was as if I were moving about in a trance. The very thought of him filled me with a strong sensation. Only then did I realize that was my first love. But now, where were the sweet tenderness and peaceful bliss? Where were they?

Falling in Love Again and My Marriage

After I lost Yin, Mother's next step was trying to make her wish come true, that I would marry V, my cousin, her nephew. V had abundant family property and yet did not have those bad habits typical of children from rich families. He was very talented, very honest and sincere with people, well-versed in literature, and was called the child prodigy in his clan. We saw each other often and were very close, but I did not love him, nor did I want to love him. Both our mothers desired the marriage. The year after I lost my love, we became quite infatuated with each other for a while because of frequent contact. Still, in the end I did not marry him. I anticipated that if we were to marry, neither I nor he would be happy. The reason was very simple: our beliefs were too far apart. My background was that of the second generation of a declining family transforming into a revolutionary family; and he was an inheritor of a wealthy family's property. The things that I imagined and aspired to would never enter his mind. That being the case, our souls and flesh could not possibly be in agreement. I had no use for his wealth, as I did not care for the enjoyment of material life. If I wanted to invest a large sum of money into the realization of my ideal, his family would definitely object to it. Even he himself would probably dislike it. Speaking of his personal needs, as he is the only son of a rich family with its own customs and relations, he should marry a virtuous woman, someone who understood the way of the world and was apt in society. But I was a self-centered girl who treated herself as the starting point in all things. Heaven knows! How were we to match? So, naturally it did not succeed. And later on I met Gengbai, with whom I got engaged and then got married.

Gengbai and I met the year I arrived in Nanjing. Before that, I had read a lot of his writings and knew his personal history very well, especially his love affair with a certain lady which had caused a sensation in the entire city of Nanjing. He was my father's friend. Every time I read his poetry and essays, I always thought that it was rare for a man of his age to have such progressive thoughts. And no wonder he had a romantic relationship with a modern young lady. I met him first at an older woman friend H's home. It was an autumn night. A man wearing a yellow jacket and silver gray pants came to visit. Only after the introduction of our hostess did I know that he was the well-known Mr Lin Gengbai. I was very surprised at his youth and easy grace. He spoke fluent Mandarin and nobody would have assumed that he was from Fujian. After our little chat, we kind of took to each other. A man who believed in socialism and yet at the same time was good at fortune-telling, that was a funny combination. My curiosity caused me to give him the time and date of my birth, asking him to tell my fortune. In less than a week, he sent me a letter with a poem and my fortune attached. The first line of the poem was: "My old friend has a daughter whose features resemble that of her father." His remarks on my fortune were quite novel and had a touch characteristic of our era. But judging from his beliefs, there was still a very big contradiction. And for that reason, I became very interested in him. Later, he often came to H's home to visit me. On a certain official holiday, he invited me to see a cartoon exhibition, and that night he invited me to dine with him alone for the first time. During dinner, he talked about his old flame and all of a sudden burst into tears. I was so shocked that I was at a loss for words. From then on, this Mr Contradiction gave me yet another impression: an infatuated lover. Our contact increased, but all along I took him as one generation older than me and always politely addressed him as Uncle Bai. That was why later some people mistakenly spread the rumor that I married my uncle. After that Gengbai came to see me everyday, and was very attentive to me. But he never hindered my life as a student. Each week he would write me three or four letters, and after he knew that I wrote poetry, he also sent me poems. His letters were rich in content, and vivid with smooth fluidity. His poetry fully expressed his hopes and genius. His poems and letters never bored me, no matter how many he sent. It can be said that I admired his words more than I did his person. He was indeed very sharp, witty, knowledgeable. He had a thorough understanding of various social problems. Each time he talked about the diseases of society and their cures, he would grasp my entire soul. The cold society and crisis-laden world which we lived in compelled me to construct an ivory tower with him. I often thought, if the power of my love could help resolve his contradiction, invigorate a man crushed by his time, and inspire him to contribute to the creation of a brand new world, then, why should I withhold it? Motivated by this, I accepted Gengbai's entire love in the spring of 1937. On March 7 we were engaged in Shanghai. The ceremony was simple and solemn, our tea reception was joyful with more than one hundred relatives and friends attending. It was not until March 3 that I sent an express letter to Mother to inform her of my engagement and to invite her to the ceremony. I did not ask Mother's permission for my engagement, as once I had my heart set, nobody could change my mind. Gengbai was a divorced middle-aged man with five or six children, and I knew for certain that he would not fit with Mother's ideal. But I also knew that Mother loved me and would forgive me, so I took the liberty to decide for myself.

After our engagement, I returned to Chongde, and on the way I went to Shanghai to get medical treatment for my tonsils. During summer vacation I accompanied Mother to West Lake to escape the summer heat. Gengbai came to visit us a few times; he and Mother got along very well. The gunfire of August 13[33] drove Mother and me back to Chongde, and Gengbai rushed to Nanjing to attend legislature meetings.

I lived in Chongde. Now that my dream of going abroad vanished, I might as well go back to college to study. But Mother did her best to stop me, stressing that the war would definitely not last long and I had to make sure to be with her during the war. So I had to stay in Chongde temporarily. I recorded the war news from the radio and wrote for wall newspapers, doing whatever work there was in the rear. Some time passed in that way. I was bored to death and the war on the front line stirred every single cell in my body. "I can not postpone any longer, I want to participate in the mighty torrent of this grand age," I thus expressed my determination to Mother. Meanwhile Gengbai wrote to me that he had decided to move to Nanjing from Shanghai. His excitement and joy filled me with new hope. So I left home, and left Mother.

I first went to Shanghai. During this time, the Chinese forces fought many winning battles. Yet all the universities in Shanghai were preparing to move west. As I had no suitable school to enroll in, I went to Nanjing with Gengbai. I always thought that there must be something more meaningful than studying to do, so we often discussed the war, as well as political and social improvements. We both held grand hopes and wanted to fight together for the final victory of the country. To make our daily life easier, we got married with a simple wedding on September 26. Our witnesses were Mr Chen Zhenru, and Chen Gongbo who has now unfortunately become a traitor to China. It was held at the Nanjing International Association.

Honeymoon Under Heavy Bombs

After we got married, we lived at the Hotel Capital. At that time the devils (gui zi)[34] were bombing the capital, so each day we experienced a few hours of bombing. But we never went to the basement to hide.

During this time, the full-scale resistance war seemed to have been launched only on the military front, so that we found no place for the service of all of us who were determined to do our part. There were many military strategists, diplomats, politicians, celebrities, and important people in the Party staying at the Hotel Capital. Each day we spent all our time in self-criticism and more self-criticism. We learned from one another and encouraged one another, convinced that when we could put ourselves into service soon.

VI. Going West

Good-bye, Nanjing!

Human, material, and financial resources were all moving west due to the on-going war. Gengbai, like everybody else, received three months worth of salary and was told to find his own livelihood. We did not go by car, as during that time of emergency a drop of oil equaled a drop of blood. So we took something anybody could afford — the train.

It was the Christmas of 1937. All institutions were relocated, even workers in the hotel had moved to live in the International House of Refugees. In our hotel only the manager (who was soon to work at the House of Refugees) remained along with a couple of workers. Our food had changed from western cuisine to egg fried rice. And that night there was only one bowl of egg fried rice left for each person. Clearly we would have to eat plain rice the next day! On the street stood a few policemen, and the defense cannon of Nanjing was already set up. The city seemed utterly desolate and quiet, except for Xiaguan Railway Station, where abandoned luggage piled up and the labor class masses who did not have a chance yet to retreat lingered. The two of us walked back and forth on the streets quite a few times with a strange feeling. We only hoped to see that behind the silence would appear some calm resistance, and that the firing of the cannon would crush all the invaders. But reality told us that was only wishful thinking. Only then did we realize that if we continued to stay there, we would only become captives of the devils. We decided to leave. The next morning, we had to take the express shuttle train of a certain aviation corps as there were no passenger trains running. At last, like the laborers who could not let go of their luggage, with a final glance at Nanjing we took leave.

In the train were the aviation corps members, their families, Gengbai and me, and another fellow traveler — Miss S, Gengbai's former lover. She had found him a few days before and wanted to come with us to move west. She was originally a left-wing woman. At that time she was passionately pursued by an important figure in Guangxi and was doing administrative work at a certain war zone. During the trip, she and Gengbai played out quite a few episodes of a lingering passion. All those fully demonstrated the contradiction in a literary man and politician, as well as a woman during a time of transition from a feudal society to a new society.

How We Got to Hankou

For the first part of our trip, the train rolled along Jin-Pu Railroad, the enemy bombers following us the whole time. Our train would often go back a station or two in order avoid enemy planes. At this speed, it took us an entire week to get to Xuzhou from Nanjing. During that week, there was no dining service and we had to fill our stomachs with roast chicken and quench our thirst with soybean milk. Because we took to the road empty-handed, we had to endure the cold. We only had ourselves to blame, as we were so accustomed to having our luggage carried by a porter!

After arriving in Xuzhou, we parted with the aviation corps to take a passenger train. Miss S parted ways with us for a certain mission. She climbed out of the train from the window and left with a member of the aviation corps. Gengbai and I stayed at China Travel Service for three days, and we spent those three nights waiting for a train in the station. It was not until the fourth night that we caught the passenger train of Long-Han Railway. We bought first class tickets and packed into the second class car. In our society order did not exist under normal circumstances, not to mention during war time. We could only blame ourselves for not being good at pushing and shoving. It took us more than ten days by train to get to Zhengzhou. We ran around in the streets of Zhengzhou for one night without finding a hotel with a vacant room. The next day we had fish balls in a Fujian restaurant and bought water to wash our faces, but after that we again met with the wanton bombing. All the houses around were destroyed and Zhengzhou was thrown into disorder, with corpses all over the place. We narrowly escaped from the hand of the God of Death. That evening, with the help of a bank manager, we bought two passenger tickets on the Ping-Han Railroad. I felt comfort and satisfaction that I had never felt before riding in that first-class compartment.

We arrived in Hankou on the New Year's Eve of 1937. Neon lights shone on the streets of Hankou and firecrackers lit up the sky. It almost made me forget why we came to Hankou.

Life During the War

Were we not fit for our time or did our time have no use for us? Although the war had already spread to Xuzhou, and newspapers, slogans or periodicals were all calling to "concentrate human, material, and financial resources," Gengbai could not find anything to do. I, too, was idle all day long, and lived a traveler's life with him. The legislature had earlier given salaries to its employees as travel fare to move west for the suspended period. The three months' salary we had drawn had long been spent on our travel expenses, and whatever property we had left behind in Nanjing had gone to the devils.

When we arrived in Hankou, we encountered a severe winter, but we could not afford coats and cotton quilts along the way. We could not give up the façade typical of our class for the war, so in daily life we still had to maintain our respectability. As prices were skyrocketing, our expenses were paid off first with Gengbai's leftover cash, later with my savings. Still, days came and went. At this time, our personal war was not targeted against the Japanese devils but against our own financial problems. We could not make a fortune out of a national crisis by doing business or similar jobs. The easiest way left was to write. But there were multiple difficulties. If we wanted to appeal to the general society in writing, we would definitely have to go against our own wills. Neither Gengbai nor I could do that. If we followed our wills, then our writings would not sell. Perhaps no publisher would take them even for free. So we could only lead a frugal and simple life while struggling to keep up appearances. I began to wear dresses made of decent-looking cotton fabrics, not silk *qipao*, and Gengbai Chinese tunic suits, not western style suits. We lived in moderate hotels, ate set meals at restaurants or bread (one piece for twenty cents) in our own room. We were quite reconciled to the circumstances for a long period of time in Hankou. Once I was a reporter at the front, but this new life did not bring me new hope or excitement, so I retreated along with the military. Meanwhile the legislature sent out announcements to resume its meetings, summoning us back to Chongqing. This time, we were obliged to the head of a certain bureau who gave us a sum of money. As if discovering some new goal we took the Minyuan Steamer and charged forth toward Sichuan.

For the four years we lived in the foggy city of Chongqing, we ran around to find shelter during air raids. The quality of our daily life was badly affected by the soaring prices and insufficient housing. Other than that, we seemed to have little to do with the war anymore! Children, servants, water, rice, and coal occupied my entire mind. By then I already understood very well that my life was being consumed day after day.

VII. Flying South

Going to Hong Kong Island

We received boarding passes on November 28. On December 1 we took a flight on Emei of China Airline to Hong Kong. We arrived at midnight.

Dying for Righteousness and Encountering Disaster

We lived in Jiulong [Kowloon] for but seven days before devils started The Pacific War. At that time our housing was not yet settled, so we stayed at the Hotel Clymon on Koston Road. The day after the war broke out, we thought about crossing the water to Hong Kong with our friends Jinduo, Chengzhu, Yunchuan and Manshi. But because we could not receive the proper passes, it did not work out. On the eleventh, we moved to the Yuexian Building to stay at Shuyi's home to avoid trouble with the devils. But the relentless devils shot Gengbai and injured me (for details, read about Gengbai's death on the *Guilin Daqian Magazine No. 1*).

One Year in the Sickbed

After this disaster, the enemy's headquarters dispatched an army surgeon for me. While he dressed my wound, to my surprise, he tried to comfort me, and he spoke fluent Chinese. I did not feel any pain then, but felt indignation and hatred.

Since the night of the nineteenth when I was injured, my nerves were aching acutely. The Japanese surgeon persuaded my roommate to find me an orthopedist to treat my broken arm. For heavy bleeding, my life was in grave danger.

Shuyi crossed the sea to Hong Kong and never returned. This time, the only person who helped me was Mrs Shen, that is, Ms Qian. With her fluency in Japanese, she found me a Chinese doctor who had studied in Japan. His surname was Gui. He claimed that he used to be a director of sorts at Zhongshan University and a bone surgeon. After two days of Doctor Gui's treatment, he decided that I must stay in the hospital for further diagnosis, so my roommate and a few of Gengbai's colleagues' wives decided to send me to Gui's Clinic the next day.

This was indeed a blessing in the middle of misfortune. The day I entered the hospital, A Kuan found Manshi who rushed over to take care of me at the news. Those who took me to the hospital included Ms Qian, Manshi, and four factory workers who were very kind to me. This had been arranged one day ahead of time with Dr Gui. Unexpectedly, Dr Gui had gone out on a professional call when we arrived. A tall doctor received us (later we learned his surname was Cui), and he declared that Dr Gui had not notified them about this. He was going to close the door on us. After a long negotiation, we placed in his hand the one hundred and fifty Hong Kong Dollars we had prepared, and only then did he show a grin. He opened the door slightly and said, "In that case, carry her to the corridor to rest for now, and then we'll talk it over … ." Once I was carried in the corridor on a stretcher, Dr Gui came back. I was moved into one of their tiny hospital rooms. That afternoon, Manshi came to see me again. He told me to rest quietly and not to worry.

In the hospital, I was in good spirits except that I constantly missed Gengbai. At that time everybody concealed the truth from me, claiming that Gengbai had also been injured and had been taken to Queen Mary Hospital. Because the bullet went into my arm first, I believed them. Manshi came to see me everyday and that in fact I became a burden to him, because the truth was that Gengbai had already died, and all our money had been robbed. Although Dr Gui accepted one hundred and fifty Hong Kong Dollars, his clinic did not serve food and we had to pay for all kinds of expenses out of our own pockets. Right then the war broke out in Hong Kong and almost all the businesses along the streets closed. Worst of all, large paper bills were no longer in use. Manshi was busy finding food items and small change and small bills. I lived very comfortably in his affectionate care, and had a constant supply of milk, canned food and fruit, cured meat, and even beer.

I recuperated well. I did not have a fever or inflammation in the wound. I gradually recovered my spirits. One afternoon, I sat up for a while on the doctor's orders, with my maid and nurse A Ying supporting my arm. Because of that, my bone ruptured a blood vessel, and later that night the wound started bleeding without stopping. Later the blood coagulated. I fainted twice that night. The next day when Manshi came, I had already lost all my energy. I could not open my eyes, could not speak, but my mind was very clear. Blood was still oozing. So, I had to get a few hemostatic shots, hematic shots, and cardiotonic shots on a daily basis. According to what the doctor had said to Manshi, if we wanted quick results and reduced cost, the only thing to do was to cut off my arm and replace it with an artificial hand in the future. But Manshi firmly rejected the idea. He asked the doctor to do his best to preserve my arm, and he would pay for all the expenses. They discussed this behind my back, but I had long foreseen the situation and I only wished to die with minimal pain. We continued this way for more than a week, and my arm was finally preserved along with my life. But I had lost more than three to five washbasins of blood. After that I was constantly at my last breath and extremely exhausted in spirit. My nerves ached acutely and almost all the time I was groaning. Manshi as usual came to see me everyday, but each time he came in quietly and returned home quietly. I had no strength to talk. It was all I could do to suppress my moaning, for I did not want to reveal too much of my pain in front of friends. Two months passed that way. When I was out of danger and recovered a little mentally, Manshi had to leave for the inland. This was a great blow, for from then on I would lose my only intimate friend, and would have to lead my hard life in unknown surroundings. I longed for Gengbai. I had no idea whether he was alive or dead. I thought of my children, whom I could not entrust with anybody. My mother and my old acquaintances far away … . All night long I shed tears. Manshi found Gengbai's poetry manuscripts for me, and gave me money for my medical and board expenses. He found someone to look after my children and introduced his friend Mr Wu Chuanshi to take care of me. Upon his request, Mr Qiu also came to tend me. He promised to try to accompany me back to the inland. Because Manshi arranged things for me too carefully and too well, it made me suspect that perhaps Gengbai had died. Heavy, dull pain attacked my heart. I really would rather be dead than alive. But, as a person confined in bed, I was even deprived of my freedom to take my own life.

My body became stronger each day, but my arm was still bound and could not move. For that reason my worry and pain increased each day. I often cried until my tears ran dry and my eyes hurt, but still my indomitable life would not end.

Mr Wu and Mr Qiu visited me often. They brought me invaluable help and consolation. Sincere friendship moved me deep and gradually revived my courage to live.

My health did not restore as smoothly as I had hoped. Although my wound healed little by little, Dr Gui's promise to Manshi of full recovery in two months has not fulfilled. And after three months, four months, my wound did not heal. Then the doctor went back on his promise and started calculating my medical expenses by Japanese military coupons instead of Hong Kong Dollars. That being the case, I still owed him money after having thrown in the food money that Manshi had given me in order to pay for my medical bills. His attitude toward me changed day by day. The humiliation from snobs, life's pressures, painful memories, and my endless recovery process bothered me. Fortunately Mr Wu and Mr Qiu insisted on paying my expenses. The doctor never told me for sure when my broken arm could be connected and when my wound would be healed. The three of us all knew that we had been taken in by this quack, and perhaps I would never recover if we stayed with him. But if we wanted to change to another hospital, we could not afford to pay a new admission and treatment fee. In between, I sought help from quite a few people and also wrote many letters to Shuyi who had already returned to Shaoguan. I asked her to report the condition to the Chongqing authorities and send us some financial aid through her husband's influence as the head of the seventh district relief unit. In February, the seventh district issued me five hundred dollars of *fabi*,[35] noting that Shuyi and her husband wanted me to return to the inland. Each time they brought me hope that the government had agreed to pay for my medical expenses, it was all in the form of verbal checks. Finally, thanks to Mr Wu's negotiation with Dr Gui for one month, we agreed that Mr Wu would pay for half of the debt through a loan. I was then transferred to Guanghua Hospital. Dr Hua, the head of the hospital, treated me personally. Only then did we know that the quack had not connected my broken bones in the first place and had only hastily used medicine to grow my flesh. Finally my flesh grew but the broken bone was still inflamed inside, which threatened to disable my right hand and leave my wound forever unhealed. According to Dr Hua, I was lucky not to have inflammation which would spread all over the body.

After diagnosis through X ray, Dr Hua said that the nerves in my arm remained well and intact. There was a good chance that my hand would be saved. But my physical condition might be too weak now for bone connecting surgery. Assuming that everything went smoothly, the surgery could be completed in six weeks and I could leave the hospital in two months. This news brought us great relief. Later, Mr Wu ran around everyday managing to pay for my expenses in advance. He also managed to get me some nutritious food before the surgery. With the doctor's diagnosis and careful treatment, as well as assistance from my friends, daily life became much easier. Thanks to Mrs Yang Yunshi's enthusiastic effort, I received from the government a relief of two hundred and seventy Hong Kong small bills (equivalent to four hundred large bills). It paid for only one tenth of my debts to Gui's clinic.

When it rained, it poured. One month after I entered Guanghua Hospital, I discovered that I was pregnant. For that reason, my surgery postponed to the undefinable future. It was no use worrying and crying, and I could only struggle to survive. But in that scorching hot summer, each time I saw how Mr Wu worked for my sake, I was so filled with apology that my heart ached. Calm and kind, he always told me: "Just sit back! I will always think of a way for you. Someday you will recover and return to our homeland. By then, if you write me a letter with your right hand, I will be ever so delighted." Alas! What noble friendship! How should I thank you!

Having learned about my condition back in April, Mother wrote me many letters with pain and sadness. It was at that time I was officially informed of Gengbai's death. I was almost destroyed by bereavement, but a strong idea seized me tightly. Gengbai's posthumous manuscripts had not been published, there was no one to look after our children, and my hatred for the devils was still to be avenged. I should not let my friends down for their support and expectations of me. I must try to pull myself together, and to stand on my feet and shoulder my responsibilities. I should become a useful person in society.

During July and August, Mother managed to send me a few sums of money through many hands. With that, I bought expensive milk powder and fed my unborn child Yingtong. The thought of Mother's painstaking effort, her solitary life, and her selfless love inspired my determination to be a good daughter of China. How I wished I could be her filial, attentive daughter at the same time!

My broken bone was not connected until two months after the birth of Yingtong. I was hospitalized for eleven and a half months all together. During that time I was completely unable to turn or move, constantly moaning in my sickbed. I had tasted all the bitterness and pain of life, but had also obtained the most rare and precious friendship in life. I was not destroyed by my bad experiences. On the contrary, those tough trials and warm friendship molded my strong will. I wanted to live and strive for a meaningful future.

VIII. Returning to the Inland

A few muscle movements had proved that my arm was not disabled, so I declined Mother's kind advice that I should stay put in Hong Kong and decided to return again to our homeland. Meantime, I practiced diligently using my left hand to write. I would forever use my pen as a weapon and crush our enemies' hearts.

To raise my travel fare and plan for an itinerary, Mr Wu worked as busily as ever. I stayed at his residence temporarily to rest. Mr Wu's wife, his younger sister, his daughter, and even his father's concubine all treated me with extraordinary affection. That made me experience love that is most rare.

In late December I received Shuyi's letter that she had entrusted someone to bring to me. She invited me to Shaoguan and arranged for me to go back with the messenger. She had enclosed travel fare in the amount of two thousand dollars. But according to the messenger, that money had been robbed on the way. Since someone was to accompany me, I did not want to pass up the opportunity to go back. Still counting on Mr Wu's arrangements, I left Jiulong by train at 1:00 p.m. on December 28, 1941.

At 2:30 p.m. the train arrived at Dapu. After a few rounds of inspections and questions by the enemy puppet officers, we arrived at Shayuchong the following night. Then, after one and a half days of travel on land, we reached in our homeland — Danshui. Five days after leaving Guanghua Hospital, the head of the enemy puppet Information Agency came to look for me. With a lure of a large bonus and a threat of violence, he wanted to employ me to carry out information work. I dealt with them with both soft and hard tactics. Thinking back on this now, I cannot help but heave a sigh of relief. I have to laugh proudly. Ha! Ha! The lackey of our enemy, no matter how sneaky you were, you would never capture people with a will and a soul.

From Danshui to Heyuan we took a civilian boat. After spending five days in Heyuan, we set out for Huizhou. At that time, Huizhou was under constant attack by enemy planes and the local authority forced evacuation everyday. We were kept on the run for two days and only then took a boat to Laolong. On the following day we boarded a bus bound for Shaoguan. The following poem is a sketch of the scenery along the road.

> Attached poem — Bus Journey (Laolong to Qujiang)
> Going up and down the hill frequently,
> Traveling by car, my thoughts abundant.
> Only by enduring the fatigue of a long journey
> Can one feel the virtues of the people.
> Standing or sitting, there is no place either way
> In exile, we share one sky.
> Galloping, in order to strengthen myself
> With a single hand I support my quivering body.

IV. Today and Tomorrow

After twenty-one days of hard travel, I set foot in Shaoguan, a town of strategic significance in our homeland. In order to settle many personal matters, I temporarily unloaded my belongings at Shuyi's house. In the next few days, friends from different places wrote to me to offer consolation and encouragement. Some wanted me to work in Chongqing, some invited me to go to Kunming to engage in writing, others advised me to go to Chengdu to rest first, and the rest hoped for me to go to Guilin. How excited and gratified I was, that I could receive so much earnest friendship and warm encouragement. I wished I could fly to all these places to thank them in person. But a heavy burden lay on my shoulder. I had to raise funds to publish Gengbai's writings to let his spirit live on. In order to support my three children and myself, I had to assume all the responsibilities. After careful consideration, I accepted the kind help and arrangement of Mr Li, an old revolutionary and an acclaimed senior in the cultural realm. I accepted the earnest invitation of Mr C, the head of a certain institute as well as Gengbai's poetry friend, and arrived in Guilin at dawn on April 4. From then on, I was on my own and dealt with society directly without the protecting hands of friends. Now I am a government functionary. I go to and from work on time each day. I learn to dispatch worldly businesses, big or small. I feel that the life of a government functionary is inflexible but very interesting.

I firmly believe that the world evolves constantly and that society progresses every day. Although some things are symptomatic of backward movement, they are no more than the occasional colds and coughs in one's health. They can never prevent society from moving forward. I also believe that in tomorrow's society, the small and weak nations will surely be liberated, and that the oppressed masses will raise their heads, and that women will obtain emancipation, independence, and equality in the light of dawn. In that regard, all democratic countries in the world now have joined forces to fight the invading enemies. Nevertheless, it will obviously take more effort to achieve final victory. In our ideal future society, all people in the world do what they can and get what they need. If we want to realize this goal, we now must seize the day and strive. We women, in particular, have to do that. In today's world, only Russian women have really gained freedom, independence, and equality in politics, economy, and education. Although Euro-American and Chinese societies have made promises of equality and freedom to women, we are still far from solutions to all issues. If women want real liberation, we must work and be part of the struggle at the eve of liberation. I will cultivate myself and do research and exercise in my spare time. I am willing to contribute all my knowledge and ability to the struggle for a magnificent tomorrow. I am willing to use my pen as a weapon to crush the enemies' hearts. I am willing to use my seething blood to water the begonia of the future.

A Brief Autobiography

Peng Hui

Translated by Jing M. Wang

Peng Hui (1907–68), originally named Lianqing, was from Changsha, Hunan. She went to Changsha First Women's Normal School in 1923 and enrolled at Beijing Female Normal College (Beijing nüzi shifan xueyuan) in 1925. After becoming a member of the Communist Party in 1927, she went to Moscow to study. Upon returning to China in 1930, she joined the Chinese League of Left-Wing Writers (Zhongguo zuoyi zuojia lianmeng) and started her career of writing and translation. During the War of Resistance against Japan, Peng was a leader of women's national salvation movement. She participated in the founding of the All-China Association of Literary Resistance (Zhonghua quanguo wenyijie kangdi xiehui) in 1938. She was persecuted to death during the Cultural Revolution (1966–1976). Her novels include Returning Home (Huanjia, n.d.) *and* The Endless Tides of the Yangtze River (Bu jin Changjiang gun gun lai, n.d.). Grassland (Cao yuan, 1942) *is her Chinese translation of Anton Chekhov's original work in Russian.*

I

I am a native of Changsha, Hunan, but I was born in Anqing, Anhui, as Father held an official position there. It wasn't until I was four and Father fell gravely ill that my family returned to Changsha. Father passed away before long and left behind Mother, my three sisters, and me. That happened in the early Republican years. At the time, my elder sister was eight, I six, and my two younger sisters four and one. My sad and solitary childhood started then.

The source of Mother's eternal regret was that she did not have a son. It was also the reason why the old society bullied and mistreated her in her widowhood.

Paternal Grandfather once won the fifth place in an imperial examination at the provincial level, but he lived in poverty and left nothing for Father and Uncle. When Father died, we had accumulated a few mu^1 of land and some real estate. These all accumulated from Father's hard work as *biao tong*[2] in late Qing and Mother's careful management. As it was, we were under no obligation to share what we had with the rest of the family.

Mother, however, was a woman of traditional virtue and put too much weight on kinship. She realized that along with our core family, Uncle was also Father's loved one. Therefore, she invited Uncle over and gave him money to get married, in spite of the fact that Uncle was a middle-aged good-for-nothing. On top of that, she supported him and his wife, hoping that they would bear a male heir to continue the family line. It was as though such an act would compensate for Father's unfilialness of not having a son.

Out of everyone's expectation, getting married and living on our money did not satisfy Uncle. He wanted a concubine on top of all his debt. He bribed some of his relatives to break into our house to eat all our food. They threatened to divide up the family property between Mother and Uncle. As Father had held official posts far away from our hometown and died soon after we returned to Hunan, we always associated more closely with our relatives on Mother's side. According to the customs of the old society, however, maternal relatives did not have any say in the situation that we were confronted with. Consequently, our family members arbitrarily drafted a contract and divided our property between Mother and Uncle. Before they did that, they withdrew one third to pay for the education and dowries of my sisters and me. The contract said that Mother's share was to eventually go to Uncle's son whenever he got one. Otherwise they would adopt a son for Mother from our relatives and let him inherit her share. My sisters and I had no right to our parents' property. I cannot describe how upset Mother was over this issue. As for my sisters and me, we were not old enough to resent the loss of property, but as children, we were deeply hurt by Uncle's ungrateful acts toward Mother.

Mother was never in good health. After Father's death, especially after

Uncle's severance, sadness and fatigue further affected her health, so that she became ill almost all year round.

In elementary school, we clearly felt the sharp contrast between the liveliness at school and the desolation at home. It smelt strongly of medication in Mother's room, where she lay in bed, curtains let down. We had to talk, walk and put down our satchels gingerly and slowly. In winter and on overcast days, the room looked very dim for the lack of light. As Mother was the only person in this world who loved us, we spent most of our time in her room no matter how dreary it felt there.

Maternal Grandmother and Third Aunt lived right next door. Sometimes we wandered into their rooms and saw our cousins, all about our age, ask their father questions in their studies and act very spoiled with their mother. It was quite painful for us. I remember murmuring to myself our aunts and uncles' loving words to their children on my way home in childlike envy and sadness.

In such a lonesome and monotonous life, our utmost source of happiness was Mother telling us stories about the past and the present when her physical condition permitted her to do so. Mother was an excellent storyteller. No matter how old and trite a story was, it would become extremely entertaining when adapted and told by her. Whenever she felt well enough, she did needlework during the day and sometimes visited Grandmother. At night she would sit under the light and tell us stories, which delighted not only us but also our aunt and her maids. Everyone respected Mother as a person who had seen the world because she was literate and traveled to many provinces with Father.

Mother's stories were indeed very touching. A shining example is her version of "The Legend of the White Serpent."[3] When she got to the point where the monk Fa Hai imprisons the White Serpent under Lei Feng Tower, she described in a detailed manner the scenery around Lei Feng Tower by West Lake that she had visited with Father. She would vividly depict how the tower stood tall and soaring, and how the White Serpent stuck her head out of a small window on the bottom layer to rendezvous with her son. In this way, the audience not only enjoyed the plot but also felt as though they visited the historical sites vicariously through her.

When telling the love story of Liang Shanbo and Zhu Yingtai,[4] she repeated the fascinating dialog between the protagonists verbatim, according to the original version. She even made a good story out of a theft at our home, reenacting how the thief slipped Father's long saber from underneath the door and how he pulled a saddle clanking down to the ground. We felt as though it was an exciting anecdote, not something bad that happened to us.

Father witnessed the revolutionary Mr Xu Xilin[5] gun down Enming. I heard that it was through Father's recommendation that Mr Xu got a position with Enming. Mother knew Mr Xu in person and was well acquainted with his history. As a result, I began to admire this revolutionary hero through Mother's story before I studied history. When my history teacher glossed over Mr Xu in class, I felt that this martyr was deeply wronged. I wished I had the courage to stand up to tell the class of Mr Xu's glorious deeds.

Sometimes we borrowed fairy tales from school for Mother to read so she could tell the stories to us. Even though we knew them quite well, it was much more fun hearing them from her. I remember one adaptation of "Heir Apparent Exchanged for a Leopard Cat."[6] When my elder sister and I first read it, we did not quite understand it. Mother rendered it a completely different story. In her version Renzong's mother was exiled from the Song court, but Renzong's filial piety was such that he continued to lick at his mother's blinded eyes until she could see again. When Mother got to this point of the story, I shed tears of sympathy and joy.

Prepared by Mother's fascinating tales, we later learned to read fairy tales and other forms of fiction on our own.

Even today, my most delightful memory of the past is still the four of us sitting around Mother under the light at night listening to her tales.

II

We were unfortunate, fatherless girls. It was our life's sole pleasure to enjoy Mother's storytelling under the dim light, but Mother was in extremely poor health, and we were soon to be deprived of this pleasure.

When I was eleven going on twelve, Mother's condition deteriorated every day. In the dead of winter, she passed away, leaving behind my three sisters and me. At that time, my youngest sister was but six years old. Orphaned and unloved, we began to experience all the cold realities of life.

As planned, Mother's property was claimed by Uncle's adopted son, who turned out to be older than us. Luckily, my sisters and I could live off our dowries. On her deathbed, Mother entrusted us to the care of her eldest brother. Therefore, we moved to Maternal Grandmother's house after her passing, bringing with us our old female servant. Since then, Maternal Grandmother collected our share of the land rent to pay for our food and accommodation at her house. Our education, clothing, and other expenses came from the house rent paid to our names. Thanks to Father's property, we were fed and clothed in the world, even though we did not enjoy parental care. Bereaved of motherly love, we learned to depend on each other. Indeed, our mutual attachment was stronger than that between ordinary siblings. In high school and at college, people commented that we were more like the best of friends than sisters. My elder sister was very mature for her age. She nursed Mother and did all the household chores when Mother was sick in bed. She became our surrogate mother after Mother died. In reality she was only a girl of thirteen. The trivial details of family responsibility burdened her and denied her a carefree childhood. Even today the thought of it makes me hurt for her.

I was a sickly child. Mother had worried a lot about me. After she died, it fell on Elder Sister to take care of me whenever I was ill. One winter, my old asthma relapsed. I doubled over in coughing fits during the day and was kept awake at night. Traditional herbal medicine did not work, and the Western medical doctor's prescription was no good, either. Eventually we got a folk prescription, which prescribed a kind of insect shell that could be purchased from the medicine shop. It was said that seven such shells individually roasted in the fire made one cup of tea. They should be roasted again and again after each cup. I have to drink seven cups to be cured, so dictated the prescription. Our old servant had no patience for such a chore, so my eldest sister made the tea for me personally. Fortunately, it was winter, school was out, and we had a fire pan in our room. My eldest sister sat right next to it and, without a murmur, she roasted the insect shells seven times and made seven cups of tea. I still remember her benign look as she roasted the insect shells and her kindly face when inquiring how I felt after each cup. The love on her face made me shed tears behind her back. If I coughed without stopping, she would look at me with extreme worry and concern. If I did not cough for a while, she would say before I had noticed it myself, "Look, I think you're getting better. You haven't coughed for quite some time now." I often bit my lip to hold back coughs. I did not want to wake her up in the middle of the night and frequently coughed underneath my quilt. Her loving care inspired my love for her and for my two younger sisters. This love grew deeper day by day, and it extended to all the helpless and the needy in the world.

III

Thus, with no one loving us in this world, we only had each other. I became rather anti-social, shunning all formalities with my relatives and elders. Even when Mother was alive, I was not a great favorite with everyone because of my strong personality. On top of it all, Maternal Grandfather's family was extremely discriminating against women. Maternal Grandmother expected all the children in the house to talk to her with affection and respect. Girls could only curry favor with her by regularly sitting next to her doing needlework or doing chores in the kitchen. These requirements, however, did not agree with me. So, I was often nervous with her. How I wished she had forgotten my name. During winter and summer vacations, I walked out of my room only for three daily meals. For the rest of the time, I felt quite contented reading novels in my room to the point of complete absorption. This was also true of the older one of my two younger sisters. She and I had been reading companions since childhood. My littlest sister was still too young to read, and she enjoyed other children's company. As for my elder sister, perhaps she thought she represented us in Maternal Grandmother's house and felt compelled to please Maternal Grandmother. Luckily she was more easy-going than the rest of us. Maternal Grandmother liked her all right. She served as the only connection between Maternal Grandmother and us. I often congratulated myself that I was the second daughter. If I had been the eldest, I probably would have made our situation much worse.

Since about the fifth or sixth grade in primary school, I loved reading novels. Just as most other female beginners did, we started with *tanci*[7] scripts, such as *Heaven Rains Flowers* (Tian yu hua),[8] *Twice Destined in Marriage* (Zai sheng yuan),[9] *Green Peony* (Lü mudan),[10] and read all the scripts we could lay our hands on. We knew nothing about the artistic quality of the texts, simply wanting to enjoy the stories and escape from the reality. In this way we found our highest form of pleasure. Stories like *Flowers Born of the Pen* (Bi sheng hua)[11] and *Twice Destined in Marriage* that portray women seeking adventures in male disguise particularly fascinated me. I could not wait to dress as a man myself and go out to perform some dauntless deeds in the world. I often vaguely felt in my dreams that I was no longer a girl but a boy, that I was studying to take the exams to become a *xiu cai* or *ju ren*,[12] or that I was about to secure an official post. I sometimes even dreamt of Mother proudly patting me on the head and commending me as her only son. Once when my youngest sister was ill, I woke up from one of such pleasurable dreams. In the total darkness of the night, I heard from the next bed (my elder sister and youngest sister shared one bed, and my other sister and I shared the other) my youngest sister's uneven breathing and Elder Sister checking the little one's forehead to see if her fever had come down. All of a sudden, I came back to reality. The dream contrasted with the desolateness of our life. I could not hold back my tears. When I woke up in the morning, my pillow, pajamas, and a part of my quilt were still wet.

When I read *A Dream of the Red Chamber*[13] later, I shed a lot of sympathetic tears for the sentimental and sickly Lin Daiyu. At the point where Lin Daiyu burns her poems as a symbolic gesture to end her deep love for Baoyu, tears streamed down my cheeks, and I was choked by sobs.

The older one of my two younger sisters and I were both fans of the novel for quite a while. We frequently competed to recite the poems and even prose portions of the novel. Our little sister and younger cousins often asked me to tell them stories or lend them books. Our room virtually became the cultural center for the children in this big family.

As we had many cousins, Maternal Grandmother's house always bustled with noise and excitement during festivals and the New Year period. Relatives and neighbors came in droves to extend their holiday wishes. Our cousins competed with each other in their gambling games and in lighting firecrackers. Although we had loved to do these things once upon a time, we now sat in our room reading novels with total indifference to their activities. Sometimes my elder sister urged us to go and wish the elders a happy new year for etiquette's sake. We then had no choice but to mix among our cousins and mindlessly kowtow to the elders. Awarded with our share of the sweets and other treats, we still had nothing to say. We could think of nothing but the characters in the stories that we had been relishing a little while before.

Maternal Grandfather was an honest, reserved old scholar. My male cousins had to read poetry and Confucian classics[14] in front of our grandfather every day after school. He adamantly objected to girls going to school. As for my sisters and I, we went to school for three reasons. One, we continued a tradition established by Mother. Two, we had independent financial resources and could afford our own tuition. Three, to Maternal Grandfather who strongly discriminated against women, we simply did not exist. Therefore, he seldom bothered about us (although he opposed to my elder sister's going to school shortly after Mother's death).

One summer, however, he somehow found out that the older of my younger sisters and I had been reading *A Dream of the Red Chamber*. He flew into a rage and scolded us for three days, as though we had disgraced him. Fortunately, he was a gentleman and did not use violence, but he took away the novel we never tired of reading. I still remember the distress we felt then.

I still disliked needlework. I searched for books from Father's book cases. I came upon a collection of song lyrics by Bai Xiangshan[15] and another collection entitled *Song Lyrics Composed at Shuyu* (Shuyu ci).[16] After that, I developed an interest in song lyrics, but I did not love them half as much as I did the lifelike characters in *A Dream of the Red Chamber*. I was inconsolable. I longed for another good book to make up for my loss. As soon as summer ended and school started again, I rushed to the school library to try my luck. At that time, all but my youngest sister were attending Changsha First Women's Normal School. We failed to find a good book in the library. Once I checked out a copy of *A Collection of Writings from the Ice-Drinking Studio* (Yin bing shi wen ji).[17] When I went home the following Saturday, our uncle, the husband of Mother's sister, came to our room to talk to us. He knew that we were fond of books and asked about our readings. I showed him the book I had just borrowed. I thought he would be impressed with my choice, but he shook his head and said, "This is outdated. It would be best to read *New Youth*."[18] I did what he told me, and I am grateful to him to this day. In Maternal Grandfather's living room, the bookcases were lined up in perfect order along the walls. One of them, doorless and topless, contained some neglected books, among which was a bound volume of *New Youth*. For this I had Second Uncle, Mother's brother Mr Yang Yufu, to thank. Those were his books. He was then teaching in Beiping. Maternal Grandfather looked down upon *New Youth* and neglected it. I had seen the volume a long time ago without knowing its significance. At my uncle's words, I grabbed it and devoured it. It was then about 1923, and *New Youth* was no longer new, but for me, an unguided reader of fourteen, reading it was entering an entirely new world. In the same way that we had been absorbed with *A Dream of the Red Chamber*, the older one of my younger sisters and I read and reread the volume of *New Youth* that we owned. It felt as though we had caught a ray of hope for the future society. Our joy and exhilaration were beyond words. Later, we also located journals such as *New Tide* (Xin chao)[19] and *New China* (Xin Zhongguo).[20] We worshipped Hu Shi and other intellectuals who promoted the Literary Revolution[21] as if they were idols. Their bold articles against traditional Confucian ethics deeply impressed us. In our composition class, I began to write stories in the vernacular and published them in the journal run by the Student Autonomous Society. My classmates jokingly called me the "novelist." We often discussed various new thoughts. Our Chinese professor had always thought highly of me, but because he was too old-fashioned a scholar to appreciate our new thoughts, we persuaded him to quit his job.

The female school we attended was notoriously conservative in Changsha. In a sequestered environment like an old well, our radical act put us in the spotlight in school. Two classmates, respectively named Li and Peng, and I were honored as "the three heroines." Such was the magical power of *New Youth*.

Since then, I have loved to read all mind-opening literature, not just fiction. Like all youths, I yearned enthusiastically for a better society.

The following year, Mr Sun Zhongshan's effort to unify China, his passing, and the May 30 Tragedy[22] enraged all patriotic youths. We were no exception. The patriotic fervor of Li, Peng, and me reached the apex. We organized propaganda and fund-raising teams to work outside campus. In the meantime, we put together all the money we had and launched a small journal. Though still teenage girls, we did all the work ourselves: writing, editing, printing, publishing, and marketing with a bookstore. The contents of the journal were all inclusive, for example: patriotism, liberation of colonized countries, women's issues, and new literature. I drafted the introduction for the issue. After the journal's publication, a few progressive professors praised our work and especially commended my introduction. When I returned home, the uncle who introduced me to *New Youth* also spoke highly of me. After only three issues, however, we left Changsha for Beiping to go to school.

The reason is as follows: Running the journals, our desire for knowledge grew increasingly strong. I became more and more dissatisfied with our school. We did not want to wait even though it was only one year before we graduated. Therefore, Li, Peng, and I came to Beiping together during the summer and subsequently started our college career.

IV

When I attended school in Beiping and abroad, I did not major in literature, so I do not have much to say here about this period. My effort in literature began in the year of the September 18 Tragedy.[23] At that time, I was teaching in Shanghai. For the first time I lived away from the older of my younger sisters, my reading companion since childhood. I missed her very much and wrote poems to send to her. At the same time, a few friends died. Then, my youngest sister fell in love and got married though she was too young. These events put me under the sway of strong emotions. I often wrote to give outlet to my sadness. It was at this chaotic time in my life that I seriously took up literature, something that I had a passion for since childhood. Therefore, when I had spare time from teaching, I began to write fiction. My past experiences were great material for fiction, but I could not organize them well on paper. Whenever I finished a piece, I hid it at the bottom of my suitcase, too embarrassed to read it again. My first story was published in *The Big Dipper* (Beidou)[24] after the January 28 Incident.[25] In the following year I married Mutian. Housework and childbearing are indeed thorns on a woman's career path. During pregnancy and nursing, I did not write anything at all, nor did I read much. After my child was weaned, Mutian and I made a study plan. He began to translate Balzac, while I read classical Russian literature. Nekrasov's poetry and Chekhov's[26] fiction were among my favorites. Whenever I discovered a good piece, I translated it into Chinese. Some of my translations were published in literary journals. This was the beginning of my work in translation. During this period, my husband and I quit all work, focusing on reading and translating. Although some people had reservations that we were out of step with society, we believed that it was necessary for us at that time to give ourselves more training in literature. Further, such experience laid a solid foundation for our translation later.

My translation of Chekhov's *Grassland* (Cao yuan), published in 1942, was among the work I did during this period. A novella of about one hundred thousand words, it took me as long as ten months to complete. Such a prolonged process was because the child was often sick, Mutian had a serious illness, and I had a miscarriage. Now, when I see my translation of *Grassland*, I often remember the fetus that I lost while working on it.

As soon as I finished translating *Grassland*, the cannons fired against the Japanese invasion of Shanghai on August 13.

The tide of resistance against Japanese aggression excited us, so we could no longer continue to read and translate in our little private world. We planned to go to the interior of the country to take up cultural propagation work. Therefore, we decided to give up the life in our comfortable home in Shanghai with our now two children (I still mourned over the loss of my other child). We moved to Wuhan, where Mutian and his fellow poets published a poetry journal and organized poetry recitations. Zi Gang,[27] Song Yuan,[28] and I, along with several others, started a women's journal. As my colleagues all liked to write essays in *belle lettre* style, they elected me to write theoretical articles. Meanwhile, I was invited by a bookstore to edit a collection of essays on women's issues. Then I returned to my hometown and taught for a few months at a cadre school. During this year I did not write much, but I composed some poems that I still like today, because I wrote these poems with the excitement and enthusiasm of the early stage of the War of Resistance against Japan. The one in memory of the children snatched away by a Japanese boat was written in Wuhan. The occasion of the poem is as follows: In an international women's press conference on anti-aggression held in Hankou, Mr Shao Lizi[29] exposed the fact that a Japanese boat in Shanghai had captured some Chinese children to send to Tokyo. Mr Shao's voice trembled with excitement. Listening to his report, I was reduced to tears in public because of the motherly love I felt for those children. I was so upset that I had to walk out of the meeting. On my way back from Hankou to Wuchang by boat, I drafted the poem in my mind with tears in my eyes. When I got home, my child was already asleep. Her peaceful breathing made me think of the children taken away by the Japanese. The thought of them kept me awake for the entire night. I committed the poem to paper.

Wuhan fell. Our family moved to Kunming. I wrote most of the stories in my colllection *Returning Home* (Huanjia) there. Then Mutian and I both got teaching positions at Zhongshan University. The bad weather in the north of Guangdong took a toll on our health. During those two years, we took a lot of medication besides inhaling chalk dust. In the summer of 1942, we decided to quit our jobs at Zhongshan University and resume translation in Guilin. Within less than a year, I translated stories by Leo Tolstoy and Chekhov, a total of three hundred thousand words. I will edit and send them to the press soon. During that year, as I did not have help at home, I did not achieve my goal of thirty thousand words per month. I always regret it.

Right now, I teach at Guilin National Normal College. Although Mutian and I always consider teaching as a secondary profession, I take my classes seriously. Whenever I have excellent students, I feel very gratified. Their progress urges me to work harder. I plan to put together some reading notes while teaching.

From now on, I want to serve my country and my people through writing.

At the midpoint of my life, I have not accomplished as much as I have hoped. I feel guilty at the thought. Fortunately, being an optimist, I often encourage myself with the motto "Work hard at middle age." When I grow old, I will motivate myself with the motto "Keep up in old age."

For the sake of my country's prospects, my mother's suffering, my children's future, and for myself, how can I possibly slacken my efforts at work?

October 17, 1943
Guanyin Mountain, Guilin

Midpoint of an Ordinary Life

Xie Bingying

Translated by Shirley Chang

Xie Bingying (1906–2000), originally named Xie Minggang, was born in Xinhua, Hunan. She started to write in 1921 when she entered Hunan First Female Normal School in Changsha. In 1926 she became a cadet at the Central Military Political School in Wuhan and joined the Northern Expedition army the following year. She studied at Waseta University in Japan in 1935 and returned to China at the outbreak of the War of Resistance against Japan in 1937 to do her part for her country. She organized a women's service team in Hunan on the front and also edited a journal called Yellow River Literary Journal *(Huanghe wenyi). After the war, she became a professor at Beijing Normal University (Beijing shifan daxue). In 1948 she moved to Taiwan to teach at the current National Normal University. She retired in 1971 and relocated to the United States in 1974.*

As a prolific writer, the corpus of her writing includes novels, short stories, essays, and travelogues. War Diary *(Cong jun riji, 1828) and* Autobiography of a Female Soldier *(1936), her most well known works, have been translated into many different languages.*

I. My Family

Xieduo Mountain was a small village. Right next to the road linking Anhua and Xinhua, it saw travelers come and go all day long. Especially in July and August in the lunar calendar, villagers heading for Mount Heng to worship the Sage King of Southern Yue would walk by in groups, chanting songs of worship all the way. In the quiet of the night, their singing would occasionally wake us up. There was a long street in this village where meat, liquor, and other food items such as candy could be purchased. Customers who frequented these stores were mostly men, and women as a rule did not go to market.

This was a beautiful place. The village itself was surrounded by little hills, and a winding river, like a belt, murmured a rhythmic song all year round. The river was so clear that you could see tiny shrimps swimming in it. In spring, girls picking tea leaves melted your soul with their singing. Those women were all farmers who did not go out usually, so during this time, they covered their heads with kerchiefs of blue or other colors, exposing only their faces. When they saw men, they lowered their heads and quickly walked by like shy brides. In the whole village you could not find even one woman with natural feet, as everybody had their feet bound, pointed as small red peppers.

"Women should all bind their feet, a big-footed woman will never be married off." Old women all said so.

I grew up in such an environment.

My father, my grandfather's only son, was a *ju ren*[1] during the Qing dynasty. He was naturally intelligent and had an especially good memory. In his eighties, he could still remember things that had happened in his childhood and recite poems he had read as a child. Some of his students called him *Kangxi Dictionary* (Kangxi zidian),[2] as he always had ready answers to their questions about literary allusions. He was taciturn but kind. However, if he got angry over something, he would lose his temper with no restraint. He never told a lie in his whole life and never harmed others to benefit himself. Mother, like Father, also won esteem from everybody in the village. She was smart, ambitious, and hardworking. She did not have much education, but had sharp perception of things. When she married into the Xie family, she was only sixteen. My father was teaching elsewhere all year round, so the burden of running the household fell on Mother's shoulders. She had six children. Her first son died when he was only three. My second brother died in Nanjing in the year of the Northern Expedition.[3] My sister died two years ago. And now only my eldest surviving brother, my third brother and I are here to mourn my late parents. Come to think of it, how sad it is!

"Parents love the youngest; grandparents love the eldest." This was a common saying of my hometown. Since I was the youngest child in the family, I won my parents' special tender care. Even when I was ten years old, my father still often held me in his arms. In winter, he would sleep next to me, keeping me warm me with his leather coat. My grandmother also paid me a lot of attention. Whenever she had treats like candy or fish, she would always give me some. I loved fish and shrimp as a child. Once, I went to catch fish in the river barefooted. Fearing that my mother would get angry if I took the fish and shrimp home, I dug up a hole in the ground as stove, used a piece of broken tile as wok, collected some leaves and broken branches to make a fire and cooked them. Even with no salt or oil for flavor, it came out very tasty.

I was a tomboy with no trace of any girlish habits. I enjoyed playing with boys. Whenever we played soldiers holding sticks in hands and lining up for training, I would always give watchwords and directions, so that they all called me the commander in chief. I often dreamt of leading an army when I grew up. I would bravely gallop across the battlefield on horseback, wearing a shining officer's sword and carrying a pistol. I was against foot binding and ear piercing. I had no idea what equal rights between men and women meant. I only knew that since both were human beings, why was it that men did not have to have their ears pierced and their feet bound? Why did they leave all those sufferings to us women? And why did men have the right to go to school but not women?

Father loved me dearly. He started teaching me to read poems by the women disciples in the Sui Garden (*Sui yuan*)[4] and *Three Hundred Poems of the Tang* (Tang shi san bai shou)[5] when I was only five or six years old. I had an amazing memory and once I read a poem I could recite it right away. Because Mother would not allow me to go to school, I went on a hunger strike for three days. Later when she saw my pathetic face after crying so hard, she let me enter a private school. After one year in the private school, I transferred to Datong Women's School.

The school was founded by the town government of Datong. There was a men's school and a women's school, with only a hill and a street in between. Normally students from these two schools had no contact. Only on Sundays when we were all out playing boys and girls might see one another on the hill or at the end of Three Brooks Bridge. Girls always avoided looking at boys in the face and lowered their heads while walking. But once the boys had passed by, girls would turn around to look at them, exchanging comments as to who was handsome and who looked silly. If a girl had a fiancé at the men's school, other girls would make that material for delightful talk.

"Minggang (my name), we've seen that one of yours. He is twice as tall as you. When will you invite us to your wedding banquet?"

They joked with me, but I considered that a great humiliation and ran to the toilet to cry my heart out.

How humiliating that my mother arranged my marriage when I was only three. My fiancé also went to Datong School, in the men's division. Although we did meet once informally, I had such a bad impression of him that I knew I would never marry him.

My feet, bound by my mother, weren't untied until I entered Datong Women's School. The two red threads inserted in my pierced ears were taken off and replaced with two small tea leaf stems then. This was an order from my mother, so that I could wear earrings when I got married. As for my feet, she objected to unbinding them. But because the school did not allow anyone in with bound feet, she could not rebind them. So she called us barbarians.

Ever since my days in Datong Women's School, I loved Chinese. Whenever we had composition class, the teacher would write the topic on the blackboard. Some classmates would think for a long time without coming up with a single word, but I was always the first one to finish and turn it in. Mine were the longest, too.

During winter and summer breaks, Father always taught me to read the *Four Books* (Si shu),[6] but Mother often urged me to learn how to embroider, spin, and weave. Almost every day she would nag, "You'll be married off in a few years and yet we have not yet begun to prepare your dowry. Are we really going to send you off on a sedan, with nothing but your person? You may not feel embarrassed, but I still want to save face!"

Hearing this, I hurt in silence. I thought: Am I really going to marry that stranger?

At that time, my eldest brother was teaching in a middle school, my second and third brothers both studying in the County Middle School where my father worked. Even during vacations, they had to listen to Father lecturing on *Records of the Grand Historian* (Shi ji)[7] and study the *Five Classics*[8] (Wu jing) everyday. I showed even more enthusiasm for studying. I wanted to finish elementary school, middle school, and go on to college. But such fantasy was the last thing that Mother allowed me to indulge in. She always stressed that women had no use for learning. She would often interrupt my reading with needlework, such as embroidering and weaving. This planted seeds of bitterness in my young heart, and I could no longer be as happy as other children.

II. From Elementary School to Middle School

After one year at the Datong Women's School, I transferred to Xinhua County Women's School, which had a higher academic standard. A few faculty members were recruited from Changsha. Our Chinese teacher You Ruoyu recently graduated from Women's Normal University with honors. She strongly encouraged us to read classical Chinese, but did not object to our writing in the vernacular.[9] It was then that I started reading modern fiction. My second brother, studying at Shanxi University, sent me a copy of A Collection of Short Stories (Duanpian xiaoshuo ji) translated by Hu Shi.[10] It interested me intensely, so much so that I wanted to try my hand at fiction in imitation of the stories therein. But after reading Hu Shi's essay "On the Short Story" (Lun duanpian xiaoshuo),[11] I lost the courage.

Our school put much emphasis on the training of public speaking, but I would stutter whenever I got on stage. One time I managed to articulate my title but could not utter another word after that. Ashamed, I wanted to kill myself. But for a classmate who discovered me, I might have taken my own little life. But after that blow, somehow I became more and more courageous, and I no longer stuttered.

Due to my father's influence all my siblings loved to read. Even on Sundays I would cross the river to study Classical Chinese with Father. At that time, Father was the principal of the County Middle School. He served for thirty years in that position.

The next spring, I transferred to Good Faith Women's School at Yiyang, more than four hundred li[12] from my home. It was a missionary school which strongly emphasized English. Our principal was a Norwegian woman, unmarried at over forty years of age. When I transferred there, I should have been enrolled in the second year class, but the placement test put me in the second semester of the first year.

The school was located on the other side of the Peach Blossom River. When I ran up to the balcony for fresh air every morning, I could see fishing boats floating lightly on the mirror-like tranquil river, like sea gulls flying. Across the river was a dense forest, dark green, enveloped in the dim light of dawn. The sun gradually rose above the surface of the river, quite like a ball of fire. Then its radiance shone all over the earth, coloring the river red. I watched these exquisite morning scenes with such delight that I often missed roll call and morning prayer. Speaking of praying, it was such a headache. I am not against religious beliefs. On the contrary, I advocate freedom of beliefs. But I do not approve of idol worshiping. Jesus agreed to be crucified by the Jews for the happiness of all people. We could admire his self-sacrificial spirit and his glory as much as we wished, but we did not have to pray all the time. Especially before every meal, we had to lower our heads, close our eyes, and pray: "Heavenly Father, may all people worship you ..." I found that meaningless.

Because I did not attend those religious services and because I organized a demonstration against Japanese Imperialism on May 9, National Shame Day,[13] I was expelled from school at the end.

That summer, I passed the entrance examination to Hunan First Female Normal School in Changsha. Mother by then had become more open-minded and did not object to my going there. Father even personally accompanied me by boat from Lantian to Changsha. From then on, my life was settled. As a fourteen-year-old, I grew more and more interested in literature. Apart from attending classes, I spent all my time in the library. For a time I worked as a librarian so that I had a chance to read more fiction. Every time new orders arrived, I always had the first opportunity to read them. I worshiped authors like Guy de Maupassant, Emile Zola, Leo Tolstoy, Fyodor Dostoyevsky, and Alexandre Dumas fils, etc. Fairy tales by Oscar Wilde and Vasily Eroshenko were also among my favorites. Among classic Chinese novels, I liked *Water Margin* (Shui hu)[14] and *Romance of the Three Kingdoms* (San guo yanyi)[15] most. Although *A Dream of the Red Chamber*[16] is a famous novel, Lin Daiyu's tears failed to win my sympathy. As for Jia Baoyu's silly manner and his sole ambition to hang out with girls, I called him "no good."[17] I once had a big fight with Mother over *Water Margin*, and that is especially worth recording here. When I was in elementary school, I went home for summer vacation. I spent entire days reading that torn, thread-bound copy of *Water Margin*. In the evening when everybody sat outside enjoying the cool air with a fan in their hands, I would entertain them with episodes from the novel as if I was a professional storyteller. Most enchanted by the stories, my grandmother often announced at the beginning of dinner: "Hurry up finish your dinner, so we can listen to Minggang tell us stories."

Hearing that there was going to be a story session, men and women, old and young, all came. Some held their rice bowls in their hands, and others a long-stemmed tobacco pipe or simply a cup of tea. At the climax of some stories, I often got so carried away that I started acting them out. For instance, in the middle of the episode on Wu Song killing a tiger,[18] I accidentally kicked over a small child sitting right in front of me. But the child did not cry. Instead, he laughed heartily.

Mother resented my fascination with novels. One day she took away my *Water Margin* and hid it under the floor. Not knowing where it was, I got so anxious that I started crying. When I finally found it, I dared not read it in front of her anymore. I would wait until late at night when everybody was sleeping and then stealthily get up, light the oil lamp, and relish it. Pretty soon I ruined my eyesight. They hurt so much that I could hardly keep them open. Mother scolded me for that and I replied, "You can not prohibit me from reading novels. I will read even if I turn blind."

Mother still considered *Water Margin* an evil book. If I had not purposely omitted Pan Jinlian's flirtations with Wu Song in my storytelling sessions,[19] I could not have continued with impunity.

I was naturally inclined to fiction with tragic and heroic elements. Even in movies and theater, I would prefer tragic to happy endings. Goethe's *The Sorrows of Young Werther*, Dumas's *Camille*, Su Manshu's *Records of the Scattered Wild Geese*[20] (Duan hong ling yan ji) and Zhu Shuzhen's *Heart-Break Poems* (Duan chang ji)[21] became my favorite readings. I had two good friends who studied literature, and one of them — Shu Ruiyu — even had a tragic love affair with my second brother. We wrote many stories, prose, and modern poems, but did not show them to our Chinese teacher. We also kept diaries, but that was highly private and none of us shared it with others.

During the five years in school, we only had three Chinese teachers who had varying emphases on classical Chinese and the vernacular. It was the second year in high school that I started writing fiction. "A Flashing Impression," my first piece, critiques how a teacher's wife once bought a maid and then solicited our comments on that girl over dinner. Filled with indignation, I ran back to school to write that piece without eating. That story was published the very next day in the literary supplement in the *L'Impartial* (Da gong bao).[22] From then on I became more fascinated with literature and I wrote often. But I did not entertain the idea of becoming a writer. When Mr Sun Fuyuan[23] published my *War Diary* in *The Central*

Daily News[24] in Wuhan and then Mr Lin Yutang[25] translated it into English, I felt greatly flattered and uneasy. I was afraid that I would fail their high expectations and the readers' enthusiasm. And from that point on, I began to develop a critical standard for literature, not just reading for enjoyment. I practiced writing more and more studiously.

As an old-fashioned Chinese man of letters writing both essays and poetry, Father loved to teach us to read works by the Eight Great Prose Masters of Tang and Song.[26] He often said to me: "Child, you must become the second Xie Daoyun[27] and the second Ban Zhao.[28] I place all my hope on you."

Looking back, I feel so heartbroken. I have not accomplished anything in my study, and yet, both my parents have been buried under the merciless, cold, yellow earth.

III. Joining the Army

Mine was an entirely feudal family. All five children's marriages were arranged by Mother when we were young. My second sister-in-law was an ugly shrew. Second Brother was disgusted by the mere sight of her, not to speak of having any tender feelings for her. He had long wanted a divorce. But Mother said: "If you want a divorce, first kill me with a knife." Second Brother was most filial, so he would rather sacrifice his personal happiness than hurt Mother's feelings. It was hard to resolve the contradiction. He loved both Mother and me. While he dared not rebel against his arranged marriage, he urged me to escape from mine that was impending. He read in the newspaper that the Central Military Academy was recruiting female cadets, so he rushed to my school and insisted that I apply immediately.

"If you don't join the revolution, you will be forever confined in the misery of your marriage, nor can you develop your literary talent. For the sake of your future, join the army right now! It is your only way out."

How grateful I was to Second Brother! I was enlightened to see a new life. In the winter of 1926, I plunged into the mighty furnace of the revolution. I started strict military drill and political training in the Military Academy's sixth year class. The next year, I joined the Northern Expedition,[29] and *War Diary* was written during that period.

There were over two hundred female classmates training with me. They all joined the army without the knowledge of their families and their schools. Among them were the most progressive and bravest women in China. Many had their feet bound once just as I did. Now, they donned military uniforms and leggings, and carried guns on their backs and cartridge belts on their waists. When they walked, they looked like swaying ducks. When we drilled, not only did the onlookers find them funny-looking, even they themselves admitted that their bound feet matched poorly with the uniforms. And yet nobody felt ashamed. Rather, they said, "we're the women of the time." Frankly, that represented all of us. Our instructors commended us every day that we were distinguished women. Among us were daughters of wealthy parents, wives, even mothers of three or four children. Most marvelously, there was a mother and daughter training together. Although a gap of twenty years existed between them, the fully armed mother looked no more than an elder sister to her daughter. We all gave up the comfort at home and the easy life at school for the tempering of a stronger body and mind under the iron-like discipline in the army. We came here to learn to endure hardship. Our male classmates all thought we were not tough enough and many would quit halfway. The fact was, by graduation day, only one woman had left, and that was shortly after entering the school. She did not live up to our expectation and we all called her a coward among women and a wretch among human beings.

Our school was located at the famous Two Lakes Academy of Classical Learning (Liang hu shu yuan). The men's troop and the women's troop were divided by only a wall, but the exchange of love letters was not possible without the help of the postal service. There was an interesting episode of exchanging love letters. Whenever we went over to the men's troop for weekly memorials, the male students all paid special attentions to our badges. Some of them remembered only one name, and some quite a few, and then they wrote love letters addressed to those names at night or when they had spare time. One woman with a pockmarked face received a letter that said: "You are as beautiful as angels in Heaven. How can I help loving you?" That enraged her so much that she jumped up, thinking the sender was ridiculing her. In fact that boy did not see her very clearly. He merely remembered her name and sent her a formulaic love letter.

Our life could not have been more joyful. Be it a snowy winter or blazing summer, we drilled, just like regular soldiers. But nobody felt it was any hardship. It was even more interesting when we joined in the Northern Expedition. When we marched, we walked eighty to ninety *li* on average during the day, and at night, we often slept on door planks[30] or on straw.

Strong and energetic, I often wrote during breaks and sleep time. Without a desk and bench, I sat on the ground using my lap as a desk.

Besides writing at every opportunity, I also engaged in the women's movement. In those days, women's greatest oppressions included foot binding, seclusion from school, and arranged marriage. Wherever we went, we met with young women wishing to join us. But in fact it was impossible for them. Like the story I wrote of in "An Evening Guest" (Wanjian de lai ke), many women eventually sacrificed their lives.

Living in that grand age, I forgot that I was a woman and I never thought about personal things. All I wanted was to devote my life to the revolution, wipe out the warlords, and relieve all the people in China from suffering. I only wished to shed my blood in the battlefield. Never again did I fret over the so-called "marriage" of mine.

IV. Escaping from My Marriage

As if in a dream, I dragged myself home with two swollen legs after the dismissing of women's regiment.

Mother heard different rumors while I was in the army. Some said I had died on the front and some said I was seriously injured. Seeing me, Mother was at once joyful and resentful. She was happy that I finally returned home alive and reunited with her. She was angry that I deceived her. I was at the front, but purposely sent letters to a friend in Changsha. She then mailed them to my mother. That way I kept my mother posted about my life "in school." But later I stopped writing altogether. She got so worried that she prayed to Buddha all the time. In fact, that was not the major reason of her resentment, either.

"A woman soldier in the company of men who talk of nothing but freedom! How outrageous! You have ruined our family's reputation and shamed your in-laws. Now I have to marry you off right away, and if there's any problem, let's just see what face you have to go on living!"

So Mother was most angry at my joining the military.

This was a critical moment that would decide the happiness of my whole life. If I surrendered to feudal forces, then all my life would be over! Ever since the baptism of revolution, I resolved to relieve not only my own but also other people's suffering. I could not obey my parents' order. I had to break off the engagement with the Xiaos. Seeing that Mother fixed a date with the Xiaos for my wedding, I grew so agitated that I lost sleep. I ran away three times and three times Mother hunted me down. Finally I had no choice but to take part in the puppet show. I acted as bride and allowed them to carry me off in a red sedan chair, which was more like a kidnapping. Fortunately my fiancé was very understanding. He knew that nothing good would come out of forcing the marriage. So after being nominal husband and wife for a few days, I ran away. From then on I was free. I won my battle against traditional marriage. Despite that I broke Mother's heart and incurred condemnation from my villagers, I was very proud of myself. "Where there is a will, there is a way." I forgot all the pain of imprisonment by Mother. I only saw that in front of me lay a smooth, open road.

IV. College Life in Poverty

After running away from home, I was imprisoned at one time, taught in elementary school to support myself, and suffered more shocks and pain than I had from my family. But I was never discouraged. I believed that as long as I worked hard and continued fighting against the hostile environment, I would eventually triumph.

I took Aizhen with me and wandered to Shanghai. She ran away without a penny on her also to flee from her arranged marriage. I had only one odd dollar left by the time we arrived in Shanghai. Fortunately Mr Sun Fuyuan[31] came to our assistance and helped us in numerous ways. When I was studying at Shanghai Art University, I was almost as poor as a beggar. For the entire winter I had on nothing but a tattered cotton jacket given to me by a friend. My shoes were so worn that my toes stuck out. Once I starved for four days on end. I did not have the money to buy drinking water, so I drank from the faucet. During winter vacation, my classmates all left school for their warm homes. I stayed in the attic by myself reading all day and all night. At that time, *War Diary* had just come out and sold quite well. But Spring Tide Bookstore was short on funds. So I did not get much in terms of royalties. Just as I agonized over tuition in the future, Third Brother wrote from Beiping, urging me to apply for Beiping Female Normal College in the summer. He enclosed the travel fare. I was overjoyed. For one thing, Beiping was an old capital I always dreamt of visiting. Secondly, I had the opportunity to continue with my education. I arrived in Beiping more than three months before the scheduled entrance examination, so Xiao Lu and I edited the supplement of the *Hebei Republican Daily* (Hebei minguo ribao).[32] The newspaper was banned before long and I lost my job. Fortunately, half a month later I was admitted to the Female Normal College.

It felt as if fate worked against me. After living in peace and comfort for but half a year, Third Brother for some reason left Beiping and could no longer support me financially. That threw me into poverty again. I had to take classes and teach at the same time. I was so busy every day that sometimes I did not even have time to eat. In winter, I could not afford to take streetcars, so I walked in the one-foot-deep snow from West Town to East Town. Once my fingers grew numb from the cold and I could not hold chalk. My students urged me to warm my hands over the fire, but my fingers were browned without feeling any pain. In the middle of the night, when my classmates at the college had all gone to sleep, I was still correcting students' tests or writing in candlelight. Those essays earned me only fifty cents per thousand words. The reason I was writing them with such vigor was because I had not only myself to support, but also my poor little daughter and an old female servant.

Mr Li Jinxi was the chair of the Chinese Department. He sympathized with my situation and found me a job punctuating historical books in the Beihai Library. But finally I could not take that job as I was tied down by childcare. Hardly able to afford two meals per day, I survived on sweet potatoes and corn buns. Once, because I owed money at the kitchen, they even threatened to take away my trunk. But how would they know that the trunk was filled with nothing but novels, manuscripts, and a few worn garments. Indeed, how could there be anything of value inside?

No matter hard life was, I kept my spirits up. When I attended lectures, I heard my child crying and my own stomach rumbling at times. But whenever I walked into a study room or library, I soon forgot all about these and concentrated on studying. Yes, during that time, my only spiritual consolation consisted of reading. Apart from that, I organized a literary study group with a number of friends sharing a passion for literature. We held meetings, published journals, and performed drama, which kept me busy and inspired.

VI. Sailing East to Japan

After leaving the Female Normal College, I went to Shanghai. In my dark little room by the gulf, I wrote *A Youth Named Wang Guocai* (Qingnian Wang Guocai) and *Youth Letters* (Qingnian shu xin), both over 100,000 words. With the royalties for these two books, I set out for Tokyo. It was bad timing, because the Japanese warlords invaded Manchuria in precisely that year. Every Chinese student in Japan lived in anxiety and pain. Every day in school we would encounter some Japanese rascals insulting us by saying: "Our Great Japanese Imperial Army has occupied China!" "Chinese are too unfit, and need us to rule them!" "Pathetic slaves with no country!" Each time I heard all these enraging words, they pricked at my heart, and I was about to explode with rage. One night a female classmate from Manchuria wept holding a newspaper extra. I felt even worse watching her. How I wished I could grow wings and fly back to my country immediately and join in the resistance work! I hesitated because I had not yet studied Japanese well and the travel fare meant quite a bit of money for me. Before long, however, an opportunity to go back home presented itself. We organized a "Memorial for the Martyrs in Manchuria." During that event, the Japanese police arrested a dozen student leaders. They also tore up our elegiac couplet and sent police dogs to drag students from the stage in the middle of their speeches. They even slapped some in the face. After that, they took more precautions against us and we in turn hated them with more vehemence. Groups of male and female classmates sacrificed their studies and returned to our motherland to help with the resistance work. When I returned to Shanghai, the War of Resistance broke out in Shanghai and Wusong areas after the January 28 Incident.[33] That was an earthshaking war, and every patriotic person with a conscience was in a frenzy of excitement. I joined in the work at Baolong Hospital, organizing a rescue team to care for injured soldiers in the battlefield. In addition, I became a member of All-China Association of Literary Resistance,[34] edited a weekly journal called *The Glory of Women* (Funu zhi guang),[35] and mobilized more than three hundred woman workers to involve in war efforts. Shortly after that a truce agreement was reached and our journal was discontinued by the French imperialists. So I drifted to Xiamen to teach with a disappointed and deeply wounded heart.

Life in Xiamen turned out to be peaceful and pleasant. I spent all my time with a group of innocent young people, feeling rejuvenated myself as well. Xiamen's beach was my favorite resort. I often took long strolls by myself on the soft sandy beach, watching the tide suddenly surging and splashing all over me. Sometimes in the warm sunlight I would lie on the beach and daydream about fantastic things — waking up to find myself carried by the waves up and into Dragon King's Palace or swept by a gust of sea wind into the sky. I visualized all kinds of happiness escaping from this mundane world, but to my disappointment, I always came back to the depressing reality.

Teaching was indeed a joy. For all that people say about the boredom of correcting papers, I liked it. I took delight in helping students do literary research. In class, as a teacher, I was very serious. If I noticed anyone not concentrating on the class, I would immediately order the student to leave the classroom. But once the class was dismissed, we became good friends and spent time together like siblings. Perhaps because I related to students very closely in every school, my departure never failed to reduce some of them to tears.

People in love with literature are like gardeners, eager to spread seeds at all times. Xie Wenbing, Fang Weide, Guo Mangxi, You Jiemei and I edited a monthly journal called *Lighthouse* (Deng ta),[36] the only literary journal in Xiamen then. But unfortunately we only published two issues before we had to stop. Before long, our genius poet Weide passed away, and then Jiemei and Mangxi were also nowhere to be found. Life could be unpredictable. It sometimes made me feel extremely helpless.

After returning to Changsha, I lived at Miaogao Peak and wrote all the time behind closed doors. *Autobiography of a Female Soldier* was completed then. Shortly after that I sailed again to Japan to continue where I had left off with my ambition. I wanted very much to focus on reading for a couple of years and study European literature systematically. After entering the school of arts and humanities at Waseta University, I took many courses with Hisao Honma. I rented a room in the Otori Apartments at Shitame District, living with Japanese only in order to practice the language. I exchanged Chinese classes with Mr Taketa for Japanese grammar and Japanese fiction. I brought my diary with me to Tokyo, which I kept writing for eight consecutive years. This was for an agreement I made with a bookstore to publish a selection of my diary. Surprisingly, as I started with this project, I met with the gravest blow of my life — I was arrested on the night of April 12 in 1936! During the three weeks in prison, I endured cruel punishment, hunger, and all kinds of humiliation. (I would rather not go into details here. Please read my book *In a Japanese Prison* (Zai Riben yu zhong)!) From then on, I saw even more clearly the true colors of the Japanese warlords. I vowed that as long as I lived, I would fight with the Japanese imperialists. I wanted to avenge myself, and moreover, I wanted to wipe away the disgrace of my country.

I am always grateful for the great kindness with which Mr Yazi[37] and his entire family received me upon my return to China. As Third Brother telegraphed me to go to Guilin, I took a detour by way of Hong Kong and Jiulong, where I spent two days in leisure. There I became close friends with three people at the first meeting. During my entire summer's break, I saw all the famous tourist spots in Guilin, Liuzhou and Yangshuo. These pleasure trips relieved me from memories of the wounds I had suffered physically and mentally. In August, I assumed my new appointment at Nanning Middle School teaching two sections of Chinese. But for my severe head injury, I fainted very easily. I only taught for one semester, and could not hold out any longer.

Back to Hunan, I put a dozen essays into a collection entitled *Wind of Hunan* (Hunan de feng) to be published with North New Book Company (Bei xin shu ju). I was just about to take a good break when I received a telegram informing me that Mother was gravely ill. On the seventh day after I arrived home, Mother died in my arms. The pain and sorrow I felt at that moment was beyond words.

Over my marriage issue, I broke Mother's heart. Later she came to see my point and showed me special love and concern. On the day she died, she kissed me many times. Even though she had a condition that caused her to lose the power of speech, she managed to tell me, "My child, you've lost weight!" Her voice was full of tenderness and maternal love. Even today, whenever I think of Mother in her sickbed, this voice comes to my mind.

Since Mother's death, my insomnia relapsed. I could not bear to look at the things left by Mother, so I went to Mount Heng to recuperate. I had scarcely been there for two months before the roar of cannons at Marco Polo Bridge[38] rushed me from my sickbed to the frontline. This was a major transition as well as the beginning of the most fulfilling life since the Northern Expedition.

VII. After Resistance War

For three years I lived in field hospitals, which were reeking of blood and constantly under gunfire, all over the Yellow River and Yangtze River areas. I collected a great deal of stories of heroism that would touch anyone's heart. I related to the millions of people at the rear the patriotic deeds of those unknown heroes who protected our nation with their lives. Later I edited *Yellow River Literary Journal*[39] in Xi'an for three years. Those days are well worth remembering. I often took my manuscript to the kitchen table, holding my baby with my left arm and writing with my right hand. Now I live like that again, and worse, as I now have another child, Little Lili. For the sake of my two children I cannot work outside of home for the time being. Yet, I consider it my natural duty, the duty of all women, to raise the next generation for our nation. I must try to make time to write and read among my full engagements.

In the first half of my life, I suffered great pain and shock over the issue of marriage. Yet I stopped fretting about it, because I came to consider career and learning the most important things in life, not love and marriage. What a pity that I am in bad health, and I have to work for a living, which distracts me from writing. I have not accomplished anything. What a shame!

What is there to write about? I am too insignificant and too ordinary. I have wasted half of my life, disappointed my deceased parents, failed the expectations of my relatives and my friends. Nevertheless, I will not give up. For as long as I live, I will work hard and strive!

In Chengdu, on the night of October 30, 1943

My Autobiography

Ye Zhongyin
Translated by Jing M. Wang

Ye Zhongyin (1912–?), also known under the penname Ye Zi, was from Dacheng, Hebei. When she enrolled at Beijing Female Normal College in 1928, her career in drama performance began. In 1935 Ye studied drama at the National Drama Training School (Guoli xiju zhuanke xuexiao) in Nanjing and became a professional actor after graduation. During the War of Resistance against Japan, she played a very active role in spoken drama for national defense. She once served as director of the Spoken Drama Section of Beijing People's Art Theater (Beijing renmin yishu juyuan). Ye was a member of China Association of Dramatists (Zhongguo xijujia xiehui).

I. My Childhood

I grew up in the countryside. My family was fairly well-to-do in the county as my ancestors had been very diligent for generations. When Grandfather was a young man, he and his brother worked closely together, so the family prospered. Grandfather toiled away all year round in the fields alongside his hired laborers and eventually died from constant exhaustion.

Granduncle owned a private bank in a neighboring town. When I was a child, he brought us delicacies and pastries every time he came home. He gathered us around him, and we all enjoyed the treats. In the meantime, we watched him stroke his mustache and sip his wine with content. He told us stories from town. He was a smart man and often helped friends and family resolve difficult situations. For that, everyone respected him. Thanks to his prestige, no one disobeyed his orders whenever he chose to give any.

Father attended school in town. He married Mother when he was eighteen. Before Elder Sister was born, he had left for Japan to continue his education. He was a handsome man. Unlike most children of farmers, he had a fair complexion and good-looking features. Everyone adored him as a child and agreed that he would become a high official. To see this prophecy fulfil, the family did not allow him to follow the plough and sent him instead to a private family school to be a scholar. In Japan, many young Japanese women liked him, calling him "the handsome man from China."

Grandmother was an extremely warm-hearted lady with fluffy hair and a benign face. Kind and generous to everyone, she always put other people's interests before her own and tried her best to help others. As a result, all family members and friends respected her. Seeing that Mother had to live apart from Father soon after their wedding — because he went to Japan — Grandmother gave Mother extra attention and love. Instead of burdening her with household chores, Grandmother just let her stay in her own room doing embroidery and needlework, while Grandmother herself did all the housework. Grandmother not only bore the pain of separation from her favorite son, but also comforted her daughter-in-law. She faced her brother-in-law's displeasure, as he only grudgingly agreed to pay Father's tuition in Japan and often complained about it. But Grandmother remained calm and resolute. She worked tirelessly for the family, as it was a labor of love.

Mother was a quiet and demure young woman, Maternal Grandmother's youngest daughter. As Maternal Grandmother was born and raised in a literati family, she taught Mother refined manners early in life and helped her read some literature as well. Mother seldom stepped out of her room to socialize with people, keeping to herself every day. She won much admiration with her excellent needlework, and was particularly known for her tiny bound feet.

Father studied in Japan for ten years, only visiting at home a few times during summer vacations. I was born during his absence. Mother did not have any milk to breast-feed me, so I howled all day long. My elders fed me wheat gruel. Sometimes they took me to other people's houses so I could get some spare milk from other nursing women.

At that time, I learned to use crying as a means to get what I wanted, especially attention and comfort. I loved Grandmother and Auntie Tian most, as they cared for me day and night. Although I got a wet nurse later,

I would not let Auntie Tian out of my sight for a minute. I still vaguely remember that one night I started to cry suddenly. Both my wet nurse and Mother tried to hold me, but I wanted neither of them. At the end of their wits, they woke up Auntie Tian. She held me in her arms, paced the floor in the main room, and hummed lullabies gently. She continued in this manner until I fell back asleep in the warmth of her bosom. By then, it was already dawn.

When I was four, Father returned from Japan and obtained a position in Beiping. He wrote and sent for us to join him there. When the letter reached us, we were all sitting in the courtyard enjoying the cool evening air. After we read it, Elder Sister cried out and jumped around the courtyard with joy. Our cousins all surrounded us and congratulated us on our good fortune. They all agreed that Beiping was a heavenly place where no ordinary rural people could go. But I sat on my little bench in silence, feeling sad about having to say goodbye to Auntie Tian. Auntie Tian was Granduncle's daughter. Granduncle was tied down to the land by his responsibility to take care of the family property. Seeing what was on my mind, Auntie Tian came over and said, holding my hands: "Aren't you happy? You're going to be in a place where emperors lived."

"I'm not going. I don't want to leave you."

"No one would cook for you here," she said smiling.

"I'll cook for myself then." I knew she was just joking.

At last I took leave of Auntie Tian and moved to Beiping with the rest of my family. Now, in place of Auntie Tian's smiles, I constantly noticed Father's stern, iron-like face. I had to follow the adults all day long. Their lack of energy and monotonous ways bored me to death. I found life in this house dreary and lonesome. Each day passed just like every other. Oh, how I hated this death-like solitude and suffocating silence! It was a pity that I could no longer roam in the open fields with my friends and enjoy Auntie Tian's gentle attentiveness — I missed her so very much. Feeling like a bird suddenly shut up in an iron cage, I was so frustrated that I often burst into tears. Father found my crying annoying and always threatened to punish me. I thought he was very unsympathetic and inconsiderate. Gradually I began to defy his authority. The more he tried to stop me, the louder I cried. Once I so infuriated him that he hit me with his cane. However, as stubborn as ever, I refused to give in. Mother anxiously urged me to be quiet but did not dare utter a word to check Father's rage. Mother was never brave enough to criticize what he did or said. Having heard Father's uproar, Grandmother hurried over and cried: "You're scaring the child! Why are you so nasty to such a young girl? What if you injure her?" She took me away in her arms. Father stormed: "You've both spoiled her. That's why she's so impossible."

After this incident, Grandmother became my savior every time Father hit me. Father once told me angrily, "If you cry again, just get out of this house and never come back again." So I did get out. Grandmother followed me and tried to drag me back. I struggled with her and refused to budge. At last my strength gave way, for after all I was much smaller than her. As soon as she relented, I tried again to get away. We went back and forth quite a few times until Grandmother said: "Come to my room and stay with me. Keep away from your parents." It was only then that I followed her into the house.

Since childhood, I had the impression that the word "father" meant cruelty. The sound of the word made me nervous and scared. I thought he did not love anyone. I never saw him laugh heartily or chat with anyone in the family. He had an air about him that demanded obedience and distance. I did not know if he was at all interested in family life. Therefore, I was melancholy as a child. I was often lost in thought and shed tears for no reason. I never spoke of how I felt or what I wanted. Small things, no matter now trivial, saddened me, yet I contained my feelings, nor did I ask anyone for anything. Still less did I try to curry favor or scheme to make circumstances work my way. That would have hurt my pride. I had a heart of gold and would not harm even a person I hated. I thought it was cruel to do that. In retrospect, I find that I am not tough enough to deal with today's society. I feel like a failure and am very disappointed in myself.

When I was five, Father hired a private teacher for Sister and me. After that, we worked on our lessons all day in the study under this old scholar's supervision. As I saw Father's long face less and less, I sensed a pressure being lifted from my chest. I became relaxed. But the old teacher was relentless in making us read and write. That was virtual abuse for children our age. I got out of one cage only to find myself trapped in another. My once lively spirits suffered under such constraint.

On hot summer days, I felt drowsy and dozed off frequently, not knowing at all what I was reading. Sometimes it took nothing less than the angry teacher thumping the desk with his fist to wake me up. Fortunately he allowed us to go out for a walk every now and then. I tried to linger outside for as long as possible. Occasionally, I saw him putting on his long gown, as if about to go somewhere. Then my heart leapt with joy. I could not wait for him to leave.

My elder sister's diligence perplexed me. After each day's work, she never failed to recite all the lessons that we had learned previously. One day, the teacher asked me to repeat one lesson from memory and promised to give me an apple if I did well. Honestly, I was so tempted that I could not focus on the text at all. Seeing that I disobeyed him, he turned pale with rage. Silently, tears rolled out of my eyes. At last, he put that big, red apple in my hand.

Luckily, this kind of life ended when I enrolled in school the following year. I qualified as a first grader, and Sister as a fourth grader. Since then, I found real freedom, like a prisoner newly released from her cell. I was so glad to be able to enjoy life. I played games with my school friends every day until the bell rang for school to close. Then we still loitered until the bell man came personally to urge us to leave. I always saw Grandmother first when I got home. As she had already looked for me half a dozen times at the door, I had to put up with her kind nagging: "Can you ever have enough fun? I was so worried about you, but you don't care. What's so fascinating about school anyway?"

Sister came home earlier than I every day, because she could not wait to finish her homework. I often stood next to her desk watching her draw objects and maps, practice calligraphy, or write essays. Under her influence, I did well on these subjects, too.

Since I went to school, I rarely set eyes on Father. He became more involved with his work and spent much of his time socializing. When I left for school each morning, he was still in bed. He did not get home until midnight, and by that time I had already gone to sleep. I was so happy not to see him at all. On Sundays, he occasionally offered to take us to some historical sites or parks, but no outing seemed to be worth an entire day's constriction. I spent most of my time on Sundays with Grandmother. I played cards with her, watched her smoke her long pipe, and listened to her stories about "the long hair"[1] or about her life as a young woman. Then we went to bed.

II. My Love for Music, Dance, and Drama

At school, I enjoyed physical education most, because we competed, sang, and danced in that class. I loved these activities and distinguished myself as the best dancer of all my fellow students. Every time we practiced, the teacher would ask me to demonstrate for the whole class. I proudly walked up and stood in front of them. Under their scrutiny, I sometimes felt scared, but once I focused on the movements, I forgot about their stares completely. When I finished, I returned to my place amid their applause. A thrill of joy sent my heart racing.

Chinese was also a delightful class. The teacher understood youngsters' love for fun. Whenever we read a good story, he would appoint several students to perform it. One text was about the *Titanic*. We dramatized a ship sailing on a turbulent ocean. Using our desks we formed the decks of the ship, and cabins were benches. We used teachers' pointers for paddles. All of a sudden, the ocean roared with a gust of raging wind, which frightened the passengers. At this moment, the boat hit on a reef and was totally wrecked. A huge torrent dashed into the ship and tilted it. In chaos, some screamed, some held their children fast, and others tried to clutch onto their possessions. All of them were too frightened to know what to do. Someone in the audience suddenly cried out, "Get the water out, you fools!" He grabbed an ink jar and jumped onto the *Titanic* to frantically scoop out the water. Everyone else followed suit. Some grabbed blackboard erasers and others inkstones as tools. At this point, the teacher commanded: "Stop!" The frenzy gradually relented. The teacher smiled and asked: "Where did you all get the tools? How did you cross the ocean to the ship?" At that, we burst into laughter.

We often staged our performances at weekly gatherings and anniversaries. On stage, I attracted the most attention, which contributed much to my career in drama performance later in life. Back then, I had no idea that drama would become my lifelong passion. I was just driven by the desire to be the best in my class. I excelled in other courses that required physical performance, such as drawing, calligraphy, and handcrafting. My works were often exhibited.

From the time I fell in love with singing and dancing, I no longer cried when depressed. These art forms served as personal expression for me. I gained emotional balance in the lyrics and in the movements. Thus, I felt that they had a hypnotizing effect that distracted people from everything else.

In middle school, many of us graduated from the same primary school. We became interested in Li Jinhui's[2] musical dramas. We asked our music teacher to teach us Li's melodies, and then we designed our own dances.

We spent an enormous amount of time practicing and making costumes. In *Three Butterflies* (San hudie) we made dresses out of crepe paper of all colors and butterfly wings out of wires and laces which we colored afterward. In *Spring Joy* (Chuntian de kuaile), we each created our own personal costumes. For wings of orioles and swallows, we found gauze material. We pulled out the cross thread and used the remaining part to make tassels. Then we attached them to wings cut out of cardboard. The various colors applied to the wings vividly resembled real feathers. We also tailored and sewed dance costumes. We kept the raw material in our drawers and in every narrow space we could find underneath our chairs and desks. We finished the projects in our spare time, and, of course, we stole a few minutes in class every now and then when the teacher was too preoccupied to notice us. In the small school auditorium, we performed with all our hearts and souls. We felt fulfilled and proud of ourselves. The teacher also commended our work and appreciated our voluntary spirit.

In addition to musicals, we also came to perform drama. Because we had difficulty finding scripts suitable for young adults, we composed our own. One person wrote down the story, and we all took part in dramatizing it. One play depicts a naughty girl who played a practical joke on her elder sister-in-law that caused enough misunderstanding for a divorce. Later, the girl regretted her actions, explained the situation, and brought the couple back together. Of course, having neither a professional director nor decent props, we relied on our own resources and used our own discretion in the whole process. When we felt that we had rehearsed enough, we decided to stage the play on a Saturday afternoon in the school stadium. We did not attend classes that day, trying to get ready for the performance the whole time with much excitement. We set about very early putting on our so-called makeup — no greasepaint to speak of. Amusingly, I played a male role in this play. What seemed especially funny was the set of borrowed Western-style suit and pants that were too big for me. When the curtains opened, I walked to the center of the stage, so unnerved by the big audience that I forgot my lines completely. Fortunately, I managed to articulate the main ideas without making any noticeable mistakes. But somehow my body became so tense that I had no control over my voice and my movement, which felt very constrained and mechanical. My hands and feet turned into obstacles for my performance, and I put my hands in my suit pockets. Later I had no idea what I said and did on stage. As soon as I finished, I ran back to my bedroom extremely embarrassed. The teachers, however, spoke highly of our performance. Our geography teacher rushed to our dorm in great delight and congratulated us in his crisp Sichuan dialect, "That was fantastic! I'll give you each a doll." He meant that he would give us each a picture of a doll. We felt very encouraged. Later we printed the script in a single volume titled *The Younger Sister's Fault* (Meimei de cuo). In addition, we published a literary journal to open up a space for our creativity.

One summer, when I was feeling very bored at home during the long warm days, my elder sister and I discovered an art institution not far from our house by accident. It was called Art Society, organized by a group of interested youths. It included sections such as music and dance, painting, literature and art, photography, spoken drama, traditional drama and so forth. My elder sister and I both joined. I was elected head of music and dance section. My sister was with the spoken drama section. Before long, I recommended my younger sister to my section. We took part in this organization without our parents' knowledge. We went out secretly every day after lunch when our parents were taking their daily nap. By the time we came back, they had already left for work.

The Art Society was based in a two-storied Western style house. We rehearsed on the second floor. I often saw a girl standing next to the staircase watching us. Her big lively eyes and athletic figure attracted my attention. Soon she became one of us and participated in our work. Her name was Ying Fengzhen.[3] She renamed herself Ying Yin later in Shanghai. I could tell instantly that she was a natural dancer, and she had received very good training. I was delighted to make her acquaintance and work with her. We choreographed a few dances together, which we presented when Art Society gave public performances. We performed "Bathing in the Ocean" (Hai yu wu) and "Tango" (Tan ge wu). My sister performed solo "A Doll's Dance" (Wa wa wu). Three dancers did "Bathing in the Ocean." They all wore pink bathing suits, which was quite shocking then in most people's eyes. Ying Fengzhen and I danced "Tango." She dressed as a man while I appeared in a woman's costume.

Shortly afterwards, Fengzhen was admitted by Tomorrow Song and Dance Troupe (Mingri gewu jutuan)[4] through careful screening. I often admired her freedom. She left Beiping for Shanghai, and we had to say good bye. Later I saw her twice, once in Nanjing, the other time in Chongqing. Recently I learned that she committed suicide in Shanghai. I felt very sorry for this friend of my younger days.

The public performances earned us some fame and visibility. Many schools invited us to their gatherings. Father hired a martial arts teacher for my younger brothers. They practiced everyday. My uncle had a passion for magic. He made quite a few props of different sizes with his own hands. Influenced by our intense interest in performance, my brothers sometimes took part in our activities, even the martial arts teacher. In this way, our entire family became a performance troupe of sorts. Later we gave our performance troupe a name and made a banner and a few small badges. Each of us got a stage name, with one character in common in every name. This, however, all happened behind my parents' back.

One day, Father came to the room shared between my elder sister and me, his face crimson with rage. He threw a pictorial on the table and said, "Look at this for yourselves! Your pictures are published in the pictorial. How disgusting! None of those who place their pictures here are decent people. Don't you know better? Look at your bare arms and legs! Don't you feel ashamed? I never expected that you would degrade yourselves this way. Why don't you aspire to higher goals? Do you want to become lowly actors?" This volley of angry words so shocked us that we did not have the courage to utter a sound. We knew that the pictures of us performing "Bathing in the Ocean" were also published. No wonder Father flew into such a rage. Mother had to take the blame and suffered much for our actions. Since then, we did not dare participate in such performances for a long time.

The next time we performed, we staged *The Revived Rose* (Fuhuo de meigui)[5] at an anniversary commemoration in college. Ever since then, the male lead would repeat the line "The rose has revived, but the woman's beauty will fade" to me every time he saw me. Later we performed a few one-act plays, such as *Comrades in Arms* (Zhanyou)[6] and *Infanticide* (Ying er de shahai)[7] and so on. We always worked with joy. Because of such experiences I fell in love with drama. Some of my friends and I often gathered after class and discussed drama-related issues. We even planned to set up our own amateur drama performance troupe. We all worked hard in order to draft the basic guidelines, print our manifesto, and prepare the paperwork for registration. But it all turned out to be a vain effort, as we failed to get registered because of the strict censorship of the government. For quite some time we felt frustrated.

III. My Career in Drama

After graduation from college, I taught school in Tianjin for six months. I was not at all interested in teaching, for I had to conceal my real self beneath a moral mask and apply a rational rule to everything in life. Such rationality was a hypocritical social norm, not an honest expression from one's own conscience. True feelings were molded into a stiff matter to be suppressed. Such mechanical life meant oppression to me. I felt as though my lively personality was constricted, and my energetic body confined. I needed the kind of youthful joy and spontaneous manifestation of feelings. For this reason, I quit my job at the end.

Fortunately, I went to many plays during this period, which made my life more bearable. When I saw the public performance of China Travel Drama Troupe (Zhongguo lüxing jutuan)[8] in Tianjin, I admired them very much for what they did, but I did not have the resolve yet to become a professional actor.

My elder sister wrote to me from Nanjing at this juncture and asked me to visit her there for a short while. Although I had been to Nanjing once before, it felt like the first time, as I had scarcely seen anything during the previous visit. This time I fully enjoyed the natural beauty of the south and did a lot of leisure reading as well. One day, I saw the enrollment advertisement of National Drama Training School[9] in the paper, which aroused my interest. What would be the curriculum? What would the students do every day? My dream was rekindled. I wanted to attend this school and discussed my idea with my sister. She fully supported me, as she knew that drama was my passion. I was admitted. Out of one thousand applicants, sixty passed the exams. I felt lucky.

Meeting my classmates on the first day of school, I sensed immediately that this class was quite extraordinary. I felt slightly uneasy. Some of us were very young, while others seemed to be middle-aged. Most were quite unkempt. Among the male students, some looked like high school kids from impoverished families, some humble clerks, others romantic artists, still others hard to categorize, and a few were college graduates. Among the female students, some behaved like housewives, some young students, and others social butterflies. Suddenly I spotted a classmate from college. She majored in education then. I was surprised that she and I actually shared the same ambition! It was only later that I gradually learned that these students had all had experience in drama, and many even had acted as leaders of amateur drama troupes for a number of years.

The school was small and dilapidated. Only the gate could be called decent. As all students were expected to live on campus, I had to comply and moved into the extremely crowded dormitory. Fortunately, my room was not big enough to allow more than three people. Of my two roommates, one was a college graduate and writer, the other a straightforward, likable high school graduate.

The students in this class were at different levels, which made it difficult for the instructors to choose suitable textbooks. As for me, I did not have to take some of the introductory courses. Therefore, I always read other books in class, which was against the rule. I liked afternoon rehearsals best, because the class size made it necessary to divide us into three groups. Each group had an instructor to guide us through a one-act play.

My group was to present *Mutiny* (Bing bian).[10] We spent about three months rehearsing it. We started out assigning roles, and then the actors practiced reading their lines. When we read through the sentences and individual words, our instructor corrected us until we articulated every sound and tone accurately. For example, we must clearly express emphases, moods, intentions, and the characters' status and personality. We worked deliberately through the play line by line. Then we changed roles and started all over again until every actor had a chance to play all the roles. By that time we were quite familiar with the lines of all the roles and could repeat them from memory. Formal rehearsal began from here.

We roughly designed the stage, put out the props, and set about rehearsing. At first the director did not prescribe moves and positions, so the actors improvised. We had no idea what to do, and sometimes we could not keep the rehearsal going. When that happened, the director helped us position ourselves and suggest movements, which had to be changed many a time. He often lost his temper at actors slow to pick up the cues. Once he was so rude to a female actor that he reduced her to tears. We all felt displeased with his personality. Gradually he became aware of it and controlled himself. He came to be gentler and showed more patience in helping the actors better comprehend the play. That worked much more effectively.

During rehearsals, we played the roles in turns. It was not until then that I began to vaguely understand the techniques of acting. Previously I just depended on my intuition without giving any thought to communication with the audience and their reception.

When we were well-rehearsed, we decided to informally present the play on the small stage in the school auditorium. With the cast set, we went about preparing for the performance.

The three groups would perform their plays on the same day, so that we could demonstrate our entire semester's work to the faculty and the guests. The stage was set, and the scenery installed. My classmates and I had already put on makeup. The scenery and props were piled up everywhere in and outside the dressing room. Everybody walked to and fro getting ready. I fidgeted in the dressing room, as if an important event was impending.

All of a sudden, the hubbub in the auditorium quieted down. I knew the curtains were about to open. There was complete silence. Such an austere atmosphere calmed me down, and I experienced the kind of serenity that resembled one's inner tension before facing a formidable enemy.

At last it was time for us to present *Mutiny*. When the scenery was being changed, my heart began to pound wildly. I felt as though it was a critical test that would determine my career in drama.

The curtains opened. On the stage, my lover and I stood behind a chair, looking at each other in silence. With our eyes we communicated what was on our minds. In the spotlight, I felt that I had turned into a transparent object to be dissected by the audience in any way they pleased. I felt slightly at a loss for a while, and then the focused attention from the audience calmed me down. I carried out every detail the way we rehearsed it without deviation. But what impression did I make? How was my performance? These questions kept ringing in my mind, but I dared not ask. I knew some people would try to offer me insincere compliments, while others might boost their own ego by criticizing me. It was hard to tell the true from the false. The most obvious problem for actors is that we cannot see ourselves. Otherwise we would not have so many doubts.

When the performance ended, we returned to our dormitory, too excited to feel the fatigue. Some said *Mutiny* was a better show than the other three plays, because we started well and made it smooth for characters that appeared later in the play. I felt relieved hearing such comments. At least I did not fail.

In bed I tried to recall how I had done on stage. I reflected on what I could have expressed more explicitly and more precisely, when I fully captured the character's feelings, and how the audience responded at different points. I also pondered over what I would do differently if I were to perform the same play again. These thoughts and scenes played and replayed in my mind, so I did not fall asleep until dawn.

A classmate came to see me the next morning. She said, "You did such a great job last night. How did you manage to become one with the character? Could you share your experience with me? I will be playing the younger sister in *The Artist* (Yishujia).[11] I don't know what to do. I am getting really anxious." I felt quite uneasy. I had little to tell her, for I had no idea then about techniques. I asked her to bring over the script and we worked on it together.

That night I sat among the audience watching the show. We demonstrated our plays for three days. In order for all the students to have a chance to present, we played many roles in turns. Three groups performed *Mutiny*. A different student played the character that I had played the day before. Along with some other students, I would play in the last show on the following day.

Having different actors play the same roles put everyone on the competitive edge. The thought that I had failed bothered me. Although my classmates agreed that I had done a better job than the other actor playing the same character, I felt that I could learn a lot from her. When the next day came, I tried to act the same character more fully. But contrary to my expectation, I could not focus on the character and articulate the lines fluently. The more I tried, the more inadequate I felt. In the course of the entire show, I was simply too self-conscious and lost the feel and concentration. Annoyed with myself, I finished the play very frustrated.

Obviously, the instructors were quite pleased with our work. They agreed that we were ready to stage the plays to the public officially. It was decided that we should perform the plays openly six times, about once a month during the second half of the academic year. We started with *An Inspector* (Shicha zhuanyuan),[12] which was adapted from Gogel's *An Inspector Calls*. Our principle, Mr Yu,[13] directed the play himself. We started rehearsing in the previous winter vacation under his strict supervision. I was elected to play a role. All the students in the cast felt greatly honored. The person in the role of the county magistrate did an excellent job. As his speech and manners befitted a corrupt bureaucrat, the audience received him with enthusiasm. Our performance turned out to be a great success. The next show was *The Liars* (Shuo huang zhe)[14] directed by Mr Ma Yanxiang.[15] It had a totally different cast. This time, the scenery and the costumes were both finely produced, the scenery being the most realistic and beautiful I had ever seen and the costumes custom-made. Experts were hired to add adornments and laces to create harmony in colors and atmosphere. However, because they had little time rehearsing, their performance came out less than ideal. The third show included three one-act plays collaborated between students who had no roles in the other shows and the special class majoring in drama.

After the three public performances, all of us had gained experience on the stage. With a clear idea of one another's performing ability, we knew who would probably make good actors and who would succeed in management. Everyone had a path to follow.

In our fourth public performance, we put on La Tisbe (Di si niang)[16] directed by Mr Wang Jiaqi.[17] To take extra precaution with the cast, two actors were picked for every character in the play. The final elect would come out of the rehearsal. I was one of the candidates for La Tisbe. I really admired my competitors' diligence. She read her lines aloud everyday and rehearsed her moves in front of the mirror. I was certain that she would get the role. I tried to deny my defeat by being sluggish and expressed my passivity by negligence. On the day we formally rehearsed, Mr Zhang Daofan,[18] who adapted the play, was there. Many students watched. Afterward, some classmates told me that my expression of fine emotions and my deportment were both superior to my competitor, which meant I still had hope. It was announced the following day that I was to play La Tisbe.

During rehearsals, I often used falsetto unintentionally. The director corrected me every time, and I would start again. I was careful to set the pitch before I opened my mouth, but I always lost it before I knew it.

The time for public performance was drawing near. Mrs Yu enthusiastically helped us design costumes. Everything was ready to go. I saw the scenery and the props being transported to the theater in a train. The entire class worked feverishly trying to get ready. I began to feel a bit nervous with a sense of heavy responsibility on me. If I failed, I would dampen the spirit of the cast and ruin the entire show. I tried to keep my heart up and was determined not to disappoint my fellow actors and the audience.

I had a long nap in the afternoon and got myself mentally prepared. Then I went to have my hair curled before heading for the theater. By the time I arrived, the managing staff from different sections had put everything in perfect order. Small as the theater was, the back stage was fully equipped, with big mirrors hung on the four walls of the dressing room, a lamp installed at every seat, makeup spread on the counter along the walls, and the changing room partitioned with velvet curtains. There was even a flush toilet! Nowhere else in China could one enjoy such backstage facilities.

The curtains opened. The military governor and I walked across the garden, through the arch, and onto the stage. We introduced our family backgrounds by way of a rather lengthy dialogue. Concerned that we might send the audience to sleep, I added various emphases and gestures in the first scene. In the second scene, as the action developed, the audience appeared to be more involved. I felt calmer on stage. When I was shot in the fourth scene, I heard exclamation from the audience. I thought this was perhaps what was called "capturing the audience's attention." I breathed out my last words, feeble and low, to the audience clearly and audibly. I thus died on the long sofa. As the curtain closed, the audience burst into applause. Then the curtains gradually slid open again. I bounced up from the sofa and dropped a curtsy to the audience together with all the other actors. I did not know if it was a good idea to do this. I suspected that it might destroy the atmosphere of the play. Maybe for this reason we no longer responded to curtain calls at later public performances.

The next day, a director advised me to use fewer dance moves in the first scene and fewer gestures in the fourth scene to heighten the sense of tragedy. I tried to follow his advice in the evening performance. But once I was on the stage, I found it impossible to bear the total silence in the theater, because actors always wanted to do their best to engage the audience. That was why Stanislavsky claimed that it was not easy for actors to achieve "solitude in public."

In the fifth public performance, the special class presented *Crows* (Qun ya)[19] directed by Mr Chen Zhice.[20] In the sixth show, Mr Ying Yunwei[21] had intended to put on *Roar China* (Nu hou ba, Zhongguo).[22] But the script was not adopted. He had to change plans and staged three one-act plays. I played in one of them called *The Worth of the Minister Extraordinary and Plenipotentiary of the State of Qin* (Qing gongshi de shenjia).[23]

We were all relieved at the successful completion of the six public performances during the semester. We decided that the first play for the next season, which was Mr Zhang Daofan's *Saving Oneself* (Zi jiu),[24] would be staged at the beginning of the new academic year. The cast was chosen, and we were each given a copy of the script and instructed to begin practicing our parts during the summer vacation.

I stayed at a friend's house in the summer. It was quiet and cool there. We lived in a two-story Western style building with one or two other housemates at different times. Thus, I could do my own work as planned. I trained my voice in the morning in a corner on the stairs. There my voice met the wall and bounced back, so it sounded clear and crisp. There was a balcony nearby. Light breezes blew this way and that, cooling everything upon touch. After practice I read books of my interest without any distractions. At dusk I read the script out loud on the balcony, articulating each word slowly and deliberately. I memorized the whole play before school started.

We gave seven public performances during the second academic year, one by freshmen, one by the faculty, and the rest by the other classes. The plays include *Saving Oneself, Blue Dragon Pool* (Qing long tan),[25] *An Enemy of the People* (Guomin gongdi),[26] *Sunrise* (Ri chu),[27] and *The Merchant of Venice*.[28] Of these, the only one I did not participate was *An Enemy of the People*. According to the general consensus, I played Chen Bailu in *Sunrise* and Portia in *The Merchant of Venice* best. I agreed with them, but the quality of my performance depended on the quality of the scripts, because my comprehension surpassed my creativity. In *The Merchant of Venice* I used two different voices, starting out very soft-spoken and switching to a thick and impassioned voice when I played the lawyer in the court. Some people did not appreciate the change. I went to seek Mr Yu's advice. He actually thought I could have used a thicker and more masculine voice. When I ran into Mr Yu on another occasion, he talked with me for a little while and told me that I had still another voice offstage. I did not understand why my voice often changed.

From our performance of *The Merchant of Venice* at graduation, we earned some money to make uniforms. We all wore nice outfits at commencement. I got two honor certificates, one for the first place in accumulated grades, and the other for the third place in conduct. Personally, however, I did not feel that this was a great honor. I should get good grades as a matter of course since I had received better education before.

School life came to an end. The principal wanted very much to organize an alumni drama performance troupe. I was invited. It was a hard decision for me. On the one hand, I did not want to part with our beloved Principal Yu and my classmates. Yet on the other hand, two other professional drama performance troupes had cordially invited me to join them. When the July 7 Incident[29] occurred and the situation became increasingly tense in

Nanjing, there was still no definite news about the alumni drama performance troupe. Therefore, I accepted the offer from Raging Tide Drama Society (Nu chao ju she)[30] under Xingying Film Section (Xingying dianying gu)[31] in Wuhan. I arrived in Hankou together with a few classmates. The head of the troupe was Mr Wang Ruilin.[32] He was very nice and caring to us. We staged *The Night Before* (Qian ye)[33] under his direction. By this time Xingying Film Section had become China Film Studio (Zhongguo dianying zhi pian chang). A studio stage was established and there were always one or two films in the making. Raging Tide engaged in propaganda work under its administration. Often we rode in a truck through the streets, the audio amplifier playing the national song "March of the Volunteers" (Yiyongjun jinxingqu)[34] interspersed with speeches and slogans until we reached the site of our performance.

Once we presented the most popular play at that time *Put Down Your Whip* (Fangxia ni de bianzi)[35] in the open at Zhongshan Park. The bleachers in the basketball court in the park were filled. As we had never performed in such a physical setting, we had to shout at the top of our lungs for our voices to carry. We did not always succeed – because we had grown accustomed to facing the audience on three sides from the stage. But in the park the audience sat on all four sides, and we had no facilities for such a setting. All we could do was to move around as much as possible. As we all had to speak with our back to the audience some of the time, it was impossible for all of us to be heard. We had three different groups presenting in turns, one group on each day, so obviously competition was going on.

Our group put on makeup at my house and then headed for the park in a truck. As we got off, the audience surrounded us, making it difficult for us to move. When we pushed our way to the basketball court, more audience was waiting for us. We hastened to get ready and started. In the middle of the show, when Sister Xiang, the part that I played, fainted from hunger, people from the audience on all sides threw coins toward me. I was quite unprepared for this. One person seemed to be crazy. He flung a lot of money at first, and then peanuts, chestnuts, and cigarettes. He threw the book in his hand onto the stage. Everyone thought this person was strange.

The audience surrounded us after the show. We retreated into a small room next to the playground, but people swarmed at the door and windows, as if watching birds and animals in a zoo. We literally had to break out of the room to get back into the truck.

This kind of performance was a unique experience. The excitement and enthusiasm made us feel involved and high-spirited. Afterward I helped the Amateur Theatrical Troupe (Ye yu ju tuan)[36] present a play called *Luminous Wine Glass* (Ye guang bei).[37] Still later I played a role in *Final Victory* (Zuihou de shengli)[38] jointly produced by all the theatrical troupes in Hankou.

As the situation in Hankou became more tense every day because of imminent Japanese occupation, our troupe decided to move to Sichuan province. I was among the first group of actors to go. We originally planned to perform some plays along the way to spread the idea of resistance. Yet, as we dreaded to have our film equipment destroyed by Japanese bombers, we hurried to Chongqing without delay. On our trip from Yichang to Chongqing, we stayed on top of the boat, there being absolutely no room to set foot underneath. The soot from the chimney covered us like a comforter. Everyone looked dirty, unkempt, and wretched. In spite of that, we held a big entertainment party on the beach on a moonlit night in order to raise money for the homeless children who were our close neighbors on top of the boat.

Once in Chongqing, we all stayed in a temple in the mountain. It was spacious, but there were not enough livable rooms. We got an additional house by the roadside at the foot of the mountain. As our colleagues gradually joined us, we started our performances. We had not had a chance yet to set the studio stage, and we could only put on as many plays as possible in the given space. The first play we produced was called *Fighting for Freedom and Peace* (Wei ziyou heping er zhan).[39] The cast included almost all the actors in China Film Studio. I soon discovered that actors from China Film Studio worked differently from the kind of elaborate rehearsal I had known before. They often had to make concentrated efforts to finish work as fast as possible, with no time to plan, prepare, and rehearse according to schedule. All business was dispatched at a speed like lightning. As we rehearsed, we took care of logistics at the same time. Sometimes actors made do with intensive rehearsal at night, and we usually had no more than a week to stage a multiple-act play. Such performances required that actors be very energetic and able to improvise to deal with unexpected situations on stage. The entire crew had to complete the whole process under extreme tension, not allowing actors to be meticulous about grammar and gestures. Needlessly to say, we adopted the "star system,"[40] a commercial system that I was not quite accustomed to. Coincidentally my Alma Mater also moved to Chongqing. Principal Yu invited me to work with him. Mr

Huang Zuolin[41] and Jin Yunzhi[42] were also eager to have me on board for the alumni drama performance. Therefore, I quit my job with China Film Studio without hesitation and returned to my former institution. However, the small number of people among the current faculty who could perform placed a limit on the scripts we adopted. To get around this problem, Mr Wan Jiabao[43] suggested that we put on a twelve-act play by Eugene O'Neill. He was going to translate it orally into Chinese, and my job was to transcribe it. But we gave up after only one act, for we soon discovered that it was simply unfeasible to stage such a long play under the present circumstances. We had no time and energy. We were busy teaching during the day, and whatever time we could squeeze out of evenings and weekends was far from enough. We all agreed that it was a hopeless cause. During this time I accepted an invitation from China Film Studio to play a role in *Long Live China* (Zhongguo wansui).[44] Later Raging Tide Drama Society became Long Live China Drama Troupe (Zhongguo wansui jutuan)[45].

I received a letter before long from Mr Wang Ruilin[46] from Chengdu, asking me to join them at Biaozheng Drama Troupe under Sichuan Province Drama School (Sicuan sheng li xiju xuexiao).[47] Unfortunately I had just returned to work for my Alma Mater. Even though I did not occupy any important position there, I found it hard to tell the principal that I wanted to leave so soon. I felt quite depressed about it. Mr Wang sent me a telegram urging me to go, as his drama troupe was waiting for me to start rehearsing *Qin Liangyu* scripted by Mr Yang Cunbin.[48] I became very worried about any further delay. But I was too embarrassed to broach the subject with Mr Yu, for I felt that I would let him down if I quit my job in this manner. At last Mr Yu himself saw my conflict. I told him everything on my mind. He understood and agreed let me go without any hassle.

In Chengdu my new colleagues and I were very happy to see each other, as we were all old friends from China Film Studio. Mr Yu wrote a few times to ask how I was doing. I was so grateful to this old mentor.

We started rehearsing. I portrayed a military officer who ages from his youth to sixty in the course of the play. It was a new experience for me. I was determined to work hard at it so as not to disappoint my colleagues. During the first audition, all the students were there to audit. I realized that they were all watching me, because they knew that I was the one the other actors had been waiting for. The students attended all later rehearsals.

Time was drawing near for dress rehearsal. Experts designed our costume. Then material was purchased and sewing began. A big classroom was emptied where the tailors installed their sewing machines. They were up to the eyes in work all day long. The designers frequently explained the patterns to them. Several experts were on call to answer questions. Under the eaves stood spears and helmets bright with silver and gold glitter. We rehearsed on the newly set up stage in the center of the courtyard. Every now and then we went to the sewing room to try on the costumes. The day before the show, some accessories were still to be made, and some armor to be altered. With so many odds and ends to do, we did not get to bed until midnight.

Before formal rehearsal the next day, I discovered that I misplaced a lace I had carefully made with my own hands. I threw a tantrum like a capricious child. I laughed at myself later and regretted losing my temper.

I used three voices in this play. When Qin Liangyu lives as ordinary woman at home, I used my normal voice; when she serves as a military general and issues orders to soldiers, I used a heroic and strong voice; when she is an old woman, I used a senile and heavy voice. I found the heroic and strong voice unsuitable for me, for I sounded dry and not broad and smooth enough.

Even though this was a fine public performance, it was a financial failure. We invested too much money in it, making it difficult for the drama troupe to operate later. We were all very frustrated. Although we performed jointly with drama professionals in Chengdu later, including plays like *Death of a Famous Actor* (Ming you zhi si),[49] *Tiger Killing Valley* (Da hu gou),[50] and *Demons Dancing in Revelry* (Qun mo luan wu),[51] we never performed independently again. Sichuan Province Drama School received notice before long to relocate to the countryside. Biaozheng Drama Troupe went along. Many people had quit by this time, with only a few remaining. Eventually we disbanded for lack of funds. I transferred to Sichuan Province Drama School where I co-directed a couple of plays with Xiong Foxi[52] and co-edited a monthly journal called *Drama Post* (Xiju gangwei).[53] Later I played in *Sai Jinhua*,[54] which was a collaboration between the faculty of Sichuan Province Drama School and the drama circle in Chengdu. The costumes were exquisitely made. The colors of the costumes and the lace matched perfectly. Some of the laces were found in antique clothing stores, and others custom embroidered. The vests were embroidered in gorgeous Hunan style. It was an unprecedented, spectacular event. After this I lived in rural areas for a long time and was not involved in drama performance for at least six months.

Foxi rented a small theater later in Chengdu and raised some funds to get started. At this juncture Chengdu was being evacuated on official order, so all the theaters discontinued their shows, which shattered our efforts from the start. By the time we had permission to proceed, our funds had been almost exhausted. In such financial straits, we staged play after play in order to cover the expenses. We rehearsed new plays as we presented the old ones while doing numerous small chores. This not only affected the quality of our shows but also physically fatigued the actors and the staff. We put on new plays without sufficient rehearsing, for we had no time to absorb the characters' personality, inner thought, and life experiences. Sometimes we barely memorized our lines. Seeing the crises in this line of profession, I accepted a friend's invitation from Chongqing and joined the Experimental Theatrical Company (Shiyan jutuan)[55] under the Central Propaganda Department (Zhong xuan bu).

In the small theater in Chengdu, I played in *Qin Liangyu*, *Christmas Eve* (Sheng dan zhi ye),[56] *Sunrise*, and *Parasitic Grass* (Ji sheng cao).[57] Fortunately, I knew these plays well and did not have too much pressure. After I became a member of Experimental Theatrical Troupe, I played the same character in *Parasitic Grass*. Before I left Sichuan for Guilin for a personal commitment, I joined China Art and Drama Society (Zhongguo yishu jushe)[58] and played in *Sorrow for the Fall of the Ming* (Ming mo yi hen),[59] *The New Laura Murdock* (Xin Mei Luo Xiang),[60] and *Peking Man* (Beijing ren).[61] I also played in one-act plays such as *The Woman in National Calamity* (Guo nan fu ren),[62] *Cherry Blossom Dinner* (Yinghua wanyan),[63] and *Ran Na*.[64] Subsequently, China Art and Drama Society disbanded, and I joined the Province Art Center. With the Province Art Center, I played roles in *This is Just Spring* (Zhe buguo shi chuntian),[65] *The Spring and Autumn of the Heavenly Kingdom* (Tianguo chunqiu),[66] and *Nation First* (Guojia zhishang).[67]

From my experience, I perceived a serious problem in the contemporary drama profession — the lack of inspiration and ambition. Actors sometimes do not take it seriously. As a result of extremely limited resources, we have to make do with poor scenery and low quality costumes at the expense of the harmony of colors, lines, and atmosphere on stage. In the end we sacrifice the aesthetic effect in drama as a whole. These problems urgently need to be addressed.

Can This Also Be Called an Autobiography?

Zhao Qingge

Translated by Jing M. Wang

Zhao Qingge (1914–99) was from Xinyang, Henan. Graduating from Henan University (Henan daxue) in 1932, she became a well-known novelist and editor, and continued writing until the 1980s. She played an active role in the theater for national defense during the War of Resistance against Japan, including playwriting. When playwrights and actors were forced to retreat to the countryside by Japanese occupation, they catered to the taste of the rural populace and turned to traditional theater forms, such as musical drama. Zhao's writings include essays, diaries, fiction, drama, and film scripts. As a prolific writer, she produced more than twenty plays, not the least of which are spoken drama series A Dream of the Red Chamber *(1943–46) and* Peaches and Plums in the Spring *(Taoli chunfeng, 1943). Her novella* Wind *(Feng, 1940) and long novel* The Moon Hanging in the Willow Branches *(Yue shang liu shao tou, 1946) are also well-known. Zhao compiled* A Special Collection of Fiction by Modern Chinese Women Writers *(Xiandai Zhongguo nü zuojia xiaoshuo zhuanji, 1949), which was reprinted as* Selected Fiction by Modern Women Writers *(Xiandai nü zuojia xiaoshuo xuan, 1950). She also compiled textbooks, such as* An Introduction to Art and Literature During the War of Resistance *(Kangzhan wenyi gailun, 1939) and* Victory of Counterattack: Propaganda Plays During the War of Resistance *(Fangong shengli: kangzhan xuanchuan wutai ju, 1940).*

Northern China was lovely. In autumn, it was not too cold nor too warm, the sunlight soft and pleasant. Oftentimes, a gentle breeze passed, lightly caressing my lonesome heart like a mother's hand. Fallen leaves swirled and drifted in the fields. The earth acquired a brownish color. Crickets sang their clear, lusty, and melodious tunes. I always had special feelings for such a landscape. Wherever I went later in life as an adult, I insisted that autumn in Northern China was simply beautiful.

At about nine years of age, I began to know melancholy. I seldom spent time with other children. At school, I did nothing but read and never had a good time with my classmates. When I came home, I dreaded to see the way that my cousins cuddled with their mothers. I often thought that an orphan should not mingle with children who had mothers, for whenever they quarrelled, these children would use their mothers to put on a show of power. Even at times of peace, they could not help displaying smug feelings about the fact that they had mothers. Take, for example, my fifth cousin, a daughter of a maternal uncle. She never failed to brag to me about a new garment or some candy. She would say, "Look, my mother made me new clothes again." Or, "I got this delicious candy. My mother bought it for me." These jarring words often reduced me to tears in my best of moods! Because of this, I had to avoid these children and keep to myself. Having grown accustomed to my own company, I came to dislike excitement (I still have the same personality now).

Once, I found a good friend who not only kept me company in my solitude but also comforted me in my sadness. It was not a human being. It did not talk but sang songs of different tempos and pitches. During the day, its songs had a fast rhythm and a high pitch, as if to break the oppressive atmosphere around me and to inspire me to brave it all. At night, they became measured and subdued, as if to send me into sweet dreams as my mother would have. At first, I let the mystery be, not seeking to know its residence and its name. As time went by, however, I found it increasingly difficult to contain my curiosity, so that I thought of nothing but meeting this creature. After all, we could not make friends without meeting one another. Once I made up my mind, I traced the origin of its songs and found myself at the stone pot of chrysanthemums in front of the window. I removed the pot gingerly and saw a little black insect less than an inch in length with two long feelers on its head. Its eyes were sparkling bright. At the end of its tail stuck out three short hairs. In a wink, it jumped out of sight before I had a chance to do anything with it. Deeply disappointed, I stared blankly and remained speechless for a moment. Then I burst into tears!

I startled Grandmother, the only person who loved me. She thought someone picked on me again! She asked kindly, "Why are you crying, Xiao Qing? Did your father and your stepmother give you a hard time again? Tell Grandma, and I'll go scold them!"

Upon being asked, I felt even more heartbroken. I cried my heart out in my grandmother's arms. When at last I told her what had happened, she laughed heartily. Gently patting me on the head, she said, "Silly child! I thought it was something awful. So, it's just a cricket. Crickets are very competitive creatures. They live in the soil. Even if you had caught it, you wouldn't be able to keep it alive. When your grandfather was alive, he also liked crickets. He often kept two of them in separate little bamboo cages. Whenever he had them fight, neither of them showed any signs of weakness. As soon as one was defeated, the victor would start singing at the top of its voice to flaunt its strength! Sometimes your grandfather picked his stronger cricket to compete with one owned by a friend of his. He often thus encouraged your father: 'A person should be competitive and persistent like crickets!' You should also remember this. If you keep crickets, take good care of them and don't hurt them. Do you understand?"

I absorbed what Grandmother had said. After that, I completely forgot about my woe from a moment before and became fonder than ever of crickets. But how I longed to catch the one I had seen! Following Grandfather's teaching, I felt the need to observe and get to know my cricket at closer range. With my mind set, I began to ask Grandmother about ways to catch and keep crickets. I made a little cage with my own hands. Using a knife, I cut very narrow chinks on one end of a bamboo tube for ventilation and an opening on the other end as the entrance. I also went out and bought some vermilion. I heard that crickets sang louder if you mix vermilion in their food. When I got everything ready, I set about looking for my cricket. To my disappointment, it stopped singing. For two days on end, it kept quiet.

Thus, I fell back into melancholy. Sometimes I felt so upset that I regretted having disturbed it in the first place! I could only blame my lot, that I could not even have a cricket for a friend. I tried to resign myself to my lonesome life.

It was perhaps the eve of a midautumn festival. After she gave Father and Stepmother chestnuts, walnuts, dates and other treats, Grandmother turned to me and placed in my hand a little glass box. She said, all smiles, "Take a look! I have a lovely gift for you!"

I took it, looked at it, and jumped with delight, as if I had gotten a treasure. Now, guess what? It was what I missed day and night — a cricket!

I hastened to put it in the cage I had made and fed it rice with vermilion. At first it did not utter a sound. By night time, however, it began to sing in its robust voice. I tried my best to take care of it, and it gradually looked settled in. Slowly, we got to know one another better. I carried it in my satchel to school during the day, and kept it by my pillow at night to keep me company. I felt extremely grateful to Grandmother for the cricket, for her loving care.

A few days later, I decided to test my friend's "fighting will" to see if it deserved to be my role model. I caught another cricket from the debris in the back garden, and put it in the same cage with my friend. Lo and behold! My friend chirped, flickering its wings. The other cricket followed suit. Neither wanted to yield to the other. Outraged, my friend opened its mouth that had two clips to it and declared war on this stranger. The stranger resisted unflinchingly. At the end of every combat, the victor would sing out loud. This provoked the loser to fight back ever more fiercely! The stranger's combating spirit never relented, not until its last breath. This testified to the truth of Grandfather's words. Later, I tried the same experiment again and again. My friend came out the winner without fail. I enjoyed this friendship until one day in mid-October, my fifth cousin, jealous of my friend's valiance and fighting skill, challenged my friend with an unusually strong cricket. After about ten rounds, my aging and exhausted friend died heroically. I felt very sad and hated this cousin more than ever.

My friend died a tragic death, with one of its legs snatched off by its enemy. I shed tears when I buried it! To appease its soul, I put its remains in a coffin made of a match box and buried it under the osmanthus tree that I had planted with my own hands. I also laid some chrysanthemums at its tomb. Thus ended our friendship.

Since then, I made friends with crickets and buried them every autumn!

By the time I was seventeen, I had graduated from high school in Kaifeng. I became friends with Miss Wen, a teacher there. I stayed on campus and waited for work, because I did not want to burden my family with my tuition lest I upset my stepmother (she took charge of financial matters). I worked part-time while preparing for college entrance examinations. That summer, I had a meal plan at a restaurant. Little Mahu, who delivered my meals, was a very personable boy from a poor family. One day, I heard a familiar music coming out of his rather worn bag. I knew instantly that it was a cricket's song! Overwhelmed by a childlike delight, I asked to see it. Sure enough, it was a very healthy cricket! It began to twitter with all its might at the sight of me! I was so exhilarated that I went out with Little Mahu every evening since then to search for crickets along the walls of the stadium. Often, we heard their vigorous songs, but they would shut up at our approach. We went on like this for days without any luck. We always returned home smeared with mud. Perturbed, I would sit blankly at the foot of the wall.

One day, when Little Mahu brought my lunch again, he missed me. Leaving the food on the table, he came to find me at the foot of the wall. At this moment, I was gazing intently into a little hole, listening to a cricket's wispy, whistling songs. When I saw Little Mahu, I whispered, "Little Mahu, come over quick! There's one here!"

Little Mahu picked a blade of cricket grass. If you rubbed the end of the leaf, you would get soft white tassels with which to tease crickets around the mouths. I could not tell whether they enjoyed or hated this, but upon contact with it, they were sure to bite on it and start singing. We children called it "cricket grass." On tiptoe, we gently wiggled the grass into the hole. Sure enough, a black creature leapt out before long. As it jumped on the ground, Little Mahu and I jumped behind it. We did not know how many rounds we went along the stadium before Little Mahu caught it with his hand. Overjoyed, I knocked Little Mahu on his cleanly shaved head. It so hurt him that he gave me quite a stern look. We have been good friends since then. Although our lives were different, we felt that friendship knew no class distinctions.

We returned to my room and set the cricket in a little cage. Then I invited Little Mahu to eat with me as a way of saying thanks and celebrating the occasion. This made him so happy that he smiled from ear to ear. Miss Wen saw us together, and without a word, she brought a mirror and placed it in front of us on the table. Two funny faces dirty with mud appeared in it. Especially noticeable were the blackened tips of our noses. Instantly, our busily chewing mouths froze. We looked at each other and burst into laughter!

From the time I lost my grandmother to the time I met Little Mahu, a period of eight years had passed. Since I lost touch with Little Mahu, eight more years elapsed.

In Sichuan's spring, there are also crickets chirping. I often hear their familiar tunes floating into my room in the quietness of sleepless nights, which returns me to my life sixteen years ago and eight years ago. Sometimes I cry over it, and sometimes I laugh over it! What I used to call my hometown has now fallen under the enemy's iron hooves. And Grandmother and Little Mahu are nowhere to be found!

I had a child's heart sixteen years ago. I kept my naivete eight years ago! But today, although I am pure as ever, my child's heart and naivete have deserted me!

I do not have the leisure any more to visit crickets, catch crickets, watch cricket fights, or bury crickets. Nor does anyone give me crickets or catch crickets with me. Even if I returned to my hometown and saw the northern autumn again, I could never more enjoy my grandmother's warm love and Little Mahu's delightful company!

Today, I still like solitude. I don't have many friends. I get pleasure out of my own quiet times instead of going to rowdy parties. Crickets are my role model and Grandfather's teaching my life's principle: Forever maintain your ambition and fighting spirit!

Ten days before my twenty-ninth birthday, in Beibei

Postscript:

Ms Baoxun wrote and asked me to write an autobiography. Sister Bingying also wrote, and she said I had to do it! Now, this put me in a difficult situation. To begin with, I boast of neither the seniority nor the accomplishments to write an "autobiography," as those who qualify must have rich life experience and high literary status. A person like me, a beginner in art and literature, how could I deserve an autobiography? I am not being modest. I am just telling the truth. Secondly, when I received their letters, I was just recuperating from a caecum surgery. It was hard to write a simple letter, not to mention anything serious! Besides, I had little to say about myself in the first place!

Although I have engaged in writing for over a decade now (from my first publication up to the present time), I am just learning the trade every time I lift my pen. I never have the audacity to call myself a "writer," nor do I think of my impulsive rhapsodies as "literature." If I recover from my illness, I am willing to devote my life to art and literature, forever learning, forever aspiring to higher goals. I would like to achieve something in the end as my loving friends have expected of me! This is the ambition that I cherish in my heart.

In compliance with Baoxun's kind invitation and Sister Bingying's urging, I picked a short narrative from a collection of my fiction to fill the gap. Having no proper title for it, I will just call it "Can This Also Be Called an Autobiography?"

Midsummer 1944, Yubei

Self-Criticism and Self-Encouragement: A Short Autobiography of a Journalist

Zi Gang

Translated by Jing M. Wang

Zi Gang (1914–88), born Peng Xuezhen in Beijing, started her career in journalism at the outset of the War of Resistance against Japan. Her writing covers ordinary people as well as important political figures and events, not the least of which is the negotiation between Mao Zedong and Jiang Jieshi (Chiang Kai-shek) held in Chongqing in 1945. In 1957, she was condemned as a rightist and not reinstated until 1979. She continued to write and publish until the end of her life.

I. Roaming in Wonderland

I have been a journalist for four years now, and will probably continue with this job. Yet I feel compelled to say that I became a journalist accidentally. A person without long-term plans and foresight, coincidence is the story of my life.

Women often ask me how I made a journalist of myself, just like I ask clerical staff how to dispatch certain business. In recent years, being a journalist is a dream for many young women. Even though chances of becoming journalists are slim, this job remains attractive to them.

It happened like this. I helped out with a magazine publisher for over a year. Sometimes I was assigned to interview people and conduct surveys about social change, which constituted all my training in journalism. On

the first day, I had no idea what to do. A business card with the title
"Journalist of a Newspaper Office" decided my job. I felt uneasy about this
"promotion." How would people perceive me now? I had more responsibility
toward interviewees.

I never studied the basics of journalism. I found it too embarrassing to
ask an editor how to go about doing my job. Relying on my courage, the
feature stories I had read, and my small circle of connections, I began to
collect news about people, organizations, and events.

It was the second year of the War of Resistance against Japan. In
Wuhan, the heart of national defense at the time, patriotic passion reached
its peak (not without ups and downs). To help save the country, numerous
organizations were formed and meetings held. People performed heroic
deeds. I worked mostly with wounded soldiers, refugees, and young men
and women making speeches, putting up wall posters, and teaching
illiterates the basics of reading and writing characters. I met Zhou Jiangjian,
the mother of a wounded soldier. I also made the acquaintance of leaders
of guerrilla warfare from the front and occupied areas, and patriotic workers
from remote provinces. Of course, I made friends with the youngsters in
the Children's Theatrical Troupe (Haizi jutuan)[1] of Xi'an. Later, the
bombings began. Every time the enemy planes left, I was among the
numerous journalists to cover the happenings in Wuchang and Hanyang
in the heat of summer. Appalled by the bloody slaughter, we poured our
wrath into our stories.

Yes, I wrote a lot out of enthusiasm and excitement as a new journalist.
In retrospect, my writings then were not up to standard, for I knew nothing
about length and readability. I just went out searching for news every day.
When I came back, I sat down and committed the material to paper.
Steeped in patriotic enthusiasm, I worked with students, workers, wounded
soldiers, among others.

I call this year "roaming in wonderland."

II. Making Progress in the Midst of Struggle

We lost Wuhan to the enemy and had to retreat to Chongqing. In part
we covered similar subjects as before. But as the war turned out to be long
and drawn-out, we had to try to accomplish more with our limited resources.
"Production and construction" were the catchwords of the day. As part of

the field personnel, we journalists shuttled back and forth between factories and workshops. If we were to elect some labor heroes, they would surely emerge out of these working men and women.

As a result of unfamiliarity with the production sections, increased censorship, and fatigue, I began to write less and less. Reflecting on my past work, I suspect that much was a waste of words, and much signs of ignorance. I learned to think twice before doing a feature story or commenting on an event. Indeed, my worst headache was feature stories. Some people wanted to get written up for fame and honor. They would say, "Please write a feature story about me!" I would force a smile. I detested such exaggerated profiles. No wonder sometimes people ridiculed feature stories as inferior journalism for its frequent overstatement. Therefore, I began to report on events in a simple and straightforward style.

I began to be dissatisfied with roaming. I wanted to improve.

Like an actor reexamining the roles she had played, I felt conflicted about many things and began to see more and more of society's darkness and hypocrisy.

On the one hand I did not have enough administrative power, on the other hand I had no total control of my own pen.

Every time I was among the oppressed, I felt deeply concerned that my *qipao*[2] would form a barrier between them and me. Was I qualified to speak for them? Did I deserve their trust? Did I have the capacity to represent their interest? A soldier's helpless family could regard my help as an act of charity; a groaning wounded soldier could look contemptuously at condoling visitors; a female worker toiling away for twelve or thirteen hours a day could turn away from a fair-skinned interviewer. Naturally, wearing a mask was of no use. This is what I began to suspect. I wanted to say that these unprivileged people were truly kind. I seldom had any bad experiences with them. But since I came to understand their situations more, I rarely sought a personal interview at meetings held in honor of soldiers and their families. If a journalist wearing a pair of thousand-yuan shoes asked a wounded soldier, "How much do you get paid every month?" it just sounded to me like a cat crying over a dead mouse.

I saw this problem and its causes; but under the present circumstances, I could only live with the situation. I hated myself for not being able to do anything and tried not to playact like a hypocrite.

I came into contact with the rich and powerful. Journalists had to visit both heaven and hell without alarm. "Dissipation coexists with diligence."

Life always reminded a journalist with a good conscience of this statement. All the luxury, waste, lust, corruption presented themselves clearly to journalists' eyes, yet we did not have the power to expose them. This was the source of our satisfaction and frustration. Yet, it was miserable for a journalist to go to another job for the confinement. I find it interesting that the word "news" consists of the first letters of "north, east, west, and south" in English.

III. Never Be Complacent

"To live, to learn." This saying applies most to journalists. A big knowledge base is necessary, especially for lack of a clear division of labor because all newspapers reduced in scope during war times.

If we do not consider attending tea parties an honor, not feel smug about being in journalism, and not assume our duty to be fulfilled with some sketchy interviews, then we must keep an open mind and update our knowledge about the world every day! Perhaps due to traditional constraints and perhaps a lack of studiousness, I must admit that female journalists often do not measure up to male journalists in professional capacity, just like women usually are not as learned as men. Therefore, female journalists in general lag behind their male colleagues in gathering news despite some exceptions. Male journalists are more prone to misconduct, however. For example, some try to make a fortune using their professional privilege or engage in sideline business.

Learning on the job is always required of a journalist, as well as curiosity, a sense of justice, resilience, information-gathering skills, and excellent writing skills ... All right, I must stop all this preaching. After all, I am only a novice.

It takes time and energy to keep abreast of the happenings in the world. It is hard for women most of the time. We are not as physically strong as men. Long distance travel and battlefront interviews prove challenging for women to say the least. We need strong bodies to acquire skills necessary for journalists, such as horseback riding, swimming, and driving.

I must raise women's issues here. The home, the kitchen, and the family are all fetters for female journalists. The need to be mobile, a characteristic of journalism, makes these fetters even more acutely felt. I myself am no exception. Because I cannot do it all, I often feel sad about the compromises I have to make.

As a journalist, I mostly covered events in cities where I lived. I traveled very little and set foot on the battlefield only once during the war years. Perhaps I will regret it for the rest of my life. I realize that war is happening not only at the front but also in every corner in the rear. This makes it easier for me to do my part, and I feel better.

Learning foreign languages is also a must for journalists, and many of us are making time for it.

Above I shared my heartfelt self-criticism and self-encouragement. I am not good enough to be a role model for other women.

January 15, 1943

Notes

Introduction

1 Tu Wei-ming has convincingly refuted this assumption. He envisions the Confucian individual self as "a series of constantly expanding concentric circles," "an open system," and "a dynamic process" that reach out to the external human world and to the entire cosmos. See Tu 1985, p. 133; Roger T. Ames, et al., 1994, pp. 180–3.

2 Using a section separate from the main body of the text as a way of inserting authorial self-account was practiced in the West as well. See Georg Misch pp. 307–25.

3 A complete translation of the biographies included in Liu Xiang's compilation is found in Albert R. O'Hara, 1971.

4 Recent scholarship has examined how laudatory accounts of women's lives in some of the histories served social functions. See Katherine Carlitz and T'ien Ju-k'ang.

5 See Gui Youguang, pp. 267–8.

6 See Wu Meicun, pp. 1014–7.

7 See Zhang Xuecheng, pp. 56–8.

8 Allegedly written around 1809, an incomplete version of the book was first published in 1870. The World Book Company claimed to have published it in its entirety in the 1930s. It is an account of the joys and sorrows in Shen Fu's romantic and artistic life with his wife. Leonard Pratt and Chiang Su-hui observe that, instead of writing chronologically, Shen "takes particular topics and follows them each through his life, one at a time ..." They describe his six separate narratives as "layers" that Shen maps onto his "floating life." See Introduction to Shen Fu, p. 14.

9 Lu Yin's autobiography narrates the abuse the subject suffers as a child and her growth and achievement as a writer.

10 *Autobiography of A Female Soldier* tells the story of the young Bingying's pursuit of education, struggle against foot-binding and arranged marriage, and

experience in the Nationalist army. It was first translated into English by Adet Lin and Anor Lin as *Girl Rebel: The Autobiography of Hsieh Pingying* in 1940. Tsui Chi's version, *Autobiography of a Chinese Girl*, came out in 1943. The most recent translation is *A Woman Soldier's Own Story: The Autobiography of Xie Bingying* by Lily Chia Brissman and Barry Brissman published in 2001.

11 *My Tragic Life* focuses on the subject's battle to survive a destructive relationship and sexually transmitted disease while trying to pursue a career in literature.

12 *My Life* includes sixteen previously published autobiographical narratives that remember the young Su Xuelin's childhood, path to education, achievement as a writer and literary scholar, and political antagonism with communism.

13 *Ninety-Four Years* devotes a chapter to the subject's family genealogy with a focus on her mother and narrates at great length her research on Qu Yuan's poetry, while replaying many of the themes treated in *My Life*.

14 *Autobiography of a Chinese Young Girl* concentrates on the subject's pursuit of education from childhood to her departure for the United States as a student.

15 Encouraged by Virginia Woolf, *Ancient Melodies* presents the delights and difficulties of growing up in an upper-class extended family in Beijing with her father's wives, children, and servants.

16 *Autobiography of A Chinese Woman* was Yuenren Chao's (1892–1982) English translation of his wife Buwei Yang Chao's original Chinese text (she published under the name Yang Buwei in Chinese). The publication of the English translation preceded that of the Chinese version by two decades. When the autobiography eventually came out in Chinese, it became two books — *Autobiography of a Woman* (Yi ge nüren de zizhuan, 1967) and *Miscellaneous Accounts of the Chaos* (Zaji Zhao jia, 1972).

17 See Dorothy Ko, pp. 29–67.

18 See Tan Zhengbi; Ellen Widmer and Kang-I Sun Chang; and Kang-I Sun Chang and Haun Saussy.

19 See Ida Belle Lewis; Jane Hunter; and Pui-lan Kwok.

20 See Yi-tsi Feuerwerker, p. 159; Wendy Larson 1998, pp. 177–88.

21 Zhang has been rediscovered in recent years as one of the forerunners of the New Culture Movement. His approach to modernize China was sexual liberation and family planning. He studied in France in the 1910s and was among the first Chinese students to have earned a doctoral degree from a Western educational institution. A partial translation of *Confessions* was published in May 1928 in Shanghai, and a complete translation in September the following year, reprinted in February 1931. See Yang Qun.

22 Lin Yutang first introduced Duncan's autobiography to China through a book review. Several different translations were published in the late 1920s and early 1930s. Yu Xijian's translation, *Wo de sheng huo*, was published in Shanghai in

1934. It was the only complete rendition at the time. Lin Yisheng rendered *Daughter of the Earth* into Chinese as *Da di de nüer*, which came out in 1932.

23 Hu Shi wrote "The Biography of Li Chao" in 1919 to promote women's rights to education and inheritance of property. Li Chao died of sickness and depression at college at the age of 24, for her family had not only pressured her to quit school and marry but also disowned her financially.

24 This novella contains the female protagonist Xingqiu's education in France, conversion to the Catholic Church, and submission to arranged marriage, closely intertwined with the narrator's nostalgic portrayal of her mother. In *A History of Modern Chinese Fiction* (1971), C. T. Hsia renders this title as *Bitter Heart*. In *Modern and Contemporary Chinese Women's Autobiographical Writing* (1998) Lingzhen Wang translates it as *A Pricked Heart*. I base my translation on this semantic explanation: "'Ji xin' is taken from a line in *The Book of Poetry* (Shi jing). 'Ji' is a tree that survives very rarely. When 'ji' is young, it is called 'ji xin.' People sometimes compare themselves to tender trees in need of a loving mother's nurture in order to grow. For this reason, love for one's mother is called 'ji xin.'" See Shen Hui, in *Celebrating the Ninety-fifth Anniversary of Professor Su Xuelin* (Qingzhu Su Xuelin jiaoshou jiu zhi jin wu huadan, 1995).

How I Left My Mother

1 The Northern Expedition was a coalition between the Nationalist and Communist forces to wipe out imperialism and warlordism. They took Wuchang, Hubei, in October 1926 and fought all the way to Nanjing and Shanghai, ending with Jiang Jieshi's (1887–1975) campaign to wipe out communists starting in April 1927.

2 One *li* equals about one third of a mile.

3 *Qipao* was a gown worn in the early Qing by Manchus of both sexes and all ages. Because Manchus are *Qiren* (Bannerman), the gown is called *qipao* (banner gown). By the 18th century, *qipao* came to refer exclusively to women's gowns, usually long, body hugging, sleeveless, and laced. When *qipao* became fashionable all over China after the Nationalist Revolution in 1911, it embodied modernity and liberation, as wearing one-piece gowns had been men's privilege previously. Eliminated in the 1950s through the 1970s, *qipao* revived in China since the 1980s.

4 This is more often known as Zhongshan Incident (Zhongshan jian shijian). On March 18, 1926, Jiang Jieshi had a gunboat named Zhongshan dispatched to the Huangpu Military Academy (Huangpu junxiao) in Guangzhou. Upon its arrival, Jiang began to purge communist members affiliated with the

academy and the Northern Expedition Army, suspecting they were plotting against him with the aid of Zhongshan and its crew.

5   *A Dream of the Red Chamber* (1791), one of the great novels in China, is a 120-chapter work, with the first 80 written by Cao Xueqin (1717–1763) and the last 40 by Gao E (1738–1815). Revolving around the star-crossed love between the talented, beautiful, and sentimental Lin Daiyu and her cousin Jia Baoyu, the novel portrays the fall of a feudal family. Baoyu is very afraid of his father, as his father often resorts to violence in disciplining Baoyu.

Jumping Through Hoops

1   An important part of Confucian gender ethics, Three Followings dictate that a woman follow her father before marriage, her husband after marriage, and her son(s) after losing her husband.

2   Ban Zhao, a female moralist and historian in the Han dynasty (260 BC – 220 AD), composed *Admonitions to Women*, the first work of feminine ethics in China. See Introduction, p. 8.

3   See note 1.

4   Four Virtues include feminine conduct, discourse, appearance, and work, respectively referring to preservation of chastity, humility in speech, propriety in dressing and deportment, and expertise in household chores.

5   Big World is the oldest entertainment venue in Shanghai, opened in July 1917. For its movie houses, theaters, dance halls, variety show rooms, and other amusement places, it is known as "China's Broadway."

6   Guan Daosheng (1262–1319) was a female calligrapher and painter in the Yuan dynasty (1206–1368).

Imprints of Life

1   *Peach Blossom Fan* (1699), a musical drama by Kong Shangren (1648–1718), treats the fall of the Hongguang reign (1644–45) of Southern Ming (see note 4), with the famous love story between Hou Fangyu (1618–55) and Li Xiangjun as the nexus.

2   *Ci*, or song lyric, is a poetic genre that originated in the Tang dynasty (618–907). *Xiaoling* is the shorter form of *ci*, the more extended form being *manci*. Because *ci* titles point to set tune patterns, the practice of *ci* composition is called *tianci* or filling in lyrics.

3   *Song Lyrics of Ming Ke* is a collection of short lyrics by the Qing poet Zhang Huiyan (1761–1802). Contrary to his emphasis on representation of social

realities, the compositions in this collection are mostly nostalgic, sentimental, and romantic.

4   Southern Ming (1644–1662) is a general designation for the reigns established in southern China by the defeated Ming court after the Manchus took over.

5   *The Fungus Shrines* is a poetic drama by Dong Rong (1711–60). Set in the reigns of Wanli (1573–1620), Tianqi (1621–28), and Chongzhen (1628–44), it describes the heroic deeds of two female generals, Shen Yunying and Qin Liangyu, in defense of the late Ming court. In the final act, when they meet at a local temple, a divine fungus (lingzhi) sprouts in a bamboo grove. With the plant they make two small shrines where they place tablets of their loved ones who died in the historical turmoil. The play derives its title from this particular detail.

6   Emperor Hongguang, Zhu Yousong (?– 1646), reigned from 1644–1645 in Nanjing after the fall of the Ming dynasty (1368–1644). He was captured in Wuhu in 1645 by Manchu troops and was executed in Beijing the following year.

7   Emperor Yongli, named Zhu Youlang (1623–62), was the last emperor of the Southern Ming. He was captured and executed by Manchu troops in southern Yunnan.

8   Qin Liangyu (1574–1648) and Shen Yunying (1623–1660) were both female military generals known for their heroic deeds in defense of the late Ming court against the Jurgens and later the Manchus. See note 5.

9   Double Nine, the ninth day of the ninth month in the lunar calendar, was a traditional Chinese festival. On that day people climbed hills or ascended heights to picnic and enjoy natural scenery. In 1930 the Nationalist government decreed that Double Nine should be September 9th in the solar calendar. The number "nine" was believed to be the extreme of longevity. Ironically, however, the subject's mother died on a Double Nine holiday.

10 Vasily Yakovlevich Eroshenko (1889–1952) was a Russian writer. Lu Xun (1881–1936) translated some of his fairy tales into Chinese in the 1920s.

11 At the Paris Peace Conference in 1919, the Chinese delegation demanded that privileges enjoyed by Germany and later seized by Japan in Shangdong province be restored to China. When the conference turned down the demand, strong opposition occurred all over China. On May 4, students in Beijing held a demonstration in Tian'anmen Square. Along with workers' strikes and boycott of Japanese goods, anti-imperialism and anti-warlordism reached a climax.

12 It is a temple dedicated to Emperor Wu of Han. During his reign (140–194 BC), one of the most splendid in the Han dynasty (206 BC – 220 AD), he enthusiastically patronized literature and Confucian learning.

13 A chamberlain of Emperor Wu of Han, Su Wu was sent in 100 BC on a mission

to the Hun court. There, he sought to assassinate Wei Lü, a Chinese renegade in favor with the Hun ruler. Su Wu was imprisoned and called upon to abjure his allegiance to the Han court. As he refused to comply, he was sent to the deserts surrounding Lake Balkash, where he tended the flocks for the Huns for nineteen years. When he at last returned to the Han court in 81 BC, he had become a grey haired old man.

14 *Women's Star Weekly* was published in Tianjin from April 1923 to October 1924 under the supervision of Deng Yingchao (1903–91).

15 Li Zhishan (1896–?) graduated from The First Female Normal School in Hubei in 1918. She became a member of the Nationalist Party in 1923 and worked for the Communist Party after 1949. At different times she was an editor of *Women's Star Weekly* and *Tianjin Women's Daily*.

16 *Minguo Daily* existed in Shanghai from January 1916 to December 1931. In 1924 it was made the official organ of the Nationalist Party, superceded later by *The Central Daily News* (Zhongyang ribao).

17 The supplement became a standard adjunct of Chinese daily newspapers early in the 20th century. At first it was a page reserved for chitchat and jokes. Since the Literary Revolution in 1917, editors began to use it as a space to discuss Western literature, social problems, and political theories for the propagation of modern ideas and practical knowledge.

18 This implies that she planned to go to Wuhan to participate in the War of Resistance against Japan, Wuhan being located in the upper reaches of the Yangtze River in relation to Shanghai.

19 *The Central Daily News* was established in Hankou in March, 1927. It was based in Shanghai from 1927 to 1929 and in Nanjing from 1931 to 1948. Official organ to the Nationalist Party General Committee, it continued publication in Taipei after 1949.

20 Sun Fuyuan (1894–1966) was actively involved in the promotion of New Literature in the 1920s. At different times he was editor-in-chief to several major newspaper supplements.

21 *Shanghai Journal* was founded by the British entrepreneur Ernest Major (1830–1908). Issued from 1872 to 1949, it is often quoted as an "encyclopedia" of modern Chinese history.

22 *Reading* was founded in 1936 with Reading Publishing House (Dushu chubanshe), which became part of Three-Associations Book Store (San lian shudian) in 1948.

23 On January 28, 1932, Japanese forces invaded Shanghai, where they were held at bay by the Cantonese Nineteenth Route army and Nanjing Fifth army for more than a month before the Chinese defenses crumbled. On May 5, 1932, a truce was arranged through international mediation, by which the Japanese agreed to evacuate the occupied areas of Shanghai and Wusong.

A Journey of Twenty-Seven Years

1   Sun Zhongshan, alternatively called Sun Yat-sen or Sun Wen, was the founder of the Nationalist Party and the Republic of China (1911–1949). The Three Principles of the People (San min zhu yi), nationalism (minzu), democracy (min quan), livelihood (min sheng), represent his major political ideal.

2   Li Yuanhong (1864–1928), a general serving under the Manchu rule, joined the Nationalist Revolution and was later made president of the Republic.

Yuan Shikai (1859–1916), the first President of the Republic of China, died shortly after he proclaimed himself emperor.

In the early years of the Republic, warlords fought among themselves for power in northern China.

3   *Zhuang yuan* was a designation of the candidate who stood first on the list of passers of the final examination in the civil service recruitment examination sequence. In the Song dynasty (960–1279) the top three passers were sometimes all called *zhuang yuan*. In the Yuan dynasty two candidates came out *zhuang yuan* from each examination. Highly coveted and esteemed, the designation usually led to a prestigious initial appointment and subsequent career in the civil service.

4   Formed in 1905 by Sun Zhongshan, the Revolutionary Alliance became the Nationalist Party in 1912.

5   Qiu Jin (1875–1907), alternatively named "Female Knight of Jianhu" (*Jianhu nüxia*), was a poet and revolutionary. She insisted on women's rights to financial independence and education. Convinced that a better future for women lay with a Western-type government, she joined her contemporary revolutionaries in overthrowing the Manchu government, for which she was executed in 1907.

6   Song Jiaoren (1882–1913) was a revolutionary in modern China. He assumed political position within the Nationalist government in 1912 and was assassinated on Yuan Shikai's order the following year.

7   *The China Times* was established in Shanghai in 1907. It moved to Chongqing in 1937 and was discontinued in 1949. It was the major rival of *Shanghai Journal* (Shen bao). Ed.

8   *Hao* refers to one's alternative name other than given name and style.

9   The Garden of Grand Vision is a garden in *A Dream of the Red Chamber*.

10 *Dao tai* was a quasi-official designation of an official in charge of a circuit (dao) in the hierarchy of territorial administration.

11 Jia Baoyu is the male protagonist in *A Dream of the Red Chamber*. See "How I Left My Mother," note 5 (p. 206).

12 *Kun qu* is a kind of musical drama once popular in Southern Jiangsu, Beijing, and Hebei. Ed.

13 Daiyu happens to be the name of the female protagonist in A *Dream of the Red Chamber*.

14 Xu Zihua (1874–1936) was a well-known poet. She met and became friends with Qiu Jin in 1906. After Qiu was executed, Xu risked her life to bury Qiu and wrote eulogies for her.

15 Cai Juemin (1868–1940), or Cai Yuanpei, was an important educator in modern China. Along with other reform-minded intellectuals of his day, he promoted women's education as well as co-education. He served as president of Beijing University from 1916 to 1926.

16 Xishi, a famous beauty in the early Spring and Autumn Period (722–468 BC), was presented by the King of Yue as a gift to the King of Wu to bewitch the latter and help bring down his kingdom.

17 On January 18th, 1915, the Japanese government presented the "Twenty-one Demands" to Yuan Shikai insisting on control of Shandong, Manchuria, Inner Mongolia, the southeast coast, the Yangtze river valley, joint operation of China's iron and steel industries, and command of several important domestic administrations. After four months of unsuccessful negotiations, Japan issued an ultimatum to Yuan demanding his signature on the treaty on May 7, 1915, deleting Article 5 but retaining demands in regard to Fujian. On May 9, 1915, Yuan accepted the demands and illegally endorsed the treaty on May 25, 1919. On this account, May 7 and May 9 were both designated as National Shame Day. *Ed.*

18 This refers to the purging of left-wing members within the Nationalist Party in 1927.

19 In Chinese, "*Hao han bu chi yan qian kui,*" a common saying implying that it is unwise to strike back when one has no equal stand in defense.

20 Liu Dabai (1880–1932) was a poet from Zhejiang.

21 Liu Gongquan (778–865) was a calligrapher in the Tang dynasty. His calligraphy became very influential in later times.

22 On the night of September 18, 1931, Japanese forces launched a surprise attack on the Chinese army stationed in Shenyang, marking the beginning of Japanese invasion of China's northeast.

23 See "Imprints of Life," note 23 (p. 208). *Ed.*

24 This refers to Japan, as the Japanese national flower is cherry blossom.

25 On July 7, 1937 Japanese troops entered Beijing by way of Marco Polo Bridge (Lu gou qiao), which marked the beginning of Japan's all-out war of aggression against China.

26 Yin is the young man's last name, which happens to have the same pronunciation as the subject's first name.

27 *Gong, shang, gongchi* are traditional Chinese music notes.

28 Autumn Society was founded to commemorate Qiu Jin, *qiu* meaning "autumn."

29 *Rudiments of Music* (1864), compiled by Zhang He (?–?) of late Qing, contains twenty melodies. *Ed.*

30 "Three Repetitions of the Yangguan Tune" is a classic farewell song in the Tang dynasty. It consists of three verses, based on Wang Wei's (669–759 or 701–761) poem "Seeing Official Yuan Er off to Xi'an" (Song Yuan Er shi Xi'an). Other poetic lines evoking sentimental feelings were later added to the song as refrains. The earliest music score dates back to the Ming dynasty. While there are many versions of the music score, Zhang He's *Rudiments of Music* contains the version still in use today. *Ed.*

31 These are lines from Wang Wei's "Seeing Official Yuan Er off to Xi'an." See also note 30. *Ed.*

32 This is the last line in the third verse of "Three Repetitions of the Yangguan Tune." See also note 30. *Ed.*

33 On August 13, 1937, Japanese forces attacked Shanghai.

34 Here, the author uses "the devils" to refer to the Japanese soldiers.

35 *Fabi*, the legal currency, was introduced by the Nationalist government on November 4, 1935. It was replaced after serious depreciation by *jinyuan quan*, the gold dollar coupons, on August 19, 1948.

A Brief Autobiography

1 One *mu* equals to 0.0667 hectares.

2 *Biao tong* is a military title in the late Qing, a *biao* being the equivalent of a regiment. An officer commanding a *biao* is called a *biao tong*, *tong* meaning "to govern" or "a governor."

3 Dating back to the Tang dynasty, "The Legend of the White Serpent" tells the story of Bai Niangzi, a woman who metamorphoses from a white serpent who longs for life in the human world. She takes her servant girl Xiao Qing, once a black serpent, and together they travel to Hangzhou. Bai Niangzi falls in love with and marries Xu Xian. When monk Fa Hai discovers their conjugal relationship, he uses his magic and imprisons Bai Niangzi under the Lei Feng Tower.

4 The legend of Liang Shanbo and Zhu Yingtai originated in the Tang dynasty. Zhu goes to school away from home disguised as a young man. She falls secretly in love with her classmate Liang Shanbo. Sometime after graduation Liang learns about Zhu's real identity and her love for him, but then Zhu's parents have promised her in marriage to another man. Liang dies heartbroken. On her wedding day, Zhu asks to stop at Liang's grave to pay respects. The grave gapes open at her approach and shuts after she leaps into it. The lovers transform into a pair of butterflies and take off on their beautiful wings.

5   Xu Xilin (1873–1907) was an anti-Manchu revolutionary along with Cai Yuanpei and Qiu Jin. He joined the Restoration Society in 1904 and participated in the planning of the 1907 rebellion with Qiu Jin respectively in Anhui and Zhejiang. Upon discovery, they took action ahead of schedule, and Xu shot and killed Enming (?–1907), governor of Anhui. Both Xu and Qiu were executed.

6   The story concerns Emperor Zhenzong of Song (998–1022), his two concubines, Li and Liu, and Li's son. Zhenzong decreed that the concubine who gave birth to a son first would become empress. Li delivered her son first. Liu conspired to have the heir apparent exchanged for a leopard cat. She convinced the Emperor that the baby was a demon, and Li was banished to the "cold palace." Liu also arranged to have the baby put to death, a task not executed. Li escaped and lived in the countryside in anonymity. The baby grew up to succeed Zhenzong as Renzong (1023–1056) at the age of eighteen. Renzong restored his mother in the palace and brought her persecutors to justice.

7   *Tanci*, or plucking rhymes, is a storytelling form composed of singing accompanied by instrumental music. It appeared in commercial cities of southern China during the Ming dynasty. By the early Qing, the genre had become extremely popular, particularly with women. Women not only read but also engaged in writing *tanci* scripts. The stories usually concentrated on romantic love and women's education.

8   *Heaven Rains Flowers*, composed in early Qing, is attributed to a woman named Tao Zhenhuai (1640?–1655?). Set in the reigns of Wanli (1573–1620) through Tianqi (1621–28), the story treats the political struggle within the court. Loyalty to the Ming dynasty informs the work.

9   *Twice Destined in Marriage* was authored by the female poet Chen Duansheng (1751–97). It depicts the love story of Meng Lijun and Huangfu Shaohua, both from prominent families serving the Yuan court. When Huangfu's father is executed for alleged treason, Huangfu runs away disguised as a commoner. Meng also escapes. Passing as a young man, she takes imperial examinations and becomes a military official. Meanwhile, Huangfu also obtains a military post in the court. After many setbacks the lovers reunite. In Liang Desheng's (1771–1845) reworking, Huangfu marries three women, which undermines the feminist position in the original story. Hou Zhi's (1764–1829) version, *Exemplary Women in the Golden Boudoir* (Jin gui jie), further curbs the feminist leanings in the work.

10   *Green Peony* attributed to Jin Yicheng (?–?) is a brilliant comedy of errors that ridicules the pseudo-intellectuals of the day. Two wealthy but mediocre students implore a talented friend to compose poetry for them, so that they could woo beautiful women, but the women outwit them and find better husbands.

11 *Flowers Born of the Pen* was written by the female *tanci* writer Qiu Xinru (1805–73). The female protagonist Jiang Dehua and her cousin Wen Shaoxia are betrothed lovers. When the court searches for beautiful women of the area, the enemy of Jiang's father volunteers Jiang. Jiang runs away and becomes a prominent official in male disguise. In frustration, Wen leaves home and marries another woman. Later, Wen also serves as an official. When the truth of Jiang's identity is revealed, the lovers reunite, but Wen keeps the other woman as a concubine.

12 During the Ming and Qing dynasties, *xiu cai* were those who had passed the elementary civil service examination and qualified to take the examination at the province level held every three years. *Ju ren* are scholars who had passed the latter examination.

13 See "How I Left My Mother," note 5 (p. 206).

14 The basic Confucian classics include Four Books and Five Classics. The Four Books are *Great Learning* (Da xue), *Doctrine of the Mean* (Zhong yong), *The Analects* (Lun yu), and *Mencius* (Meng zi). The Five Classics refer to *Book of Poetry* (Shi jing), *Book of Documents* (Shu jing), *Book of Changes* (Yi jing), *Spring and Autumn Annals* (Chun qiu), and *Book of Rites* (Li ji).

15 Tang dynasty poet Bai Juyi (772–846) was styled Xiangshan.

16 *Song Lyrics Composed at Shuyu* by Li Qingzhao (1081–1141) was named after a spring called Shuyu in front of her residence.

17 *A Collection of Writings from the Ice-Drinking Studio* contains works of Liang Qichao (1873–1929), one of the most important political and literary reformers in the late Qing and Republican China. "Ice-Drinking Studio" is the name of his study.

18 Launched in Shanghai in September 1915 as *Youth Magazine*, it was renamed *New Youth* in 1916. Edited by progressive thinkers such as Chen Duxiu and Hu Shi, it propagated Western ideas, particularly science and democracy, and attacked all aspects of Chinese traditional culture. It ceased publication in 1926.

19 *New Tide* was founded on January 1, 1919 and discontinued in 1922. Its editor-in-chief were at different times Fu Sinian (1896–1950), Luo Jialun (1895–1969), and Zhou Zuoren (1885–1967).

20 *New China* existed from May 1919 to August 1920. Hu Shi, Cai Yuanpei, and Qu Qiubai (1899–1935) served both as editors and regular contributors.

21 The Literary Revolution, launched by Hu Shi in 1917, established the vernacular as the official means of writing. Under its auspices, women's writing flourished.

22 On May 30, 1935, soldiers under British command shot several striking workers in some foreign cotton mills in Shanghai. This event led to the May 30 anti-imperialist mass movement.

23 See "A Journey of Twenty-Seven Years," note 22 (p. 210).

24 *The Big Dipper* was the organ of the Chinese League of Left-Wing Writers. This monthly journal was first published in September 1931 in Shanghai with Ding Ling (1904–86) as editor-in-chief. It was closed down in July 1932.

25 See "Imprints of Life," note 23 (p. 208).

26 Nikolai Alekseevich Nekrasov (1821–77) was a Russian poet. Anton Pavlovich Chekhov (1860–1904) was a Russian short story writer and playwright. Both writers were highly influential in China in the twentieth century.

27 See "Self-Criticism and Self-Encouragement," for biographical information of Zi Gang.

28 Song Yuan (1917–), originally named Song Deyi, is a female writer from Xiangyin, Hunan.

29 Shao Lizi (1882–67) wrote on women's issues and served as vice-president of Shanghai University and director of the political department of the Huangpu Academy in Guangzhou at different times. He joined the Revolutionary Alliance in 1908 and the Nationalist Party in 1919. After 1949, he held high-level official posts in China.

Midpoint of an Ordinary Life

1 See "A Brief Autobiography," note 12 (p. 213).

2 *Kangxi Dictionary*, completed in 1716, was compiled under the order of Emperor Kangxi (1662–1722) in the Qing dynasty. Ed.

3 See "How I Left My Mother," note 1 (p. 205). Ed.

4 The Sui Garden was Qing poet Yuan Mei's (1716–98) garden home, where he fostered the literary talents of young women. He stressed the importance of personal feelings and technical perfection in poetry, as expressed in *Poetry Talks from the Sui Garden* (Sui yuan shi hua).

5 *Three Hundred Poems of the Tang* (1763 or 1764) is a collection of Tang poems compiled by Sun Zhu (1711–78) of the Qing dynasty. Of some 130 anthologies of Tang poetry, it is by far the most widely read. Since its original publication, it has served in China as children's first introduction to the Chinese poetic tradition, while enjoying immense popularity among adult readers. Ed.

6 See "A Brief Autobiography," note 14 (p. 213). Ed.

7 Sima Qian's (145–86 BC?) *Records of the Grand Historian* is a comprehensive history of China from the reign of the mythical Yellow Emperor (2697–2599 BC) to that of Emperor Wu of the Han (140–87 BC). It is the first of *The Twenty-Five Histories* (Ershiwu shi).

8 See "A Brief Autobiography," note 14 (p. 213). Ed.

9 See "A Brief Autobiography," note 21 (p. 213). Ed.

10 Volume I of *A Collection of Short Stories* was first published in 1919, Volume II in 1933. They contain stories by European, American, French, and Russian writers that Hu Shi rendered into Chinese. *Ed.*

11 "On the Short Story," first published in *New Youth* Vol. 4 No. 5 (1918), defines the short story as a genre and briefly reviews its origins in China. It is appended to Volume I of *A Collection of Short Stories*. *Ed.*

12 See "How I Left My Mother," note 2 (p. 205).

13 See "A Journey of Twenty-Seven Years," note 17 (p. 210). *Ed.*

14 *Water Margin* is a novel of banditry set in the Song dynasty by Shi Naian (1290–1365).

15 *Romance of the Three Kingdoms* (1494?), attributed to Luo Guanzhong (1330–1400), is a historical novel about the political events during the period of Three Kingdoms (220–280).

16 See "How I Left My Mother," note 5 (p. 206). *Ed.*

17 Lin Daiyu and Jia Baoyu are the female and male protagonists in *A Dream of the Red Chamber*.

18 This is a famous episode in *Water Margin*.

19 Pan Jinlian and Wu Song are the main female and male protagonists in *Water Margin*.

20 Su Manshu (1884–1918) was a poet, novelist, and painter. *Records of the Scattered Wild Geese* is one of his famous stories on tragic love.

21 Zhu Shuzhen (1095–1131) is a female poet, calligrapher, and musician. Based on her own marriage, she wrote about women's grievances in the boudoir. *Heart-Break Poems* is a collection of such poetry.

22 Established in Tianjin in 1902, *L'Impartial* had editorial offices at different times in Shanghai, Hankou, Hong Kong, Guilin, and Chongqing. Discontinued in Shanghai in 1966, it exists today in Hong Kong. It is an important source on the 1920s and 1930s. *Ed.*

23 See "Imprints of My Life," note 20 (p. 208). *Ed.*

24 See "Imprints of My Life," note 19 (p. 208). *Ed.*

25 Lin Yutang (1895–76), a renowned essayist and novelist, was known for promoting the familiar essay (*xiao pin wen*). He played a role in introducing Chinese culture to the West.

26 The Eight Great Prose Masters of Tang and Song include Han Yu (768–824), Liu Zongyuan (773–819), Ouyang Xiu (1007–72), Zeng Gong (1019–83), Wang Anshi (1021–86), Su Xun (1009–66), Shu Shi (1037–1101), and Su Che (1039–1112). *Ed.*

27 Xie Daoyun (330?–402?) was a female poet in the Eastern Jin dynasty (317–420).

28 See "Jumping Through Hoops," note 2 (p. 206). *Ed.*

29 See "How I Left My Mother," note 1 (p. 205). *Ed.*

30   In many parts of the countryside then and until recent years, doors could be removed quite easily from the frames and used for various purposes. *Ed.*

31   See "Imprints of My Life," note 20 (p. 208). *Ed.*

32   Established sometime in the 1920s, *Hebei Republican Daily* was published by Hebei Republican Daily Press until May 1929. *Ed.*

33   See "Imprints of My Life," note 23 (p. 208). *Ed.*

34   All-China Association of Literary Resistance was a cultural coalition formed under the auspices of the Communist Party and the Nationalist Party. It existed from 1938 to 1946.

35   No further information has been found. *Ed.*

36   *Lighthouse* was founded in 1934 by the Communist Party branch at Xiamen University. *Ed.*

37   Liu Yazi (1887–1958) was a Chinese poet.

38   See "A Journey of Twenty-Seven Years," note 25 (p. 210). *Ed.*

39   *Yellow River Literary Journal* existed from February 1940 to April 1944. It resumed publication in March 1948 and discontinued in August the same year. *Ed.*

My Autobiography

1   "The long hair" is a disrespectful name given by the Manchu government to soldiers in the Taiping Rebellion (1850–64). They fought against Manchu rule and disobeyed the imperial regulation of retaining a pigtail at the back of the head. They chose to grow their hair long and wear it loose.

2   Li Jinhui (1891–1967) started his music career in the 1920s. He is chiefly remembered for his dramatic compositions for children.

3   Ying Fengzhen (1918–44), or Ying Yin, was a drama and film actor. After her lover was killed by the Japanese secret service, she suffered a major depression and took her own life.

4   No information has been found.

5   *The Revived Rose* (1924), written by Hou Yao (1900–45), dramatizes the main characters' fight for freedom to choose their own spouses. The female protagonist repeatedly attempts suicide to escape from her arranged marriage. In the end saved by her lover, they begin a new life.

6   *Comrades in Arms* (1932), written by Tian Han (1898–1968), focuses on the patriotic passion of educated youths during the War of Resistance against Japan.

7   No information has been found.

8   China Travel Drama Troupe was founded by Tang Huaiqiu (1898–1954) in 1933 in Shanghai. Staging both Chinese and foreign plays around the country in support of national defense during the War of Resistance against Japan, it

played an important role in the development of Chinese spoken drama. It was disbanded in 1947.

9   National Drama Training School was founded in 1935 by Chen Lifu (1900–2001) and Zhang Daofan (1897–1968) in Nanjing, both cultural figures representing the Nationalist Party. During its fourteen years of operation, it staged many plays against Japanese aggression. In 1949, it merged with China Central Drama College (Zhongyang xiju xueyuan).

10   *Mutiny* (1925), a satirical play written by Yu Shangyuan (1897–1970) in America, depicts two young lovers' escape from family oppression in the midst of a false alarm of a mutiny.

11   In *The Artist* (1928), written by Xiong Foxi (1900–65), the impoverished artist Lin Kemei is persuaded to feign death by his greedy wife and brother to increase the market value of his paintings. It portrays the conflict between devotion to art and materialistic temptations.

12   Also called *Xun An* in Chinese, *An Inspector* is adapted by Zhang Pengchun (1892–1957) into Chinese, based on Gogel's original play in Russian.

13   This refers to playwright and director Yu Shangyuan.

14   The English dramatist Henry A. Jones (1851–1929) wrote a play called *The Liars* (1897). Zhu Duanjun (1907–78) adapted the play into Chinese (n.d.). It is also called *Yuan huang ji* in Chinese.

15   Ma Yanxiang (1907–88) was a playwright, director, and drama theorist.

16   *La Tisbe* (1939?) was adapted by Zhang Daofan from Victor Hugo's (1802–85) *Angelo, Tyran de Padoue* (1835) which treats the actress and courtesan La Tisbe's love affairs. The adaptation was based on Zeng Pu's (1872–1935) translation published between 1906 and 1907.

17   A director and playwright, Wang Jiaqi (?–?) was one of the first teaching faculty members at the National Drama Training School.

18   Zhang Daofan, a playwright, educator, and essayist, studied fine arts in London University and returned to China in 1926. In 1935 he participated in the founding of the National Drama Training School. He was among those who established All-China Association of Literary Resistance in Wuhan in 1938. For information on the association, see "Midpoint of an Ordinary Life," note 33 (p. 216).

19   No further information has been found.

20   Chen Zhice (1894–1954) was a drama educator, director, and playwright.

21   Ying Yunwei (1904–67) was a drama and film director.

22   *Roar China* (1926) was originally a play written by Soviet writer Sergei Tretyakov (1892–1939), based on the Wanxian Incident in Sichuan in 1926 when the British navy opened fired on Chinese citizens. The Chinese version, translated by Ouyang Yuqian (1889–1962), was first staged in China in 1930. Ying Yunwei directed the play in 1933 and staged it in Shanghai on the second anniversary of the September 18 Incident.

23 No information has been found.

24 *Saving Oneself* (1935) was the first play written by Zhang Daofan.

25 *Wukui Bridge* (Wu kui qiao, 1930), *Fragrant Rice* (Xiang dao mi, 1931), and *Blue Dragon Pool* (*Qing long tan*, 1936) constitute *A Village Trilogy* (Nongcun san bu qu) written by Hong Shen (1894–1955). *Blue Dragon Pool* addresses issues of economic growth and religious belief in the course of the villagers' resistance to the building of a road through their cherry orchard and their quest for water during a severe drought.

26 *An Enemy of the People* (1927) was adapted by Zhang Pengchun from Henrik Ibsen's (1828–1908) play of the same title.

27 *Sunrise* (1935), written by Cao Yu (1910–96), is one of the masterpieces of modern Chinese drama. It revolves around the tragic life of Chen Bailu, a famous prostitute in Shanghai who witnesses all kinds of social evils. At the end of the play, she takes her own life in despair.

28 Liang Shiqiu (1902–87) translated *The Merchant of Venice* and all the other plays by Shakespeare into Chinese.

29 See "A Journey of Twenty-Seven Years," note 25 (p. 210).

30 Based in Wuhan, Raging Tide Drama Society was among many of the drama organizations founded in 1938 to engage in war propaganda by way of drama performance.

31 Founded in 1935, Xingying became China Film Studio in 1938 led by Yang Hansheng (1902–93). At different times it was based in Chongqing, Hongkong, Nanjing, and it moved to Taiwan in 1948.

32 Wang Ruilin (1905–56) graduated from the Drama Department of Beiping Art Training School in 1931. He became a film actor and held official posts in drama troupes and film studios

33 *The Night Before* (1937) is a play written by Yang Hansheng.

34 A song in the film *Children of Troubled Times* (Fengyun ernü), "The March of the Volunteers" (1935) was composed by Nie Er (1912–35), with lyrics by Tian Han. It is recognized as a classic in the history of Chinese music for its patriotism and mobilizing effect during the War of Resistance against Japan. China's acting national anthem since 1949, it was officially pronounced the national anthem in 1982.

35 Collaborated between Chen Liting (1910–) and Cui Wei (1912–79) in 1931, *Put Down Your Whip* (1936) is a famous street drama (jietou ju) produced during the War of Resistance against Japan. In the play the female protagonist describes atrocities inflicted on her homeland in the Northeast by Japanese troops.

36 No information has been found.

37 Scripted by Yu Ling (1907–1997), *Luminous Wine Glass* (1937) represents the patriotic deeds of a dance-hostess during the War of Resistance against Japan.

38 *Final Victory* (1938) was a play written by Tian Han on the theme of anti-Japanese aggression.

39 On the New Year's Eve of 1939, the drama circle in Chongqing staged a series of plays on the theme of national defense to commemorate the one-year anniversary of All-China Association of Dramatic Resistance (Zhonghua quanguo xijujie kangdi xiehui), one of many such organizations in support of China's war efforts. The plays performed include *Roar China*, *Demons Dancing in Revelry*, and *Fighting for Freedom and Peace*.

40 The "star system" refers to the making and the use of idols to increase box-office value.

41 Huang Zuolin (1906–94) studied drama at Cambridge University in the 1930s. As a celebrated director and theorist, he enjoyed a career of over thirty years teaching and directing Chinese and Western plays. He was a pioneer in combining Chinese and Western dramatic traditions.

42 Jin Yunzhi (1912–), pen name Dan Ni, graduated with a Bachelor of Arts degree from Columbia University in 1935. She went to London to study drama in 1937. After returning to China, she became an actor and professor of drama. See note 27.

43 Wan Jiabao, or Cao Yu, was a celebrated playwright in modern China.

44 *Long Live China* (1938) was a play written by Tang Na (1914–88) about how people in the occupied areas mobilized themselves to fight Japanese aggression.

45 Long Live China Drama Troupe, with Wang Ruilin as head, was affiliated with China Film Studio.

46 See note 32.

47 Sichuan Province Drama School was founded in 1938 by Xiong Foxi. It was disbanded in 1941. Biaozheng Drama Troupe was affiliated to this school, with Wang Ruilin as the head.

48 *Qin Liangyu* is a historical play written by Yang Cunbin (1911–89). See also "Imprints of Life," note 5 and note 8 (p. 207).

49 *Death of a Famous Actor* (1929), written by Tian Han, tells how actor Liu Zhensheng gives his life trying to keep his female protegé Liu Fengxian's faith in performance art and save her from temptations of the world.

50 No information has been found.

51 *Demons Dancing in Revelry* was first staged around 1936, with Shen Fu (1905–1994) as director. See also note 39.

52 Xiong Foxi was one of the earliest promoters of the Chinese spoken drama. He earned a Master's degree in drama from Columbia University in 1926 and returned to China to become a playwright, educator, and drama theorist.

53 Established by Xiong Foxi, *Drama Post* existed from April 1939 to May 1942. It published performance theories as well as literary works by both Chinese

and foreign writers. It also carried plays, including those that promoted resistance against Japanese aggression.

54 Stressing the theme of national defense, *Sai Jinhua* (1936), scripted by Xia Yan, stages the patriotism of the titular heroine Sai Jinhua (1872–1936), a famous Qing courtesan. Xiong Foxi wrote a play on the same theme in 1937.

55 No information has been found.

56 *Christmas Eve* (1940), also called *The Evil Member of the Herd* (Hai qun zhi ma), was a play written by Xiong Foxi.

57 Hong Shen adapted *Parasitic Grass* (1940) from Hubert H. Davis' (1869–1917) play *The Mollusc* (1907). Seeing the idle wives of some officials, Hong used the play to encourage women to do their part for their country. Xiong Foxi also adapted the play the same year. There is another rendition by Zhu Duanjun.

58 China Art and Drama Society was established in Chongqing in December 1942 by Xia Yan, Yu Ling, Yang Hansheng and other drama professionals at the suggestion of Communist leader Zhou Enlai (1898–1976). It played an active role in promoting spoken drama as an art form and in rallying people's efforts to fight Japanese invasion. It was disbanded in 1946.

59 Emphasizing themes of defiance and opposition during the War of Resistance against Japan, *Sorrow for the Fall of the Ming* (1940) by A Ying (1900–77) recounts the struggle of the Ming against the Qing. Zhou Xinfang (1895–1975) adapted the play to attack by innuendo the corruption of the Nationalist government through portraying the dissipation of late Ming court. In Zhou's version, when Emperor Chongzhen (1611–44) woke up to the reality, the peasant soldiers led by Li Zicheng (1606–45) had already surrounded Beijing. Chongzhen hanged himself.

60 *Laura Murdock* (n.d.) was a played adapted by Gu Zhongyi (1904–65) from American writer Eugene Walter's (1874–1941) *The Easiest Way* (1908), in which Laura Murdock is a beautiful theatrical entertainer. Named Mei Luoxiang in Chinese, she depends on a man for a living and fails to win independence. When Qu Baiyin (1910–79) adapted the play, he called it *The New Laura Murdock* (1941). Xiong Foxi directed Qu's adaptation.

61 Written by Cao Yu, *Peking Man* (1941) depicts three generations of parasitic men in a declining feudal family and envisions a better society composed of the working class and the modern educated.

62 No information has been found.

63 A play written by Hong Shen, *Cherry Blossom Dinner* (1942) exposes the corruption and non-resistance of the Nationalist government.

64 No information has been found.

65 *This Is Just Spring* (1934), a comedy by Li Jianwu (1906–82), tells how a police chief's wife, a social butterfly, helps a revolutionary to run away in spite of her unrequited love for him.

66 *The Spring and Autumn of the Heavenly Kingdom* (1941), written by Yang Hansheng, treats the internal political rivalry of the Heavenly Kingdom of the Great Peace (the Taipings). Proclaimed by the Hong Xiuquan (1814–64) in 1851, the Heavenly Kingdom started from Guangxi, marched through Wuhan, and settled in Nanjing in 1853. In 1856, power struggle within the leadership motivated Wei Changhui (1823–56) to assassinate Yang Xiuqing (1820–56). Hong issued an order to have Wei's entire family executed. Written and staged in 1941, the political significance of the play was obvious. Throughout the War of Resistance against Japan, Jiang Jieshi's priority was to wipe out the Communists. On January 4, 1941, 80,000 Nationalist soldiers ambushed a section of the Communist New Fourth Army of about 9,000 led by Ye Ting (1896–1946) and Xiang Ying (1898–1941), of whom 8,000 were killed. This is referred to as the Southern Anhui Incident (Wan nan shibian).

67 *Nation First* (1940) by Lao She (1899–1966) and Song Zhidi (1914–56) treats the tension between the Muslim and Han communities in north China and their concerted effort to fight Japanese aggression.

Self-Criticism and Self-Encouragement: A Short Autobiography of a Journalist

1 The Children's Theatrical Troupe of Xi'an, was founded in 1935. After Japanese occupation in 1937, Shanghai saw the establishment of its own Children's Theatrical Troupe which consisted of orphans deprived of home and education. In other cities appeared similar organizations that traveled around the country to perform plays on resistance themes. All such troupes were disbanded in September 1942.

2 See "How I Left My Mother," note 3 (p. 205).

Glossary

"A Brief Autobiography" "简单的自传"

A Collection of Short Stories 《短篇小说集》

A Collection of Writings from the Ice-Drinking Studio 《饮冰室文集》

A Dream of the Red Chamber 《红楼梦》

"A Journey of Twenty Seven Years" "二十七年的旅程"

A Special Collection of Fiction by Modern Chinese Women Writers 《现代中国女作家小说专集》

A Village Trilogy 《农村三步曲》

A Youth Named Wang Guocai 《青年王国材》

aijiti zajiti zixu 哀祭体杂记体自叙

All-China Association of Dramatic Resistance 中华全国戏剧界抗敌协会

All-China Association of Literary Resistance 中华全国文艺界抗敌协会

Amateur Drama Troupe 业余剧团

Analects, The 《论语》

Artist, The 《艺术家》

An Autobiography of Lu Yin 《庐隐自传》

An E (Zhang Shiyuan, Ding Na) 安娥（张式沅，丁娜）

An Enemy of the People 《国民公敌》

"An Evening Guest" "晚间的来客"

Autobiography of a Female Soldier 《女兵自传》

Autobiography of a Chinese Woman 《一个女人的自传》

Autumn Society 秋社

bai hua 白话

Bai Juyi 白居易（香山）

Bai Suzhen　白素贞

Ban Zhao　班昭

bei　碑

Beijing Female Normal College　北京女子师范学院

Beijing People's Art Theater　北京人民艺术剧院

biao tong　标统

Biaozheng Drama Troupe　表证剧团

Big Dipper, The　《北斗杂志》

Big World　大世界

Blue Dragon Pool　《青龙潭》

Bomb and the Migrating Bird, The　《炸弹与征鸟》

Book of Changes　《易经》

Book of Documents　《书经》

Book of Poetry　《诗经》

Book of Rites　《礼记》

Breaking Out of the Ghost's Tower　《打出幽灵塔》

Cai Yuanpei　蔡元培（蔡觉民）

"Can This Be Also Called an Autobiography?"　"也算自传？"

Cao Pi　曹丕

Cao Xueqin　曹雪芹

Cao Yu　万家宝（曹禺）

Central Daily News, The　《中央日报》

Central Department of Propaganda　中宣部

Chen Bailu　陈白露

Chen Duansheng　陈端生

Chen Duxiu　陈独秀

Chen Hengzhe　陈衡哲

Chen Lifu　陈立夫

Chen Liting　陈鲤庭

Chen Zhice　陈治策

Cherry Blossom Dinner　《樱花晚宴》

Children of Troubled Times　《风云儿女》

Children's Drama Troupe　孩子剧团

China Art and Drama Society　中国艺术剧社

China Association of Dramatists　中国剧作家协会

China Central Drama Institute　中央话剧院

China Experimental Theater　中国实验剧团

China Film Studio　中国电影制片厂

China Revival Society　兴中会

China Times, The　《时事新报》

China Travel Drama Troupe　中国旅行剧团

Chinese League of Left-Wing Writers　中国左翼作家联盟

Chongzhen　崇祯

Christmas Eve　《圣诞之夜》(《害群之马》)

Chu Wenjuan　褚问鹃

cifuti yu shigeti zixu　辞赋体与诗歌体自叙

Communist Party　共产党

Comrades in Arms　《战友》

Crows　《群鸦》

Cui Wei　崔嵬

dao tai　道台

Death of a Famous Actor, The　《名优之死》

Deng Yingchao　邓颖超

Devils Dancing in Revelry　《群魔乱舞》

Ding Ling　丁玲

Doctrine of the Mean　《中庸》

Dong Rong　董榕

Double Nine Festival　重阳节

Drama Post　《戏剧岗位志》

Eight Great Prose Masters of the Tang and Song　唐宋八大散文家

Emperor Wu of Han　汉武帝

"Encountering Sorrow"　"离骚"

Endless Tides of the Yangtze River, The　《不尽长江滚滚来》

Enming　恩铭

"Epitaph of Fang Mu Zhang Ruren, The"　"方母张儒人墓志铭"

"Epitaph of Pei Mu Cha Yiren, The"　"裴母查宜人墓志铭"

"Epitaph of Wang Mu Zhou Taianren" "王母周太安人墓志铭"

ershiyi tiao 二十一条

Exemplary Women in the Golden Boudoir 《金闺杰》

Fa Hai 法海

fabi 法币

familiar essay 小品文

Female Juror 《女陪审员》

Female Knight of Jianhu 鉴湖女侠

Fiction of An E 《安娥小说》

Fighting for Freedom and Peace 《为自由和平而战》

Filial Gratitude 《寸草心》

filling in lyrics 填词

Final Victory 《最后胜利》

Five Classics 五经

Flowers Born of the Pen 《笔生花》

Four Books 四书

Four Virtues 四德

Fragrant Rice 《香稻米》

Fu Sinian 付斯年

Fungus Shrines, The 《芝龛记》

Gao E 高鄂

Garden of Grand Vision, the 大观园

Glory of Women, The 《妇女之光》

gong 宫

Grassland 《草原》

Great Learning 《大学》

Green Peony 《绿牡丹》

Growth of a Labor Hero, The 《一个劳动英雄的成长》

Gu Zhongyi 顾仲彝

Guan Daosheng 管道升

Gui Youguang 归有光

Guo Dengfeng 郭登峰

Han Yu 韩愈

hao 号

Heart-Break Poems 《断肠集》

Heavenly Discussions 《天论》

Heavenly Kingdom 太平天国

Heaven Rains Flowers 《天雨花》

Hebei Republican Daily 《河北民国日报》

Heir Apparent Exchanged for a Leopard Cat, The 《狸猫换太子》

History of the Jin Dynasty 《晋书》

History of the Ming Dynasty 《明史》

History of the Northern Dynasty 《北史》

History of the Southern Dynasty 《南史》

History of the Yuan Dynasty 《元史》

Hong Shen 洪深

Hong Xiuquan 洪秀全

Hongguang 弘光

Hou Fangyu 候方域

Hou Yao 侯曜

Hou Zhi 侯芝

"How I Left My Mother" "我怎样离开的母亲"

Hu Shi 胡适

Huang Zhang (Bai Wei) 黄章（白薇）

Huang Zuolin 黄佐临

Huangfu Shaohua 皇甫少华

Huangpu Military Academy 黄浦军校

Huns 匈奴

"Imprints of Life" "生命的印痕"

In a Japanese Prison 《在日本狱中》

Introduction to Art and Literature During the War of Resistance, An 《抗战文艺概论》

Infanticide 《婴儿的杀害》

Inspector, The 《视察专员》

Jia Baoyu 贾宝玉

Jiang Dehua 姜德华

Jiang Jieshi (Chiang Kai-shek)　蒋介石

Jin Yicheng　金义成

jinyuan quan　金元券

Jin Yunzhi (Dan Ni)　金韵芝（丹尼）

ju ren　举人

"Jumping Through Hoops" "跳关记"

Jurgens　女真

Kangxi Dictionary 《康熙字典》

Kong Shangren　孔尚任

kuangzhi　圹志

kun qu　昆曲

L' Impartial 《大公报》

La Tisbe 《狄四娘》

Lao She　老舍

Legend of the While Serpent, The 《白蛇传》

lei　诔

Leifeng Tower　雷峰塔

Li Hongyuan　黎元洪

Li Jianwu　李健吾

Li Jinhui　黎锦晖

Li Ling　李陵

Li Qingzhao　李清照

Li Xiangjun　李香君

Li Yanlin　李炎林

Li Zhishan　李峙山

Li Zicheng　李自成

li　里

Liang Desheng　梁德绳

Liang Qichao　梁启超

Liang Shanbo　梁山伯

Liang Shiqiu　梁实秋

Liars, The 《说谎者》（《圆谎记》）

lie zhuan　列传

lie nü zhuan 列女传

Lighthouse 《灯塔》

Lin Daiyu 林黛玉

Lin Kemei 林可梅

Lin Li 《琳丽》

Lin Beili (Lin Yin) 林北丽（林隐）

Lin Yisheng 林宜生

Lin Yutang 林语堂

Ling Shuhua (Su Hua Ling Chen) 凌叔华

Literary Revolution, the 文学革命

Liu Dabai 刘大白

Liu Fengxian 刘凤仙

Liu Gongquan 柳公权

Liu Xiang 刘向

Liu Yazi 柳亚子

Liu Zhengsheng 刘振声

Liu Zongyuan 柳宗元

Long Live China 《中国万岁》

Long Live China Drama Troupe 中国万岁剧团

Lu Xun 鲁迅

Lu Yin 庐隐

Luminous Wine Glass 《夜光杯》

Luo Guangzhong 罗贯中

Luo Jialun 罗家伦

Ma Yanxiang 马彦祥

man ci 慢词

Manchus 满人

"March of the Volunteers" "义勇军进行曲"

Mencius 《孟子》

Meng Lijun 孟丽君

"Midpoint of an Ordinary Life" "平凡的半生"

Minguo Daily 《民国日报》

Miscellaneous Accounts of the Chaos 《杂记赵家》

Moon Hanging in the Willow Branches, The 《月上柳稍头》

mu 亩

Mutiny 《兵变》

"My Autobiography" "我的自传"

My Life 《我的生活》

My Tragic Life 《悲剧生涯》

Nation First 《国家至上》

National Drama Training School 国立戏剧专科学校

National School of Fine Arts 国立美术专科学校

National Shame Day 国耻日

Nationalism, Democracy, Livelihood 民族，民权，民生

Nationalist Revolution 民国革命

New China 《新中国》

New Laura Murdock, The 《新梅萝香》

New Literature 新文学

New Testament, The 《新约全书》

New Tide 《新潮》

New Youth 《新青年》

"Newspaper Selling Song" "卖报歌"

Nie Er 涅耳

Night Before, The 《前夜》

Ninety-Four Years of a Floating Life 《浮生九四》

Northern Expedition 北伐

Old Testament, The 《旧约全书》

"On Literary Revolution" "文学革命论"

"On the Short Story" "论短篇小说"

Ouyang Xiu 欧阳修

Pan Jinlian 潘金莲

Parasitic Grass 《寄生草》

Paris Peace Conference 巴黎和会

Peach Blossom Fan 《桃花扇》

Peaches and Blossoms in the Spring 《桃李春风》

Peng Hui 彭慧

Poetry Talks from the Sui Garden 《隋园诗话》

Postscript to *A Catalogue of Bronze and Stone Inscriptions* 《金石录》后序

Preface to *Admonitions to Women* 《女诫》序

Put Down Your Whip 《放下你的鞭子》

Qian Xingcun 钱杏村（阿英）

Qin Liangyu 《秦良玉》

qipao 旗袍

Qiu Jin 秋瑾

Qiu Lingmei 邱陵美

Qiu Xinru 邱心如

Qu Baiyin 瞿白音

Qu Qiubai 瞿秋白

Qu Yuan 屈原

Raging Tide Drama Society 怒潮剧社

Ran Na 《冉娜》

Reading 《读书》

Records of the Grand Historian 《史记》

Records of the Scattered Wild Geese 《断鸿零雁记》

Renzong 仁宗

Restoration Society 光复会

Returning Home 《还家》

Revived Rose, The 《复活的玫瑰》

Revolutionary Alliance 同盟会

Roar China 《怒吼吧，中国》

Romance of the Three Kingdoms 《三国演义》

Rudiments of Music 《琴学入门》

Sai Jinhua 《赛金花》

Saving Oneself 《自救》

Selected Autobiographies of Women Writers 《女作家自传选集》

"Self-Account of the Grand Historian, The" "太史公自叙"

"Self-Criticism and Self-Encouragement" "自愧与自勉"

Self-Narration at Forty 《四十自述》

shang 商

Shanghai Journal 《申报》

Shao Lizi 邵力子

Shen Fu 沈浮 (Introduction)

Shen Fu 沈复 (Ye Zhongyin's "My Autobiography")

Shen Ren 沈仁

Shen Yunying 沈云英

Shenzhou guoguang she 神州国光社

Shi Nai' an 施耐庵

shou cang zhi 寿藏志

shuduti zixu 书牍体自序

Sichuan Province Drama School 四川省立戏剧学校

Sima Qian 司马迁

Six Records of a Floating Life 《浮生六记》

"Some Modest Proposals for the Reform of Literature" "文学改良刍议"

Song Deyi 宋德一（宋元）

Song Jiaoren 宋教仁

Song Lyrics Composed at Shuyu 《漱玉词》

Song Lyrics of Ming Ke 《茗柯词》

song lyrics 词

"Song of the Fishermen" "渔光曲"

Song Zhidi 宋之的

Sons and Daughters of North China 《燕赵儿女》

Sorghum Has Turned Red, The 《高粱红了》

Sorrow for the Fall of the Ming 《名末遗恨》

Southern Ming 南明

spoken drama 话剧

Spring and Autumn Annals 《春秋》

Spring and Autumn of the Heavenly Kingdom, The 《天国春秋》

Spring Joy 《春天的快乐》

Spring Remains When Petals Have Fallen 《花落春犹在》

star system 明星制度

street drama 街头剧

Su Che 苏澈

Su Shi　苏轼

Su Wu　苏武

Su Xuelin　苏雪林

Su Xun　苏洵

Sui Garden　隋园

Sun Fuyuan　孙伏园

Sun Zhongshan (Sun Yat-sen)　孙中山（孙逸仙，孙文）

Sun Zhu　孙洙

Sunrise　《日出》

supplement　副刊

Taiping Rebellion　太平天国起义

tanci　弹词

Tang Huaiqiu　唐槐秋

Tang Na　唐纳

Tao Zhenhuai　陶贞怀

This Is Just Spring　《这不过是春天》

Three Followings　三从

Three Hundred Poems of the Tang　《唐诗三百首》

Three Principles of the People　三民主义

"Three Repetitions of the Yangguan Tune"　"阳关三迭"

Three-Association Book Store　三联书店

Tian Han　田汉

Tian Qi　天启

Tiger Valley　《打虎沟》

Tomorrow Song and Dance Troupe　明日歌舞剧团

Twenty-Five Histories, The　《二十五史》

Twice Destined in Marriage　《再生缘》

Victory of Counterattack: Propaganda Plays During the War of Resistance
　　《反攻胜利：抗战宣传舞台剧》

Village Trilogy, A　《农村三步曲》

Wan Li　万历

Wang Anshi　王安石

Wang Chong　王充

Wang Jiaqi　王家齐

Wang Lixi　王礼锡

Wang Renshu　王任叔

Wang Ruilin　王瑞麟

Wang Wei　王维

Wanxian Incident　万县事件

War Diary　《从军日记》

Water Margin　《水浒传》

Wei Changhui　韦昌辉

Wei Lü　卫律

Wen Shaoxia　文少霞

wen yan　文言

Wind of Hunan　《湖南的风》

Woman in National Calamity, The　《国难夫人》

Women's Star Weekly　《女星周报》

Worth of the Minister Extraordinary and Plenipotentiary of the State of Qin, The
　　《秦公使的身价》

Wu Meicun　吴梅村

Wu Song　武松

Wukui Bridge　《五奎桥》

Xi Shi　西施

Xiang Ying　项英

xiao ling　小令

Xiao Qing　小青

Xie Bingying (Xie Minggang)　谢冰莹（谢鸣冈）

Xie Daoyun　谢道韫

Xingying Film Studion　行营电影股

Xiong Foxi　熊佛西

xiu cai　秀才

Xu Xian　许仙

Xu Xilin　徐锡麟

Xu Xingzhi　许幸之

Xu Zihua　许自华

Yang Buwei (Buwei Yang Chao) 杨步伟

Yang Cunbin 杨村彬

Yang Hansheng 阳翰笙

Yang Xiuqing 杨秀清

Ye Ting 叶挺

Ye Zhongyin 叶仲寅（叶子）

Yellow Emperor 黄帝

Yellow River Literary Journal 《黄河文艺》

Ying Fengzhen (Ying Yin) 英凤贞（英茵）

Ying Yunwei 应云卫

Yong Li 永历

Youth Letters 《青年书信》

Youth Magazine 青年杂志

Yu Ling 于伶

Yu Shangyuan 余上沅

Yu Xijian 于熙俭

Yuan Mei 袁枚

Yuan Shikai 袁世凯

Yuan Wenshu (Shu Fei) 袁文殊（舒非）

Zeng Gong 曾巩

Zeng Pu 曾朴（东亚病夫）

Zhang Daofan 张道藩

Zhang He 张鹤

Zhang Huiyan 张惠言

Zhang Jingsheng 张竞生

Zhang Pengchun 张彭春

Zhang Xuecheng 章学诚

Zhao Qingge 赵清阁

Zhao Yuanren 赵元任

Zhenzong 真宗

Zhongshan Incident 中山事件

Zhou Xinfang 周信芳

Zhou Yuren 周雨人

Zhou Zhuoren   周作人

Zhu Duanjun   朱端钧

Zhu Shuzhen   朱淑真

Zhu Yingtai   祝英台

Zhu Youlang   朱由榔

Zhu Yousong   朱由崧

zhuang   状

zhuang yuan   状元

Zi Gang (Peng Zigang)   子冈 (彭子冈)

"Zi ji"   "自记"

zisong   自颂

zixu nianpu   自叙年谱

zixu   自序

zizan   自赞

zizhuan   自传

zizhuang   自状

zizuo muzhiming   自作墓志铭

Bibliography

Ames, Roger T., et al., eds. *Self as Person in Asian Theory and Practice*. Albany: State University of New York Press, 1994.

Bai, Wei. *My Tragic Life* (Beiju shengya). Shanghai: Wenxue chubanshe, 1936.

Barlow, Tani E., ed. *Gender Politics in Modern China*. Durham and London: Duke University Press, 1993.

Beasley, William G. and Edwin G. Pulleyblank, eds. *Historians of China and Japan*. London: Oxford University Press, 1961.

Carlitz, Katherine. "The Social Uses of Female Virtue in Late Ming Editions of *Lienü Zhuan*." *Late Imperial China* 12.2 (1991): 117–48.

_____. "Desire, Danger, and the Body: Stories of Women's Virtue in Late Ming China." In Gilmartin, et al., 1994, 101–24.

Chang, Kang-I Sun and Saussy, Haun, eds. *Women Writers of Traditional China: an Anthology of Poetry and Criticism*. Stanford: Stanford University Press, 1999.

Chen, Duxiu. "On Literary Revolution" (*Wenxue geming lun*). In Kirk A. Denton, 1996, 140–5.

Chen, Duo, et al., eds. *Xiong Foxi, a Modern Dramatist* (Xiandai xiju jia Xiong Foxi). Beijing: Zhongguo xiju chubanshe, 1985.

Chen, Hengzhe (Chen Nan-hua). *Autobiography of a Chinese Young Girl*. N. p., 1935.

Cheng, Jihua. *History of Chinese Film* (Zhongguo dianying fazhan shi). Beijing: China Film Publishing House, 1981.

Denton, Kirk A. *Modern Chinese Literary Thought*. Stanford: Stanford University Press, 1996.

Dooling, Amy D. and Kristina M. Torgeson, eds. *Writing Women in Modern China: An Anthology of Women's Literature from the Early Twentieth Century*. New York: Columbia University Press, 1998.

Duncan, Isadora. *My Life* (Wo de shenghuo). Trans. Yu Xijian. Shanghai: Shangwu yinshuguan, 1934.

Eberstein, Bernd, ed. *A Selective Guide to Chinese Literature 1900–1949*. Vol. IV, *The Drama*. Leiden: E. J. Brill, 1990.

Evasdaughter, Elizabeth N. "Autobiographical Closure in the Future: Women Constructing Hope." *a/b: Auto/Biography Studies* 9.1 (Spring 1995): 115–131.

Feuerwerker, Yi-tsi. "Women as Writers in the 1920s and 1930s." In Margery Wolf and Roxane Witke, eds., *Women in Chinese Society*. Stanford: Stanford University Press, 1975, 143–68.

Foreign Languages Press. *An Outline History of China*. Beijing: Foreign Languages Press, 1958.

Ge, Yihong. *A Comprehensive History of Chinese Spoken Drama* (Zhongguo huaju tongshi). Beijing: Wenhua yishu chubanshe, 1990.

Gilmartin, Christina K. et al., eds. *Engendering China: Women, Culture, and the State*. Cambridge, Mass.: Harvard University Press, 1994.

Gui, Youguang. *The Complete Works of Gui Youguang (Gui Youguang quanji)*. Hong Kong: Guangzhi shuju, 1959.

Guo, Dengfeng. *A Collection of Self-Narrations in Past Dynasties* (Lidai zixuzhuan wenchao). Taipei: Shangwu yinshuguan, 1965.

Gusdorf, Georges. "Conditions and Limits of Autobiography." 1956. Trans. James Olney, 1980, 28–48.

Hsia, C. T. *A History of Modern Chinese Fiction*. New Haven: Yale University Press, 1971.

Hu, Shi. *A Collection of Short Stories* (Duanpian xiaoshuo ji). Shanghai: Shanghai Yadong tushuguan, 1919, 89–100.

——. "Some Modest Proposals for the Reform of Literature" (Wenxue gailiang chuyi). In Kirk A. Denton, 1996, 123–39.

——. "The Biography of Li Chao" (*Li Chao zhuan*). In Hua R. Lan and Vanessa L. Fong, 1999, 89–100.

Huang, Jian, et al. eds., *Selected Works of Tian Han* (Tian Han dai biao zuo). Beijing: Zhongguo xiju chubanshe, 1998.

Hucker, Charles O. *A Dictionary of Official Titles in Imperial China*. Stanford: Stanford University Press, 1985.

Hunter, Jane. *The Gospel of Gentility: American Women Missionaries in Turn-of-The-Century China*. New Haven: Yale University Press, 1984.

Ko, Dorothy. *Teachers of the Inner Chambers: Women and Culture in Seventeenth-Century China*. Stanford: Stanford University Press, 1994.

Koozoo, Kawai. *Autobiographical Literature in China* (Zhongguo de zizhuan wenxue). Trans. Cai Yi. Beijing: Central Compilation & Translation Press, 1999.

Kwok, Pui-lan. *Chinese Women and Christianity: 1860–1927*. Atlanta, Ga.: Scholars Press, 1992.

Lan, Hua R. and Vanessa L. Fong, eds. *Women in Republican China: A Source Book*. New York: M. E. Sharp, 1999.

Larson, Wendy. *Literary Authority and the Modern Chinese Writer: Ambivalence and Autobiography*. Durham: Duke University Press, 1991.

_____. "The End of 'funü wenxue': Women's Literature from 1925 to 1935." In Tani E. Barlow, 1993, 58–73.

_____. *Women and Writing in Modern China.* Stanford: Stanford University Press, 1998.

Lee, Leo Ou-fan. *The Romantic Generation of Modern Chinese Writers.* Cambridge, Mass.: Harvard University Press, 1973.

Lewis, Ida Belle. *The Eduation of Girls in China.* New York City: Teachers College, Columbia University, 1919.

Leyda, Jay. *Dianying: An Account of Films and the Film Audience in China.* Boston: MIT Press, 1972.

Li, Daoxing. *A History of Chinese Film, 1937–1945* (Zhongguo dianying shi). Beijing: Shoudu shifan daxue chubanshe, 2000.

Ling Shuhua (Su Hua Ling Chen). *Ancient Melodies.* New York: Universe Books, 1953.

Lu, Jiye. *An Introduction to Chinese Drama* (Zhongguo xiju gailun). Beijing: Chen bao she, 1922.

Lu, Yin. *An Autobiography of Lu Yin (Lu Yin zi zhuan).* Shanghai: Di yi chubanshe, 1934.

Ma, Liangchun and Li Futian, eds. *A Dictionary of Chinese Literature* (Zhongguo wenxue da cidian). Tianjin: Tianjin renmin chubanshe, 1991.

Mann, Susan. *Precious Records.* Stanford: Stanford University Press, 1997.

_____. "'Fuxue' (Women's Learning) by Zhang Xuecheng (1738–1801): China's First History of Women's Culture." *Late Imperial China* 13.1(June 1992): 40–62.

Miller, Nancy K. *Subject to Change: Reading Feminist Writing.* New York: Columbia University Press, 1988.

Misch, Georg. *History of Autobiography.* 1907. London: Routledge and Kegan Paul, 1950.

Moses, Montrose Jonas, ed. *Representative Plays by American Dramatists.* New York: E. P. Dutton & Company, 1918.

New World Press. *A Biographical Dictionary of Modern Chinese Writers.* Beijing: New World Press, 1994.

Ng, Janet, ed. *May Fourth Women Writers: Memoirs.* Hong Kong: The Chinese University of Hong Kong, 1996.

Nienhauser, William H., ed. *The Indiana Companion to Traditional Chinese Literature.* Bloomington: Indiana University Press, 1986.

Nivison, David S. "Aspects of Traditional Chinese Biography." *The Journal of Asian Studies* 21.4 (1962): 457–63.

O'Hara, Albert R. *The Position of Woman in Early China According to the Lieh nü chuan "The Biographies of Chinese Women."* Taipei: Mei Ya Publications, 1971.

Olney, James, ed. *Autobiography: Essays Theoretical and Critical.* Princeton: Princeton University Press, 1980.

Pascal, Roy. *Design and Truth in Autobiography*. Cambridge, Mass.: Harvard University Press, 1960.

Pratt, Leonard and Chiang Su-hui. "Introduction." In Shen Fu, 1983, 9–15.

Roberts, J. A. G. *A Concise History of China*. Cambridge: Harvard University Press, 1999.

Rousseau, Jean-Jacques. *Confessions (Chanhui lu)*. Trans. Zhang Jingsheng. Shanghai: Shanghai mei de shudian, 1928.

———. *Confessions (Chanhui lu)*. Trans. Zhang Jingsheng. Shanghai: Shijie shuju, 1929.

Rowell, George, ed. *Late Victorian Plays, 1890–1914*. London: Oxford University Press, 1972.

Shanghai cishu chubanshe. *Sea of Words* (Cihai). Shanghai: Shanghai cishu chubanshe, 1989.

Shen, Fu. *Six Records of a Floating Life*. Trans. Leonard Pratt and Chiang Su-hui. New York: Penguin Books, 1983.

Shen, Hui. 1991. "A Glimpse of Su Xuelin's Early Works" (Su Xuelin zaoqi chuangzuo guankui). In *Celebrating the Ninety-fifth Anniversary of Professor Su Xuelin* (Qingzhu Su Xuelin jiaoshou jiu zhi jin wu huadan). Taipei: Guoli chenggong daxue, 1995, 12-1–12-11.

Sima, Qian. "The Self-Account of the Grand Historian." In Zhang Dake, 1992, 2127–86.

Slupski, Zbigniew, ed. *A Selective Guide to Chinese Literature, 1900–1949*. Vol. II, *The Short Story*. Leiden: E. J. Brill, 1988.

Smedley, Agnes. *Daughter of the Earth*. New York: Grosset & Dunlap, 1929.

———. *Daughter of the Earth* (Da di de nüer). Trans. Lin Yisheng. N. p., 1932.

Smith, Sidonie. *Subjectivity, Identity, and the Body*. Bloomington: Indiana University Press, 1993.

Smith, Sidonie and Julia Watson, eds. *Women, Autobiography, and Theory: A Reader*. Madison: University of Wisconsin Press, 1998.

Su, Xuelin. *My Life* (Wo de shenghuo). Taipei: Wenxing shudian, 1967.

———. *Ninety-Four Years of a Floating Life* (Fusheng jiusi). Taipei: Sanmin shuju, 1991.

T'ien, Ju-k'ang. *Male Anxiety and Female Chastity: A Comparative Study of Chinese Ethical Values in Ming-Ch'ing Times*. Leiden: E. J. Brill, 1988.

Tan, Zhengbi. *History of Women's Literature in China* (Zhongguo nüxing wenxue shi hua). Tianjin: Baihua chubanshe, 1984.

Tian, Benxiang, ed. *Chinese Spoken Drama* (Zhongguo huaju). Beijing: Wenhua yishu chubanshe, 1999.

Tu, Weiming. *Confucian Thought: Selfhood as Creative Transformation*. Albany: State University of New York Press, 1985.

———. "Embodying the Universe: A Note on Confucian Self-Realization." In Roger T. Ames, 1994, 177–86.

Twitchett, Denis C. "Chinese Biographical Writing." In William G. Beasley and Edwin G. Pulleyblank, 1961, 95–114.

_____. "Problems of Chinese Biography." In Arthur Wright and Denis Twitchett, 1962, 24–39.

Wang, Chong. "Self-Record" (Zi ji). In *Annotated Critical Essay* (Lun heng zhushi), Vol. 4. Beijing: Zhonghua Shuju, 1979, 1712–668.

Wang, Lingzhen. *Modern and Contemporary Chinese Women's Autobiographical Writing.* Doctoral dissertation. Cornell University, 1998.

Widmer, Ellen and Chang, Kang-I Sun, eds. *Writing Women in Late Imperial China.* Stanford: Stanford University Press, 1997.

Wilkinson, Endymion. *Chinese History: A Manual.* Cambridge: The Harvard University Asia Center for the Harvard-Yenching Institute, 2000.

Wong, Su-ling and Cressy, Earl Herbert. *Daughter of Confucius: A Personal History.* New York: Farrar, Straus and Young, 1952.

Wright, Arthur and Twitchett, Denis. *Confucian Personalities.* Stanford: Stanford University Press, 1962.

Wu, Hailin and Li, Yanpei, eds. *A Dictionary of Chinese Historical Figures* (Zhongguo lishi renwu cidian). Harbin: Heilongjiang renmin chubanshe, 1983.

Wu, Meicun. *The Complete Works of Wu Meicun* (*Wu Meicun quanji*). Shanghai: Shanghai guji, 1990.

Wu, Pei-yi. *The Confucian's Progress: Autobiographical Writings in Traditional China.* Princeton: Princeton University Press, 1990.

Xiao, Feng. *A Biography of Lu Yin* (*Lu Yin zhuan*). Beijing: Beijing Normal University Press, 1982.

Xie, Bingying. *Autobiography of a Female Soldier* (*Yi ge nü bing de zizhuan*). Shanghai: Shanghai Liangyou tushu yinshua gongsi, 1936.

_____. *Girl Rebel: The Autobiography of Hsieh Pingying.* Trans. Adet Lin and Anor Lin. New York: John Day Company, 1940.

_____. *Autobiography of a Chinese Girl.* Trans. Tsui Chi. London: Allen & Unwin, 1943.

_____. *A Woman Soldier's Own Story: The Autobiography of Xie Bingying.* Trans. Lily Chia Brassman and Barry Brassman. New York: Columbia University Press, 2001.

Yang, Buwei (Buwei Yang Chao). *Autobiography of a Chinese Woman.* Trans. Yuenren Chao. New York: John Day, 1947.

_____. *Autobiography of a Woman* (*Yi ge nüren de zizhuan*). Taipei: Zhuanji wenxue, 1967.

_____. *Miscellaneous Accounts of the Zhaos* (*Za ji Zhao jia*). Taipei: Zhuangji wenxue chubanshe, 1972.

Yang, Lien-sheng. "The Organization of Chinese Official Historiography: Principles and Methods of the Standard Histories from the T'ang through the Ming Dynasty." In William G. Beasley and Edwin G. Pulleyblank, 1961, 44–59.

Yang, Qun. *Biography of Zhang Jingsheng* (*Zhang Jingsheng zhuan*). Guangzhou: Huacheng chubanshe, 1999.

Zhang, Dake, ed. *The New Annotated Records of the Grand Historian* (Shi Ji quanben xinzhu). Xi'an: Sanqin Publishing House, 1992.

Zhang, Xuecheng. *Prose Writings of Mr. Zhang Shizhai* (*Zhang Shizhai xiansheng wenji*). Taipei: Wenhua chuban gongsi, 1968.

Zhongguo da baikequanshu chubanshe. *A Great Encyclopedia of China: Foreign Literatures* (Zhongguo da baikequanshu: waiguo wenxue). Beijing: Zhongguo da baikequanshu chubanshe, 1982.

Zhongguo da baikequanshu chubanshe. *A Great Encyclopedia of China: Chinese Literature.* (Zhongguo da baikequanshu: zhongguo wenxue). Beijing: Zhongguo da baikequanshu chubanshe, 1986.

Zhongguo da baikequanshu chubanshe. *A Great Encyclopedia of China: Ethnic Groups* (Zhongguo da baikequanshu: minzu). Beijing: Zhongguo da baikequanshu chubanshe, 1986.

Zhongguo da baikequanshu chubanshe. *A Great Encyclopedia of China: Language* (Zhongguo da baikequanshu: yuyan wenzi). Beijing: Zhongguo da baikequanshu chubanshe, 1988.

Zhongguo da baikequanshu chubanshe. *A Great Encyclopedia of China: Drama* (Zhongguo da baikequanshu: xiju). Beijing: Zhongguo da baikequanshu chubanshe, 1989.

Zhongguo da baikequanshu chubanshe. *A Great Encyclopedia of China: Music and Dance* (Zhongguo da baikequanshu: yinyue wudao). Beijing: Zhongguo da baikequanshu chubanshe, 1989.

Zhongguo da baikequanshu chubanshe. *A Great Encyclopedia of China: Press and Publication* (Zhongguo da baikequanshu: xingwen chuban). Beijing: Zhongguo da baikequanshu chubanshe, 1990.

Zhongguo da baikequanshu chubanshe. *A Great Encyclopedia of China: Light Industry* (Zhongguo da baikequanshu: qinggong). Beijing: Zhongguo da baikequanshu chubanshe, 1991.

Zhongguo da baikequanshu chubanshe. *A Great Encyclopedia of China: Chinese History.* (Zhongguo da baikequanshu: Zhongguo lishi). Beijing: Zhongguo da baikequanshu chubanshe, 1992.